W9-CEI-326

The BOOK *of* BOOKS

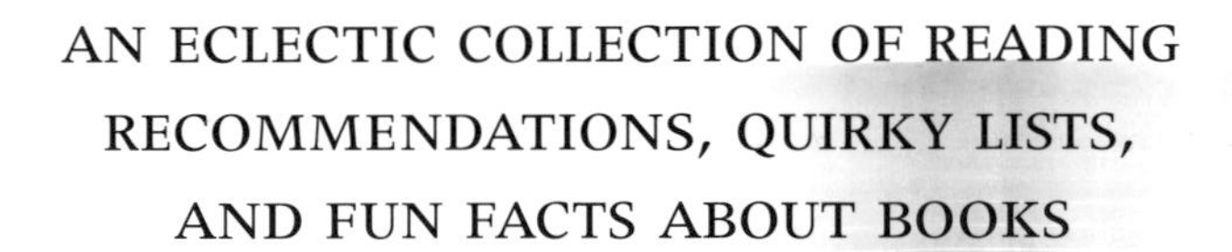

AN ECLECTIC COLLECTION OF READING RECOMMENDATIONS, QUIRKY LISTS, AND FUN FACTS ABOUT BOOKS

LES KRANTZ
***and* TIM KNIGHT**

To my parents, William and Mary Ann Knight, who instilled in me a love of reading and a reverence for language.

— *Tim Knight*

To Augusta Gottlieb ("Mrs. Gottlieb"), my first—and best—high school English teacher, who taught me about the power of words and the pleasures of books.

— *Les Krantz*

PUBLISHED BY: Wildwood Books, N2826 Wildwood Drive, Lake Geneva, WI 53147

SPECIAL ACKNOWLEDGMENT: The authors wish to thank Liz Foz, contributing writer to this work, for her thoughtful lists, attention to detail, and lively writing.

Designed by Emily Cavett Taff

FIRST EDITION

Library of Congress Cataloging-in-Publication Data is available upon request.

ISBN 0-9773632-1-X

PRINTED IN CHINA

Introduction

Finding a good book to "live in" is not easy. Nothing is more disappointing than one that doesn't meet expectations. With this book in hand, hopefully, that won't happen very often. *The Book of Books* is all about knowing what to expect from a work of literature, be it a novel, nonfiction title, or coffee table book.

When we embarked on *The Book of Books,* the prospect of creating and assembling upwards of one hundred lists of reading recommendations struck both of us as exhilarating—and more than a little daunting. That said, we then dove headlong into the process of creating a decidedly eclectic list of reading recommendations—along with an array of literary facts and anecdotes—that will hopefully pique your curiosity.

For the most part, we did not emphasize the mega bestsellers of late—the Harry Potter series, *The Da Vinci Code,* etc. Not that they are not worth reading, but there are so many, less-heralded books deserving of attention. *The Book of Books* therefore offers readers a diverse mixture of classics, overlooked gems, and intriguing new titles. And while there's no shortage of books by "dead white men," the bane of the politically correct literati, we widened our scope to encompass notable books from Asian-American, African-American and Latino writers, among others. Guilty pleasures share the pages with Russian masterpieces, illustrated children's books, political memoirs, poetry, and quirkier fare.

Whether your tastes run to William Shakespeare or Jacqueline Susann, you'll find their signature works in *The Book of Books,* which also includes excerpts from over fifty books. The result is an entertaining, provocative and essential reference for readers whose passion for books is best summed up by the following quote from the ancient Roman philosopher/politician Cicero: "A room without books is like a body without a soul."

We couldn't agree more. Enjoy!

Les Krantz & Tim Knight

African-American Novels

Stories of Twentieth Century African-American Life

When Ralph Ellison died at the age of eighty in 1994, the *New York Times* eulogized him as "one of the major American writers of the twentieth century." That Ellison merited such a glowing tribute is remarkable, when you consider the fact that he published only one novel in his lifetime. Then again, *Invisible Man* is a novel like no other—a magnificently realized portrait of a young African-American man confronting racism as he struggles to find his identity in a country that can't see past the color of his skin. Praised by Irving Howe as "a soaring and exalted record of a Negro's journey through contemporary America" in the *Nation*, Ellison's first novel won the 1953 National Book Award. His long-awaited—and long-delayed follow-up, *Juneteenth*, would appear five years after his death, but despite mostly favorable reviews, it probably won't have the shelf life of *Invisible Man*—one of eight books by African-American writers, listed alphabetically, that evoke twentieth century African-American life in all its complexity and diversity.

1. ***Another Country*** by James Baldwin, 1962 – Sensual, passionate novel about a group of Greenwich Village friends crossing sexual and racial boundaries as they search for meaning following a friend's suicide.

2. ***A Gathering of Old Men*** by Ernest J. Gaines, 1983 – In rural, 1970s-era Louisiana, a group of elderly African-American men tempt violent retribution when they stand up to racist locals, out to avenge the murder of a Cajun farmer. A finely etched and riveting novel from the author of *A Lesson Before Dying*.

3. ***The Healing*** by Gayl Jones, 1998 – An itinerant faith healer reflects on her rough-and-tumble, often bizarre life as she travels through the

rural South. A finalist for the National Book Award, *The Healing* is a virtuoso, stream-of-consciousness novel from the author of *Corregidora.*

4. ***Invisible Man*** by Ralph Ellison, 1952 – Ellison's masterpiece was chosen one of *Time* magazine's hundred best English-language novels published since 1923.

excerpt: INVISIBLE MAN:
There was a rush against me and I fell, hearing a single explosion, backward into a whirl of milling legs, overshoes, the trampled snow cold on my hands. Another shot sounded above like a bursting bag. Managing to stand, I saw atop the steps the fist with the gun being forced into the air above the crowd's bobbing heads and the next instant they were dragging him down into the snow; punching him left and right, uttering a low tense swelling sound of desperate effort; a grunt that exploded into a thousand softly spat, hate-sizzling curses.

5. ***Little Scarlet: An Easy Rawlins Novel*** by Walter E. Mosley, 2004 – Set against the backdrop of the Watts riots of 1965, Mosley's ninth book in his Easy Rawlins mystery series finds the world-weary private eye investigating the murder of a young woman known as Little Scarlet. What he ultimately learns will force Rawlins to examine his conflicted feelings about the riots. Another outstanding book from Mosley, whom former President Clinton named as one of his favorite writers.

6. ***Meridian*** by Alice Walker, 1976 – Walker's excellent second novel depicts the life and times of an educated young black woman, whose unwavering commitment to the civil rights movement ultimately takes a toll on her health.

7. ***Native Son*** by Richard Wright, 1940 – After he accidentally kills the daughter of his wealthy white boss, a young black man finds himself trapped in a downward spiral that climaxes with his arrest and trial. Sixty-odd years after Wright's debut novel ignited a firestorm of controversy, this classic hasn't lost its power to shock.

8. ***Song of Solomon*** by Toni Morrison, 1977 – Oprah Winfrey's favorite novelist won the National Book Critics Circle Award for her third novel, a masterful and poetic saga about a black Michigan family with the unfortunate last name of Dead.

American Novels

Best Fiction, 1980-2005

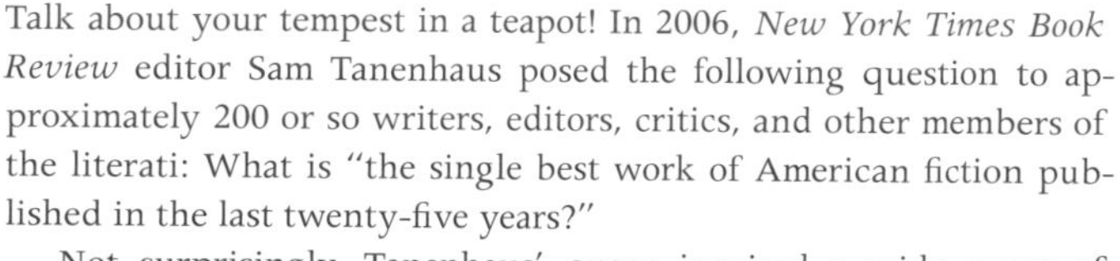

Talk about your tempest in a teapot! In 2006, *New York Times Book Review* editor Sam Tanenhaus posed the following question to approximately 200 or so writers, editors, critics, and other members of the literati: What is "the single best work of American fiction published in the last twenty-five years?"

Not surprisingly, Tanenhaus' query inspired a wide range of responses from the "judges," whose ranks included such literary heavyweights as John Irving, Stephen King, and Anne Tyler. While some refused to participate, others barraged Tanenhaus and his staff with questions regarding the criteria for inclusion. All told, 125 votes were ultimately tabulated, with Toni Morrison's Pulitzer Prize winner *Beloved* receiving the most: fifteen. It was the lone Morrison novel to receive multiple votes, whereas Philip Roth had six novels make the cut. Long rumored to be a contender for the Nobel Prize in Literature, the Newark native has been a mainstay of American literature since 1959, when his first book, *Goodbye, Columbus*, won the National Book Award.

Although the final list has generated more than its fair share of grousing, particularly in the blogosphere, here are the top five vote-getters, ranked in descending order of votes, plus five other novels, in no particular order, that received multiple votes.

1. ***Beloved*** by Toni Morrison, 1987 – An extraordinary work by the Nobel Prize winner, *Beloved* is a lyrical, emotionally shattering story of an escaped slave literally haunted by an unspeakable crime in post-Civil War Ohio.

excerpt: ***BELOVED:***

A fully dressed woman walked out of the water. She barely gained the dry bank of the stream before she sat down and leaned against a mulberry tree. All day and all night she sat there, her head resting on the trunk in a position abandoned enough to crack the brim in her straw hat. Everything hurt but her lungs most of all. Sopping wet and breathing shallow she spent those hours trying to negotiate the weight of her eyelids. The day breeze blew her dress dry; the night wind wrinkled it. Nobody saw her emerge or came accidentally by. If they had, chances are they would have hesitated before approaching her. Not because she was wet, or dozing or had what sounded like asthma, but because amid all that she was smiling.

2. ***Underworld*** by Don DeLillo, 1997 – The first of three DeLillo books to receive multiple votes (the others being *Libra* and *White Noise*), *Underworld* jumps back and forth from the 1950s to the 1990s as DeLillo examines the cold war's lingering influence on American life. Real-life events and figures ranging from J. Edgar Hoover to Jackie Gleason figure in this mordantly funny novel.

3. ***Blood Meridian*** by Cormac McCarthy, 1985 – Deemed one of the twentieth century's best novels by critic Harold Bloom, McCarthy's graphically violent western has earned McCarthy favorable comparisons to William Faulkner. Based on real events, *Blood Meridian* follows a gang of American scalp-hunters on an ill-fated expedition to Mexico in the 1840s.

4. ***Rabbit Angstrom: The Four Novels*** by John Updike, 1995 – Readers first encountered Updike's hero Harry "Rabbit" Angstrom in the 1960 novel *Rabbit, Run,* which was followed by *Rabbit Redux* (1971), *Rabbit is Rich* (1981), and *Rabbit at Rest* (1990). Spanning the years 1960 to 1990, these four novels, bundled together in 1995, vividly chart Angstrom's attempts to escape the banality of middle-class life.

5. ***American Pastoral*** by Philip Roth, 1997 – One of Roth's novels featuring his alter ego, Nathan Zuckerman, *American Pastoral* depicts the impact of the 1960s-era social unrest on Seymour "Swede" Levov, a golden boy with a beauty queen wife, whose daughter becomes a radical fugitive. An epic American tragedy, richly imagined and brilliantly written.

6. ***A Confederacy of Dunces*** by John Kennedy Toole, 1980 – Boisterous, bawdy, and side-splittingly funny, Toole's New Orleans-set farce introduces readers to the inimitable Ignatius P. Reilly, a world-class malcontent begrudgingly getting his first job at age thirty. Published eleven years after Toole's suicide in 1969, *A Confederacy of Dunces* won the 1981 Pulitzer Prize.

7. ***Housekeeping*** by Marilyn Robinson, 1980 – Two adolescent sisters, their lives shadowed by loss, come of age in the tiny, remote town of Fingerbone, under the charismatic sway of their eccentric aunt. A novel of great delicacy and emotional nuance by the author of *Gilead*.

8. ***Winter's Tale*** by Mark Helprin, 1983 – Helprin's second novel is a daz-

zlingly imaginative depiction of turn-of-the-century New York City in the magical realist mold of Gabriel Garcia Marquez.

9. ***White Noise*** by Don DeLillo. 1985 – The postmodern literary guru, DeLillo takes aim and fires satirical barbs at everything from conspicuous consumption to conspiracy theories to dysfunctional families in *White Noise,* which depicts the effect of a chemical spill on a Hitler Studies professor in the Midwest.

10. ***The Counterlife*** by Philip Roth, 1986 – Another one of Roth's Nathan Zuckerman's books, *The Counterlife* is a densely-plotted account of Zuckerman's transformative experiences while traveling in Israel, London, and New York City.

American Novels

In Search of the Great American Novel, 1900-Present

American fiction writers provide us with a unique perspective, in that their work represents a cultural divide that separates the American experience from the rest of the English-speaking world. To qualify as a "great American novel" the story should masterfully define American experiences—taking off the rose-colored glasses—and focus on the essence of American culture and its multitude of subcultures. But there's more. The literary treatment must capture the spirit of the time that the story depicts. Below are a dozen examples of books, published since 1900, that define the American experience; that is, what it is to be rich (*The Great Gatsby*), what it is to be poor (*The Grapes of Wrath*), what it is to be a liberated woman (*Fear of Flying*), and so on. The list below is alphabetical.

1. ***An American Tragedy*** by Theodore Dreiser, 1925 – The story is seeded with insights into the emotions and predicaments that can make one empathize with even the most unsavory of characters. Based on a true, high-profile murder in the early twentieth century, *An American Tragedy* tells the story of Clyde Griffiths, the son of a Kansas City evangelist, who forsakes the high ground to pursue success at all costs. In Dreiser's novel, the dark side of the American dream is unraveled with the moral ambiguities of survival as its backdrop.

2. ***The Catcher in the Rye*** by J.D. Salinger, 1951 – The wry observa-

tions of sixteen year-old Holden Caulfield tells the story of American youth's alienation from mainstream adult-culture. After being expelled from an exclusive Eastern prep school, Holden goes on a three-day odyssey, meeting hookers, nuns, old friends—his own and his mother's—getting drunk, robbed, and depressed. On his adventure, he cynically views humanity with the insight of a mature adult, yet with his own youthful brand of pessimism and idealism.

3. ***Fear of Flying*** by Erica Jong, 1973 – Humorous and engaging, *Fear of Flying* has been called everything from trash to a classic, yet it remains one of the most descriptive accounts of what it is—or was—to be a modern, educated women in a man's world as the women's movement was being born. Heroine Isadora Wing acts out her sexual fantasies, and struggles with her role as a woman and daughter.

4. ***Go Tell it on the Mountain*** by James Baldwin, 1953 – Oft described as lyrical in its use of language, Baldwin's account of a fourteen year-old black youth in Harlem in 1935 describes his coming to terms with religion, sex, and morality. Said to be semi-autobiographical, *Go Tell it on the Mountain* may be a challenging read due to its complex language and biblical references, but it is also a sensitive portrait of the black experience in pre-World War II America.

5. ***The Grapes of Wrath*** by John Steinbeck, 1939 – Though the story line is pock marked with tragedy, this chronicle of the westward journey of the Joad family is a compelling novel that describes the deplorable conditions of Depression-era migrant workers. The dream of a better life for a down-on-their-luck family escaping the Oklahoma Dust Bowl turns into an emotionally crushing experience that reveals man's inhumanity to man, yet the Joads' unfaltering hold on their own dignity is a celebration of human spirit.

6. ***The Great Gatsby*** by F. Scott Fitzgerald, 1925 – This elegantly written story of the excess, extravagance, and decadence of socialites in West Egg, New York during the Jazz Age is a study of the superficiality of life in the fast lane. The story of Jay Gatsby, a poor boy turned millionaire who falls in love with Southern belle Daisy Buchanan, gradually unfolds as Gatsby's neighbor Nick Caraway learns of Gatsby's humble origins and passion for the married Daisy. Extravagant parties, greed, and ambition are the backdrop of Fitzgerald's cautionary tale about the risks and pitfalls of the American dream.

7. ***The Heart is a Lonely Hunter*** by Carson McCullers, 1940 – Set in a Southern mill town during the Depression era, the myth of "the small-town fraternity" is exposed in this moving story of the alienation and isolation of various individuals who confide their feelings to John Singer, a deaf mute. Singer's relationships take place in a boarding house in which he is relegated to live after his companion dies an untimely death. Befriended by thirteen-year old heroine Mick Kelly, the deaf Singer is ironically the "sounding board" of a black doctor, a wandering alcoholic, and a cafe owner, whose empty lives resonant with everyone to some degree.

excerpt: THE HEART IS A LONELY HUNTER:
In the town were two mutes, and they were always together. Early every morning they would come out from the house where they lived and walk arm in arm down the street to work. The two friends were very different. The one who always steered the way was an obese and dreamy Greek. In the summer he would come out wearing a yellow or green polo shirt stuffed sloppily into his trousers in front and hanging loose behind. When it was colder he wore over this a shapeless gray sweater. His face was round and oily, with half-closed eyelids and lips that curved in a gentle, stupid smile. The other mute was tall. His eyes had a quick, intelligent expression. He was always immaculate and very soberly dressed.

8. ***In America*** by Susan Sontag, 2000 – In the late nineteenth century, Polish diva Maryna Zalezowska seeks to prove that one may reinvent one's self. In an ill-fated attempt to remake her world, Maryna abandons the theater life of New York and moves her family to an experimental utopian community in California. When that fails, she returns as an American to New York, her idealism tempered by the reality of her journey. Prosaically written, *In America* is a story about the Americanization of old-world values.

9. ***Middlesex*** by Jeffrey Eugenides, 2002 – This complex narrative weaves a picture of a Greek-American family, as seen through the eyes of Callie (and later "Cal"), a hermaphrodite. With the theme of gender identity in the background, Eugenides' novel spans eighty years of family history. The novel, which skillfully portrays one person seeing the world and his family through the eyes of both a woman and a man, won the author the Pulitzer Prize for fiction in 2003.

10. ***Slaughterhouse-Five*** by Kurt Vonnegut, 1969 – Considered one of

the great anti-war novels, *Slaughterhouse-Five* is based on the author's actual experiences as a prisoner-of-war during World War II. Peppered with science fiction overtones in the form of character Billy Pilgrim's flashbacks, the story is both funny and morbid at the same time. Billy's odyssey through the war and the fire-bombing of Dresden, Germany explores the nature of good and evil—and how one can maintain his sanity in an insane world at war.

11. ***The Sound and the Fury*** by William Faulkner, 1929 – A haunting, deeply compelling portrait of a Southern family in decline, the Mississippi writer's fourth novel is a challenging read, due to Faulkner's stream-of-consciousness style and liberal use of interior monologues. That said, *The Sound and the Fury* is a masterpiece of Southern Gothic literature—tragic and disturbing—told from the radically differing perspectives of the three Compson brothers: Benjy, an "idiot;" Quentin, a tortured Harvard student; and the oldest son Jason, a sadist with a festering grudge against his family.

12. ***Three Junes*** by Julia Glass, 2002 – This sensitive portrait of family life is divided into three summers and spans a decade in the lives of an embattled Scottish family and a young American woman. Fate brings together various members of the McLeod family and Fern Olitsky as they interact in Greece, Scotland, Manhattan, and the Hamptons. A first-time novelist who won the 2002 National Book Award for *Three Junes,* Glass vividly writes about the meaning of family and friendship in this absorbing and beautifully crafted family saga.

American West Novels

Best of the Twentieth Century

Although he never achieved the international renown of John Steinbeck, the late Wallace Stegner was often referred to as the "dean of Western writers." An ardent environmentalist and creative writing teacher whose students included Larry McMurtry, Ken Kesey, and Edward Abbey, Stegner depicts life in the American West with a singular mixture of unsparing honesty and heartfelt reverence for the landscape. His masterpiece is generally conceded to be *Angle of Repose,* a family saga that won Stegner the Pulitzer Prize in 1972.

Twenty-seven years later, this generation-spanning novel based loosely

on the life of nineteenth century author/illustrator Mary Hallock Foote would bring Stegner another, posthumous honor. In a 1999 readers' poll conducted by the *San Francisco Chronicle*, *Angle of Repose* was chosen the best twentieth century novel about the American West—just ahead of Steinbeck's *The Grapes of Wrath*, which came in second.

According to the poll's guidelines, readers could only vote for novels that met one of the following three criteria. Its subject matter pertains to the American West. The novel was written in the American West—or the writer hails from the region, which the *Chronicle* editors designated as the land west of the Rockies.

Of the 600-odd readers who voted in the poll, nearly one hundred voted for *Angle of Repose*. Here are the top ten vote-getters, listed in descending order.

1. ***Angle of Respose*** by Wallace Stegner, 1971 – Estranged from his immediate family, a retired, wheelchair bound historian assuages his loneliness by researching the life of his deceased grandmother in the nineteenth century American West. Through her journals and letters, he gains a keen understanding of his family's emotional dynamic over the years.

excerpt: ***ANGLE OF REPOSE:***
A Quaker lady of high principles, the wife of a not-very-successful engineer whom you supported through years of delayed hope, you lived in exile, wrote it, drew it—New Almaden, Santa Cruz, Leadville, Michoacán, the Snake River Valley, the deep quartz mines right under this house—and you stayed a cultural snob through it all. Even when you lived in a field camp in a canyon, your children had a governess, no less, unquestionably the only one in Idaho. The dream you had for your children was a dream of Eastern cultivation.

2. ***The Grapes of Wrath*** by John Steinbeck, 1939 – One of the authentic literary giants of twentieth century American literature, Steinbeck won the Pulitzer Prize for this magnificent account of the sharecropping Joad family devastated by the Great Depression and the Dust Bowl. Unquestionably Steinbeck's greatest novel, *The Grapes of Wrath* was subsequently adapted for the screen by John Ford in 1940.

3. ***Sometimes a Great Notion*** by Ken Kesey, 1964 – Kesey's follow-up to *One Flew Over the Cuckoo's Nest* is a richly compelling family drama set in a Oregon logging community. When the local logging union calls for a strike, the Stamper family patriarch and his equally stub-

born son ignore the union's call—and suffer grave consequences as a result.

4. ***The Call of the Wild*** by Jack London, 1903 – Praised by E. L. Doctorow as a "mordant parable," London's novella is a Darwinian-themed survival tale about Buck, a sled dog who escapes into the frozen Yukon, where he battles for a place in a wolf pack.

5. ***The Big Sleep*** by Raymond Chandler, 1939 – So complicated that even Chandler himself reportedly wasn't sure whodunit, *The Big Sleep* spins a labyrinthine web of murder and blackmail in sunny Los Angeles, the home turf of cynical, hard-boiled private detective Philip Marlowe.

6. ***Animal Dreams*** by Barbara Kingsolver, 1990 – Told in alternating voices, Kingsolver's second novel is a beautifully written story of a woman returning to her rural Arizona hometown to care for her Alzheimer's-afflicted father. Native American imagery and cultural motifs play a prominent role in *Animal Dreams,* which also won raves for its vivid evocation of the Arizona landscape.

7. ***Death Comes for the Archbishop*** by Willa Cather, 1927 – With her customary plain-spoken eloquence, Cather trades the Nebraska prairie setting of *My Antonia* for the New Mexico territory, where this unforgettable novel takes place. Based on a true story, *Death Comes for the Archbishop* portrays the struggles of a French Catholic bishop and a priest to establish a church among the Arapaho and Hopi Indians.

8. ***The Day of the Locust*** by Nathanael West, 1939 – Barely scraping by as a writer-for-hire at one of Hollywood's infamous "Poverty Row" film studios, West wrote this despairing portrait of the has-beens and wannabes seeking fame and fortune in Tinsel Town.

9. ***Blood Meridian*** by Cormac McCarthy, 1985 – McCarthy's virtuoso depiction of a nineteenth century scalping expedition in Mexico is a graphically violent novel, written in a baroque prose style. Rapturous in his praise of McCarthy, influential literary critic Harold Bloom ranks *Blood Meridian* as the reclusive novelist's masterpiece.

10. ***The Maltese Falcon*** by Dashiell Hammett, 1930 – Hammett's cynical private eye, Sam Spade, reportedly served as the model for Raymond

Chandler's Philip Marlowe. In lean, staccato prose, the former Pinkerton detective-turned writer draws you into Spade's twist-laden search for his partner's killer.

Animal Behavior Studies

Heeding the Call of the Wild

Some of the world's most dedicated scientists don't work in laboratories. They leave the comforts of city life to set up camp in remote parts of the globe and study wild animals. They learn about their subjects' means of survival, how their societies are ordered, and in many cases, their individual personalities—all the while managing to survive themselves in the animals' beautiful but often harsh environments. Here are a few informative, entertaining, and passionate books, listed alphabetically, by naturalists who have dedicated many years to studying our wild fellow creatures.

1. ***Cry of the Kalahari*** by Mark and Delia Owens, 1984 – The authors, a husband-and-wife team of naturalists, spent seven years in the Kalahari Desert on a shoestring budget, studying jackals, hyenas, lions, and other wild animals. In this book they share the dramas of learning about the animals around them—getting to know their individual personalities, and witnessing the shifting balance of interdependence and rivalry within and between the different species. Who knew that hyenas—which can crush bones as thick as baseball bats with their teeth and make a meal of the shards—could be so intriguing? There is violence and hardship in their account, but also much that is touching and inspiring.

excerpt: CRY OF THE KALAHARI:
In the early evening I was stirring my supper over the fire when seven lions came padding directly toward camp. My heart began doing flip-flops, and I quickly put the pot of stew on top of the hyena table and hurried deeper into the tree island. Peering through the branches, I could see the long, low forms gliding silently toward me, just 100 yards away. It was the same lionesses and their adolescent young I had often seen. But on the other occasions when they had visited camp, the truck had always been nearby; now I felt as vulnerable as a turtle without a shell.

2. ***Gorillas in the Mist*** by Dian Fossey, 1983 – Before Fossey went to central Africa to study mountain gorillas in the wild, not much was known about these animals. She fell in love with them and devoted her life to researching them and trying to protect them from poachers, who may have been responsible for her murder in 1985. Her book describes the gorillas' surprisingly peaceful societies, and communicates why she was willing to risk her life for them.

3. ***Hunting With the Moon: The Lions of Savuti*** by Dereck and Beverly Joubert, 1997 – Another husband-and-wife team, the Jouberts spent over two decades living in a national park in Botswana, observing and photographing the lions that live there. They followed the lions at night, and include more than a hundred full-color photos in the book. In words and pictures, the couple document the relationships of pride members, the lions' conflicts with hyenas and elephants, and much more in fascinating detail.

4. ***In the Shadow of Man*** by Jane Goodall, 1971 – One of the world's most famous naturalists, Jane Goodall shares her pioneering research on a group of chimpanzees, mankind's closest relative. She focuses in particular on one matriarch, "Flo," and her family. If you fall in love with this chimp family—which is very likely—you can find out about its next generation in Goodall's 1990 follow-up, *Through a Window.*

5. ***Listening to Whales: What the Orcas Have Taught Us*** by Alexandra Morton, 2002 – Inspired by John Lilly's work on dolphin communication, the author decided to record and analyze the noises made by orcas, also known as killer whales. She began with a pair in captivity and then set out to listen to wild orcas off the coast of British Columbia, learning their ways of life and how they "talk" to each other, using different frequencies. It's also an impressive story of the joys and sacrifices of doing research in such a rugged environment.

6. ***Never Cry Wolf: The Amazing True Story of Life Among Arctic Wolves*** by Farley Mowat, 1963 – Originally, the author was sent to the tundra of northern Canada to study the wolves reportedly menacing the caribou population. When he observed them firsthand, however, Mowat realized that the wolves were much less of a threat than had been thought. His account describes how he documented the wolves' behavior—and participated in some of it.

7. ***The Shark Chronicles: A Scientist Tracks the Consummate Predator*** by John Musick and Beverly McMillan, 2002 – Sharks are frightening, but also awe-inspiring. This book takes readers across the globe, sharing the drama of shark research. Along with discussing sharks' evolution and ecological issues affecting them, the authors cover sharks' special physiology, their reproductive lives, and some of the remarkable things that have been discovered in their stomachs.

8. ***To Touch a Wild Dolphin: A Journey of Discovery with the Sea's Most Intelligent Creatures*** by Rachel Smolker, 2001 – This is a delightful account of fifteen years with the wild dolphins off the coast of western Australia. Playful, clever, and friendly (though not always peaceable), the dolphins communicate using whistles and clicks. Smolker also observed them using tools—one of the many, amazing discoveries you'll find in the pages of this book.

Aphorists

Brevity is the Soul of Wit—and Wisdom

The literary expression of great insights into human nature can take many different forms, from epic poems to fables to complex psychological novels. A few writers, philosophers, and conversationalists have a gift for putting their most perceptive thoughts into just one or two sentences—brief sayings that surprise by their bite, wit, or expansiveness. Unpleasant and seldom acknowledged truths, upendings of conventional wisdom, paradoxes that actually make sense ... the great aphorists provide food for thought in a most concentrated form. This list, ordered chronologically, is an introduction to a few of the best.

1. **Lao Tzu,** circa sixth century BC – One of the sages of ancient China, Lao Tzu had an outlook that was anything but cynical. Some of his sayings are mystifying at first, which he freely acknowledged. "Indeed," he says, "truth sounds like its opposite!"—but he wasn't talking nonsense. One way to understand his writings is to see them as contrasting two different states of mind. On one hand, a fragmented, grasping state in which we are so obsessed with controlling things that we defeat our own purposes; and on the other hand, an open, tranquil, perceptive state much like what some modern psychologists call "flow." From the collection of his teachings, the *Tao Te Ching:*

To be empty is to be full.
He who conquers men has force; he who conquers himself is truly strong.
A journey of a thousand miles must begin with a single step.

2. **François, Duc de la Rochefoucauld,** 1613–1680 – The French nobleman sought to expose the pettiness and vanity that he believed lay beneath the surface of polite society and most human interactions. For all that he despaired of finding true virtue, humility, and selflessness, one senses that he still valued them. Perhaps he even viewed his unsparing attempts at honesty as a tonic, albeit one of very limited power against vanity and self-deception. Judge for yourself. From his *Maxims:*

   We all have strength enough to endure the misfortunes of others.
   If we had no faults of our own, we would not take so much pleasure in noticing those of others.
   We always like those who admire us; we do not always like those whom we admire.

3. **Benjamin Franklin,** 1706–1790 – Apart from being a printer, reformer, diplomat, political writer, and scientist, Benjamin Franklin was also quite a wit. Here are some of his gems from *Poor Richard's Almanack,* which was published each year between 1732 and 1757:

   Three may keep a secret, if two of them are dead.
   Keep your eyes wide open before marriage, half shut afterwards.
   Experience keeps a dear school, but fools will learn in no other.

4. **Oscar Wilde,** 1854–1900 – The author of *The Picture of Dorian Gray* and *The Importance of Being Earnest* enjoyed skewering convention, but he did it with a comparatively light and sympathetic touch. He loved art for art's sake (and wit for wit's sake), but, it seems, humanity too.

   I can resist everything except temptation. (From *Lady Windermere's Fan)*
   When the gods wish to punish us they answer our prayers. (From *An Ideal Husband)*
   A man cannot be too careful in the choice of his enemies. (From *The Picture of Dorian Gray)*

5. **Dorothy Parker,** 1893–1967 – One of the early contributors to the *New Yorker* magazine, the petite poet, critic, and fiction writer had a

sharp tongue and pen that gave her what she called her "reputation for homicidal humor." But she also had a strong instinct for self-deprecation (and melancholy). Some of her astute thoughts:

Scratch a lover, and find a foe. (From *Ballade of a Great Weariness)*
Brevity is the soul of lingerie. (Attributed advertising motto)
Men seldom make passes / At girls who wear glasses (News Item)

Arthurian Literature

The Legend of Camelot in Prose and Verse

The legend of King Arthur and his knights of the round table has held readers spellbound since at least 1138 AD, when Welsh clergyman/historian Geoffrey of Monmouth published his highly romanticized *The History of the Kings of Britain*. While most contemporary historians discount the accuracy of Geoffrey of Monmouth's book as questionable at best, he nonetheless succeeded in popularizing the story of the "once and future king," as Arthur's grave marker on the isle of Avalon identifies him, according to T. H. White's book of the same name.

Whether or not such a figure existed in Great Britain's fog-shrouded distant past, King Arthur remains a potent symbol of the Age of Chivalry—when loyal and virtuous knights defended ladies fair, ancient wizards advised kings, and magic was an everyday reality. In the centuries since Geoffrey of Monmouth's book the Arthurian romance has been told in virtually every artistic medium: verse, prose, cinema, and Broadway musical. Here are eight Arthurian romances, listed alphabetically, that evoke the swirling pageantry and mysticism of Camelot.

1. ***The Acts of King Arthur and His Noble Knights*** by John Steinbeck, 1976 – Unfinished at the time of his death in 1968, Steinbeck's neglected gem was published eight years later, with the author's letters to his agent outlining his plans for finishing it. Except for the novel's rather contemporary dialogue, Steinbeck's version of the King Arthur legend is remarkably faithful in spirit and tone to Malory's *Le Morte d'Arthur.*

2. ***Arthur Rex: A Legendary Novel*** by Thomas Berger, 1978 – The author of *Little Big Man* performs literary magic with this grand retelling of *Le Morte d'Arthur,* which Berger gently tweaks with cheeky good humor.

3. ***A Connecticut Yankee in King Arthur's Court*** by Mark Twain, 1889 – Twain's whimsical blend of time-traveling fantasy and social satire sends a nineteenth century shop foreman back to Camelot, where the know-it-all New Englander uses modern-age technology to rise in King Arthur's court.

4. ***The Hollow Hills*** by Mary Stewart, 1973 – The second volume in Stewart's enthralling Arthurian Saga, which places the wizard Merlin at the narrative center. In *The Hollow Hills,* King Uther Pendragon entrusts Merlin with the education of his son Arthur, who must pull the magical sword Caliburn from the stone to realize his destiny.

5. ***Idylls of the King*** by Alfred, Lord Tennyson, 1885 – England's Poet Laureate from 1850-1892, Tennyson dedicated this sequence of twelve, transcendently beautiful poems based on *Le Morte d'Arthur* to the memory of Prince Albert, who died in 1861.

6. ***The Mists of Avalon*** by Marion Zimmer Bradley, 1983 – King Arthur and Guenevere are supporting characters in Bradley's female-centric revisionist take on the legend. The main character is Arthur's half-sister Morgaine, aka Morgan Le Fay, who's waging a lonely battle to preserve ancient Celtic traditions in the face of Christianity. Ambitious and imaginative, Bradley's novel is a perennial best-seller.

excerpt: THE MISTS OF AVALON:

A few days later Morgaine went forth, with a few of the people of Avalon, to the crowning of Arthur. Never, in all her years upon Avalon — except for the few moments when she had opened the mists to allow Gwenhwyfar to find her convent again—had she set foot on the earth of the Isle of the Priests, Ynis Witrin, the Isle of Glass. It seemed to her that the sun shone with a curious harshness, unlike the soft and misty sunlight of Avalon. She had to remind herself that to almost all the people of Britain, this was the real world, and the land of Avalon only an enchanted dream, as if were the very kingdom of fairy.

7. ***Le Morte d'Arthur*** by Sir Thomas Malory, 1485 – The primary source for most of the novels and films about King Arthur, Malory's epic is regarded as the first English-language novel.

8. ***The Once and Future King*** by T.H. White, 1958 – An ugly, self-centered Lancelot? Merlin growing younger, not older? Those are just two of the striking revisions found in White's classic quartet of novels, that some critics interpret as a World War II allegory. *The Once and*

Future King was subsequently adapted for the screen (Disney's *The Sword in the Stone*) and stage (*Camelot*).

Artist Biographies

Lives of the Masters

The history of art is the history of many traditions and many individuals, a great number of whom are now anonymous. Luckily, we know enough about the art of the last few hundred years—thanks in part to records such as Giorgio Vasari's sixteenth century lives of the Renaissance masters—to be able to explore the lives and work of key individuals in depth. There are far too many great artists—and good books about them—for an exhaustive list of volumes, but here is a sampling of some of the best titles, listed in alphabetical order. Their pages are filled with beautiful images and remarkable stories of human accomplishment. Enjoy!

1. ***Degas*** by Robert Gordon and Andrew Forge, 1988 – The composition, palette, and psychology of Degas' work were boldly experimental, yet he never lost his exquisite sense of draftsmanship or his connection to the classical art of the past. This volume showcases his early figure studies, portraits, dancers, and bathers—plus his poetry, working methods, and prickly personality.

2. ***Frida Kahlo, 1907–1954: Pain and Passion*** by Andrea Kettenmann, 1993 – The author discusses the most salient aspects of Kahlo's life and work—how she used her self-portraits to explore her identity; her experience of physical suffering; and her relationship with the controversial, larger-than-life muralist Diego Rivera.

3. ***Leonardo da Vinci*** by Kenneth Clark, 1939 – See the Mona Lisa with fresh eyes! Curiosity, inventiveness, subtlety, and grace were just a few of the many qualities of Leonardo da Vinci, the exemplary "Renaissance man." Clark's text is wonderfully readable, and the current edition has good reproductions.

4. ***Michelangelo*** by Howard Hibbard, 1974 – A versatile and profound Renaissance genius, Michelangelo—the creator of David and the Sistine Chapel frescoes—deserves monumental appreciation. This book goes into detail about the artist's life and his work as a sculptor, painter, architect, and even poet.

5. ***Monet: Nature into Art*** by John House, 1986 – This book reveals how hard work and careful thought went into the Impressionist painter Claude Monet's landscapes, which were often developed in the studio, as well as in the open air. The end result, of course, was a feeling of spontaneity and naturalness that has appealed to generations since.

6. ***Rembrandt's Eyes*** by Simon Schama, 1999 – Centuries after they were painted, Rembrandt's portraits and other works are still amazingly touching. Schama's lively book portrays the artist's life of intense joys and troubles in a fascinating time and place—the "Dutch Golden Age."

7. ***The Ultimate Picasso*** by Brigitte Léal, et al, 2000 – Picasso was an extraordinarily prolific and influential artist. This book reproduces many works from his different phases and discusses his traditional academic training, his muses, and much more.

8. ***Van Gogh*** by Rainer Metzger and Ingo F. Walther, 1996 – Vincent Van Gogh was a much more complex person than simply the madman who cut off his ear. This book details his early life, his stunning artistic achievements, his important relationships with his brother Theo and his fellow painter Paul Gauguin, and his tragic death.

Asian-American Novels

Caught Between Two Worlds

Shunted to the margins of American popular culture, literature, and media for decades, Asian-Americans have recently emerged as a significant force in all areas of the arts. The days when actors like Mickey Rooney and Katharine Hepburn donned prosthetics to play egregious, stereotyped Asian characters in Hollywood films are long gone. In 1988, Chinese-American playwright David Henry Hwang won the Tony Award for his play, *M. Butterfly*. And Korean-American comedienne Margaret Cho blows the image of the dutiful, meek Asian woman to smithereens with her raunchy, politically charged stand-up.

It is in the literary realm that Asian-Americans have perhaps made the greatest inroads, due largely to Chinese-American writer Amy Tan, whose debut novel, *The Joy Luck Club*, spent eight months on the best-seller lists, was translated into seventeen languages, and spawned a hit film. The daughter of Chinese immigrants, Tan writes perceptively about being torn between the world of her parents and American culture. It's a theme that resonates in all of the following novels, listed alphabetically, that evoke what it means to be of Southeast Asian descent in America.

1. ***American Woman*** by Susan Choi, 2003 – Inspired by real-life radical Wendy Yoshimura, a member of the underground group that kidnapped Patty Hearst in 1974, Choi's second novel focuses on a Japanese-American militant who forms a bond with a kidnapped heiress. An ambitious and bracing finalist for the 2004 Pulitzer Prize.

2. ***The Bonesetter's Daughter*** by Amy Tan, 2001 – Another gem from Tan. A San Francisco career woman investigates the early life of her Alzheimer's-afflicted mother, a Chinese immigrant, who grew up in an isolated, mountain community ruled by superstition.

excerpt: THE BONESETTER'S DAUGHTER:
"Throughout the years, LuLing lamented in Chinese, "Ai-ya, if only your father had lived, he would be even more successful than your uncle. And still we wouldn't spend so carelessly like them!" She also noted what should have been Ruth's rightful property: Grandmother Young's jade ring, money for a college fund. It shouldn't have mattered that Ruth was a girl or that Edwin had died. That was old Chinese thinking! LuLing said this so often Ruth could not help fantasizing what her life might have been like had her father lived.

3. ***Donald Duk*** by Frank Chin, 1991 – A breezy, good-naturedly funny coming-of-age novel set in San Francisco's Chinatown. The title character is a twelve year-old boy in full rebellion mode against everything Chinese—particularly his name. However, he gradually comes to embrace his heritage through nightly dreams of building the transcontinental railroad in 1869.

4. ***The Fruit 'N Food*** by Leonard Chang, 1996 – Racism rears its ugly head for a Korean-American college student, who returns home to his economically depressed, crime-riddled Queens neighborhood in Chang's hard-hitting novel.

5. ***The Gangster We All Are Looking For*** by Thi Diem Thuy Le, 2003 – Haunting and sorrowful debut novel about Vietnamese refugees trying to let go of their traumatic past while making a new life in America.

6. ***The Love Wife*** by Gish Jen, 2004 – Clever and engaging, if overly broad, Jen's seriocomic novel depicts the travails of a multicultural family—Chinese husband/blonde WASP wife—and their adopted brood.

7. ***Native Speaker*** by Chang-Rae Lee, 1995 – Lee's brilliant first novel has been called the Asian-American counterpart to Ralph Ellison's *Invisible Man*. Feeling like a perpetual outsider in 1950s era America, a Korean-American who feels neither Korean nor American goes to work as a spy, only to suffer an identity crisis while spying on a rising Korean-American politician.

8. ***When the Emperor Was Divine*** by Julie Otsuka, 2002 – The internment of Japanese-Americans during World War II is the subject of Otsuka's restrained, quietly devastating novel.

Baseball Novels

Batter Up!

Legend has it that in the wake of the infamous "Black Sox" scandal of 1919, a heartbroken young baseball fan shamed his fallen idol, "Shoeless Joe" Jackson, with the cry, "Say it ain't so, Joe! Say it ain't so!"

Banned from the majors, Jackson retreated into obscurity, his reputation forever tainted by the scandal. Only in the pages of W.P. Kinsella's novel *Shoeless Joe*, would the former Chicago White Sox player get a chance to redeem himself, albeit as a ghost, playing in a magical baseball diamond in an Iowa cornfield. The inspiration for Kevin Costner's beloved male tearjerker, *Field of Dreams, Shoeless Joe* is one of two Kinsella novels that make the alphabetical list of great books celebrating the all-American pastime.

1. ***Bang the Drum Slowly*** by Mark Harris, 1956 – The second of Harris' quartet of Henry Wiggen novels, *Bang the Drum Slowly* focuses on the close-knit friendship of New York Mammoths' pitcher Wiggen and terminally ill catcher Bruce Pearson. Understated and poignant, *Bang the Drum Slowly* was later turned into a film starring Robert De Niro as Pearson.

2. ***The Dreyfus Affair—A Love Story*** by Peter Lefcourt, 1992 – Major league baseball shortstop Randy Dreyfus seems destined for Hall

of Fame greatness—until he inconveniently falls head over heels in love with D.J., the team's second baseman, in Lefcourt's knockabout farce.

3. ***For the Love of the Game*** by Michael Shaara, 1991 – Published posthumously, Shaara's heartfelt novella introduces us to thirty-seven year-old pitcher Billy Chapel, whose glory days are long behind him. Learning he's about to be traded, Chapel decides to end his checkered career on a high note by pitching a no-hitter.

4. ***If I Never Get Back*** by Darryl Brock, 1992 – In this clever and immensely charming sports fantasy, a contemporary sportswriter gets transported back in time to 1869, where he becomes a member of the fledgling Cincinnati Red Stockings baseball team and rubs elbows with Mark Twain.

5. ***The Iowa Baseball Confederacy*** by W. P. Kinsella, 1986 – More magical realism on the baseball diamond from Kinsella. In this time-traveling fantasy, an albino inherits his late father's obsession with proving that the Chicago Cubs played a 3,000-inning game against the Iowa Baseball Confederacy in 1908.

6. ***The Natural*** by Bernard Malamud, 1952 – Unlike the sentimental film version starring Robert Redford, Malamud's debut novel paints a far darker and much more intriguing portrait of a former baseball prodigy making a comeback with his trusty bat, "Wonderboy."

7. ***Shoeless Joe*** by W.P. Kinsella, 1982 – Blending the supernatural, baseball, and redemption story to compelling effect, Kinsella's *Shoeless Joe* has been known to make grown men cry.

excerpt: SHOELESS JOE:

As I look around the empty park, almost Greek in its starkness, I feel an awesome inarticulate love for this very stadium and the game it represents. I am reminded of the story about the baseball fans of Milwaukee, and what they did on a warm fall afternoon, the day after it was announced that Milwaukee was to have a major-league team the next season. According to the story, 10,000 people went to County Stadium that afternoon and sat in the seats and smiled out at the empty playing field—sat in silence, in awe, in wonder, in anticipation, in joy—just knowing that soon the field would come alive with the chatter of infielders, bright as bird chirps.

8. ***You Know Me Al*** by Ring Lardner, 1916 – Swollen with pride and self-pity, bush league pitcher Jack Keefe fires off a series of hare-brained yet endearing letters to a friend in this colorful, laugh-out-loud funny book from the great sportswriter/humorist.

Beat Generation

Kerouac & Company

Never a fan of "the beats," Truman Capote famously dismissed Jack Kerouac's signature work, *On the Road*, with the nasty quip, "That's not writing. That's typing." Supposedly written in three weeks flat on one long scroll of teletype paper, *On the Road* may have left Capote cold—and he wasn't the only literati to pan it—but Kerouac's "spontaneous prose" resonated strongly for legions of readers worldwide. The bebop jazz-inflected rhythms and loose, stream-of-consciousness structure of *On the Road* struck people rebelling against the rigid status quo in cold war-era America. They were the "beat generation," as Kerouac described them: weary of the routine and hungry to express themselves freely, both personally and artistically.

Along with William Burroughs and Allen Ginsberg, Jack Kerouac is revered as the patron saint of the "beats"—and *On the Road* is their bible. Here is sampling of books by and about the "beat generation," listed alphabetically.

1. ***The Dharma Bums*** by Jack Kerouac, 1958 – Disillusioned with the soullessness of everyday life in America, two young men hike the Sierras on a Zen-inspired quest for dharma, or truth.

excerpt: THE DHARMA BUMS:
Meanwhile scores of people stood around in the darkened gallery straining to hear every word of the amazing poetry reading as I wandered from group to group, facing them and facing away from the stage, urging them to glug a slug from the jug, or wandered back and sat on the right side of the stage giving out little wows and yesses of approval and even whole sentences of comment with nobody's invitation but in the general gaiety nobody's disapproval either. It was a great night. Delicate Francis DaPavia read, from delicate onion-skin yellow pages, or pink, which he kept flipping carefully with long white ringers, the poems of his dead chum Altman who'd eaten too much peyote in Chihuahua...

2. ***Gasoline*** by Gregory Corso, 1958 – A poetry collection overflowing with rich, sensual imagery and provocative themes.

3. ***Go: A Novel*** by John Clellon Holmes, 1952 – The first "beat generation" novel depicts the boozy, drug, and sex-fueled origins of the movement in post-World War II New York City.

4. ***Howl and Other Poems*** by Alan Ginsberg, 1956 – The seminal collection of beat poetry by Ginsberg, who cited Walt Whitman and English poet/artist William Blake as major influences.

5. ***Junky*** by William Burroughs, 1953 – Frank, no-holds-barred autobiographical novel based on Burroughs' own experiences as a heroin addict/dealer in post-World War II Greenwich Village.

6. ***Minor Characters: A Beat Memoir*** by Joyce Johnson, 1983 – Johnson's fascinating memoir of her relationship with Kerouac in the 1950s won the National Book Critics Circle Award for nonfiction.

7. ***Naked Lunch*** by William Burroughs, 1959 – Surreal, unsettling, and perversely witty, Burroughs' novel depicts a heroin addict's descent into a bizarre netherworld called the "Interzone."

8. ***On the Road*** by Jack Kerouac, 1957 – And the beat goes on for Kerouac's "spontaneous prose" classic about two friends thumbing their noses at conformity to savor freedom as they travel cross-country.

Big Stuff

Books About ENORMOUS Things

As mind-blowing as tiny things can be, there's plenty out there to blow the mind at the other end of the scale. Here are some entertaining and informative books, listed alphabetically, about products of nature and culture that inspire awe by their sheer enormousness. For a well-balanced mind, read them in tandem with the books listed in the entry, "Tiny Things."

1. ***Blue Whales*** by John Calambokidis and Gretchen Steiger, 1997 – Learn all about the biggest animals on earth. How did these air-breathing mammals end up living underwater? What do they eat to grow so much? How do they communicate? The book gives answers to all these questions and provides magnificent photographs as well.

2. ***Dinosaurus: The Complete Guide to Dinosaurs*** by Steve Parker, 2003 – It may seem hard to believe that such formidable creatures ever ex-

isted, but the illustrations in this book help you imagine them and their world with full-color vividness. The great predators, the duck-bills, the giants, and many other categories of dinosaurs come to life in these pictures, and the author captures the grand adventure of paleontology.

3. ***Michelangelo and the Pope's Ceiling*** by Ross King, 2003 – Michelangelo Buonarroti loved to sculpt, not to paint. But, genius that he was, when he was conscripted to decorate the Sistine Chapel he rose to the challenge. His soaring frescoes are now among the immortal masterpieces of art. This book recounts the political wrangling behind the accomplishment.

4. ***Skyscrapers: A History of the World's Most Famous and Important Skyscrapers*** by Judith Dupré, 1996 – Ogle some of mankind's most astonishing feats of architecture and engineering, from the Eiffel Tower to the Empire State Building to the Petronas Towers in Malaysia. To do justice to the amazing, black-and-white photographs of skyscrapers, this book is an unusual rectangular shape, a foot and a half high. Produced before the destruction of the World Trade Center, it includes the twin towers among its marvels. You won't want to neglect the text, which is also eye-opening.

5. ***The Stars of Heaven*** by Clifford Pickover, 2001 – All the life on our planet depends on the most familiar star, the sun, for the light and heat it generates. This book uses some amusing science fiction to help us make sense of the real-world—er, real-universe—phenomena which are even more amazing than science fiction, from our old dependable sun to black holes and supergiants.

Bird Lovers' Books

All About Our Feathered Friends

From the young woman who becomes a nightingale in the Greek legend of Philomela to Wallace Stevens' "Thirteen Ways of Looking at a Blackbird," birds have always been a theme for writers and storytellers. Yes, the dog may always be man's best friend. But various kinds of birds have charming and even awe-inspiring attributes—the gift of song, exquisite plumage, the ability to fly, intelligence, and devotion to family. Here is an eclectic list of books about our feathered friends, listed alphabetically.

1. ***The Alex Studies: Cognitive and Communicative Abilities of Grey Parrots*** by Irene Maxine Pepperberg, 1999 – Just how intelligent are parrots? We all know they can mimic human speech, but can they understand what they are saying? This book details a university professor's research with Alex, the reasoning parrot.

2. ***Audubon's Birds of America: The Audubon Society Baby Elephant Folio*** by John James Audubon, edited by Roger Tory Peterson, revised edition, 2003 – Early in the nineteenth century, John James Audubon set out to document hundreds of kinds of American birds. This edition of his prints, introduced by the respected ornithologist and bird artist Roger Tory Peterson, is expensive but well worth the money for lovers of birds and Audubon's spectacular art.

3. ***The Beak of the Finch: A Story of Evolution in Our Time*** by Jonathan Weiner, 1994 – The finches of the Galápagos Islands were the catalysts for Charles Darwin's theory of evolution by natural selection. This book recounts how two present-day scientists spent over twenty years studying these birds and documenting the evolution still taking place from generation to generation.

4. ***The Grail Bird: Hot on the Trail of the Ivory-billed Woodpecker*** by Tim Gallagher, 2005 – The adventure of searching for—and finding—a magnificent bird long thought to be extinct. An exciting and heartening true story.

5. ***Jonathan Livingston Seagull*** by Richard Bach, 1970 – An allegory about a seagull who is discontented with the mundane life of the flock and devotes himself to the art of flight.

6. ***The Sibley Guide to Bird Life & Behavior*** by David Allen Sibley, 2001 – This book is not a field guide, but it offers a wealth of information about the behavior, anatomy, and evolution of the eighty families of North American birds. Illustrated with hundreds of full-color paintings as well as many diagrams and maps, it's great for reference or browsing.

7. ***The Singing Life of Birds*** by Donald Kroodsma, 2005 – We all know and love the sound of birdsong, but why do they sing? Are their

songs purely instinctive, or does each generation of birds learn them anew? The author explains the mysteries of one of nature's loveliest phenomena and helps readers hear the songs of many different birds with sensitivity and understanding. For an aural as well as a literary experience, listen to the compact disc that comes with the book.

8. ***The Wild Parrots of Telegraph Hill: A Love Story… with Wings*** by Mark Bittner, 2004 – The subject of a recent documentary, this is the real-life story of friendship between a man and a flock of birds. The author was a lost soul living in San Francisco when he met the conures that had escaped from captivity and bred in the wild. He writes movingly about their individual personalities, and how they transformed his life.

Boarding School Novels

Top of the Literary Class

From J.D. Salinger to J.K. Rowling, writers have long drawn inspiration from the academic rigor, social hierarchy, and petty tyrannies of boarding school. These three motifs recur throughout almost every novel about boarding school life, whether they're set in post-World War II America, like *The Catcher in the Rye,* or at the supernatural Hogwarts School of Witchcraft and Wizardry attended by Harry Potter.

Although most novels set at boarding schools are coming-of-age narratives depicting the agony and ecstasy of adolescence, there are exceptions—most notably, Evelyn Waugh's wickedly funny satire *Decline and Fall,* which depicts the travails of a penniless young aristocrat forced to teach at a boys' school in Wales. Regarded as one of Waugh's best books, *Decline and Fall* heads this alphabetical list of boarding school novels that rank at the top of the class.

1. ***Decline and Fall*** by Evelyn Waugh, 1928 – It all goes comically down hill for Paul Pennyfeather after he's caught without his knickers at Oxford. Humiliated, he takes a teaching job in Wales, where things only get crazier for him in Waugh's razor sharp comedy of errors.

2. ***A Good School*** by Richard Yates, 1978 – World War II casts a looming shadow over a group of students at a posh, New England boys' school, circa 1943, in Yates' impeccable novel.

3. ***Goodbye, Mr. Chips*** by James Hilton, 1934 – A sentimental favorite from the author of *Lost Horizon*. Devastated by the sudden death of his young wife, a mild-mannered English schoolteacher finds solace in the classroom, where his selfless devotion to his students makes him a beloved figure.

4. ***The Old School*** by Tobias Wolff, 2003 – The author of the classic memoir *This Boy's Life* won raves for this elegant novel about "book drunk boys" discovering the joys and sorrows of writing at a boarding school, circa 1960.

5. ***Prep: A Novel*** by Curtis Sittenfeld, 2005 –A Midwestern teenager attending a revered New England prep school confronts issues of class and race in Sittenfeld's celebrated debut novel, one of the *New York Times*' ten best books of 2005.

6. ***The Prime of Miss Jean Brodie*** by Muriel Spark, 1961 – An eccentric, charismatic teacher at a girls' school in 1930s-era Edinburgh falls victim to her own recklessness in Spark's jewel of a novel, later adapted for the stage and screen.

7. ***The River King*** by Alice Hoffman, 2000 – A quirky, graceful mixture of mystery and magical realism about a Connecticut boarding school literally haunted by the past.

excerpt: THE RIVER KING:
A dozen years after the Haddan School was built, a public high school was erected in the neighboring town of Hamilton, which meant a five-mile trek to classes on days when the snow was knee-deep and the weather so cold even the badgers kept to their dens. Each time a Haddan boy walked through a storm to the public school his animosity toward the Haddan School grew, a small bump on the skin of ill will ready to rupture at the slightest contact. In this way a hard bitterness was forged, and the spiteful sentiment increased every year, until there might as well have been a fence dividing those who came from the school and the residents of the village.

8. ***A Separate Peace*** by John Knowles, 1959 – The loss of innocence has rarely been so sensitively portrayed as in Knowles' beautifully written story of a friendship marred by a tragic betrayal.

Broadway Books

Biographies/Memoirs of Theatrical Legends

They are giants of twentieth century American theater—the playwrights, composers, and choreographers of Broadway's "Golden Age," when theatergoers regularly clamored to see musicals penned by legendary tunesmiths Irving Berlin and Cole Porter—and serious dramas by such luminaries as Eugene O'Neill and Tennessee Williams. Although the luster of Broadway has faded somewhat in recent years, the glory days of "the great white way" come vibrantly alive in the following biographies and memoirs, listed alphabetically, that offer a veritable feast of revealing anecdotes and insights about Broadway icons, both on and offstage.

1. ***Cole Porter*** by William McBrien, 1998 – "Swellegant" biography of the most urbane and sophisticated of tunesmiths, who ran in high society's most glittering circles.

2. ***Dazzler: The Life and Times of Moss Hart*** by Stephen Bach, 2001 – Although Hart's widow, Kitty Carlisle, refused to cooperate, Bach has nonetheless written an engrossing and scrupulously researched biography of the multi-talented Hart, the 1930s-era Broadway "Golden Boy" playwright/director.

3. ***Elia Kazan: A Life*** by Elia Kazan, 1988 – Exceptionally frank autobiography from the Broadway/Hollywood icon, whose brilliant string of successes has been forever overshadowed by his decision to "name names" to the House Un-American Activities Committee during the "Red Scare."

4. ***Eugene O'Neill: Beyond Mourning and Tragedy*** by Stephen A. Black, 1999 – Taking a psychoanalytic approach to the Nobel Prize winning playwright, Black persuasively argues that O'Neill exorcised his family demons in such plays as *Long Day's Journey Into Night* and *A Moon for the Misbegotten*.

5. ***Jerome Robbins: His Life, His Theater, His Dance*** by Deborah Jowitt, 2004 – In stark contrast to his exuberant, joyous choreography, Robbins was reputed to be a sour, even hateful man widely despised in the theater and dance world. In this thorough and skillfully written biography, Jowitt reveals the vulnerability and insecurity beneath Robbins' temperamental façade.

6. ***The Kindness of Strangers: A Life of Tennessee Williams*** by Donald Spoto, 1985 – Respectful and intelligent biography of Williams, who tragically fell from critical and popular grace in the 1960s, when he plunged into alcohol and drug-fueled despair.

7. ***Stephen Sondhem: A Life*** by Meryle Secrest, 1998 – Written with Sondheim's full cooperation, Secrest's illuminating biography examines how the composer's troubled childhood informs some of his greatest scores.

8. ***Timebends*** by Arthur Miller, 1989 – An intelligent and nuanced memoir from the playwright of *Death of a Salesman* and *The Crucible.*

excerpt: TIMEBENDS:
There was also an adenoidal young assistant stage manager popping in and out whom Grosbard, incredibly, told me I should keep in mind to play Willy Loman in a few years. My estimate of Grosbard all but collapsed as, observing Dustin Hoffman's awkwardness and his big nose that never seemed to get unstuffed, I wondered how the poor fellow imagined himself a candidate for any kind of acting career. Grosbard, however, was looking not at Hoffman but at an actor, at a spirit, and this kind of naked skin-on-skin contact with essentials was what his production had in every role.

Business Books

Fortune *Magazine Recommendations*

In an article written by Jerry Useem for the March 21, 2005 issue, *Fortune* offered readers a list of "75 books that teach you everything you need to know about business" drawn up by the magazine's staffers. *Fortune* divided its seventy-five recommendations into sixteen categories—here are two of those categories, "Economics" and "Investing," with brief descriptions of the books, listed alphabetically.

Economics

1. ***Capitalism, Socialism, and Democracy*** by Joseph A. Schumpeter, 1942 – This book discusses the links between economics, politics, and social values, suggesting that they cannot be fully understood in isolation from one another. *Fortune* suggests skipping right to Chapter 7 ("The Process of Creative Destruction").

2. ***Everything for Sale: The Virtues and Limits of Markets*** by Robert Kuttner, 1996 – Kuttner outlines the dangers and pitfalls—both internationally and here in the United States—of blind faith in the benevolence of free markets.

3. ***The General Theory of Employment, Interest, and Money*** by John Maynard Keynes, 1936 – One of the most influential works on economics ever written, this book argues for measured government intervention to ward off violent booms and slumps. *Fortune* suggests that you focus on Chapter 12, "a timeless, witty, crystalline account of why financial markets confound and bewitch us."

4. ***Pop Internationalism*** by Paul Krugman, 1996 – "Pop internationalism" is the author's term for the conventional wisdom about international trade, which he believes has little to do with reality. A controversial approach to globalization that may inspire you to take the pundits' rhetoric with a heaping grain of salt.

5. ***The Wealth of Nations*** by Adam Smith, 1776 – In this pioneering work on the value of free markets, Smith lays out the fundamental assumptions of his vision of how economies function, offers clear, concrete examples to illustrate his arguments, and discusses what he sees as the proper role of government and taxation.

Investing

1. ***The Essays of Warren Buffett: Lessons for Corporate America*** compiled by Lawrence Cunningham, 1997 – Learn from one of the most successful investors of all time in this selection of Warren Buffett's annual letters to shareholders of Berkshire Hathaway. He shares principles learned from his teacher and mentor, Benjamin Graham, and from years of his own experience and decision-making.

2. ***Fooled by Randomness: The Hidden Role of Chance in the Markets and in Life*** by Nassim Nicholas Taleb, 2001 – Taleb is both a hedge fund manager and a professor of mathematics. His book is less an enumeration of strategies than a broad perspective on the nature of the stock market—and many other aspects of life in which dumb luck plays a bigger role than you might have thought.

3. ***The Intelligent Investor: A Book of Practical Counsel*** by Benjamin Graham, 1949 – The author is the teacher and mentor of Warren Buf-

fett. The fact that this book remains so well respected by successful investors over fifty years after Graham wrote it is a testament to the soundness of his concept of "value investment."

4. ***Moneyball: The Art of Winning an Unfair Game*** by Michael Lewis, 2003 – This is the story of Billy Beane, the general manager of the Oakland A's, and his success, based on creative thinking, hard study of statistics, and a willingness to stray from the proverbial beaten path.

Canadian Novels

Noteworthy Fiction from North of the Border

With the possible exception of Robertson Davies, no other Canadian novelist has attracted greater international renown than Margaret Atwood, who's regularly mentioned as a potential contender for the Nobel Prize. In the thirty-seven years since she published her first novel, *The Edible Woman*, Atwood has skillfully mined the emotional and psychological terrain of her characters in novels ranging from the dystopian cautionary tale *The Handmaid's Tale*, to the light-hearted and wryly funny *Lady Oracle*.

Shifting effortlessly from poetry to fiction to nonfiction, Atwood is arguably the greatest living writer in English-speaking Canada. That said, she is by no means the end and be-all of Canadian literature. Here are eight novels, listed alphabetically, from some of the leading literary lights of "The Great White North."

1. ***Alias Grace*** by Margaret Atwood, 1996 – Atwood's fictionalized portrait of a real-life, nineteenth century housemaid imprisoned for a grisly double murder is a fascinating inquiry into aberrant behavior. Was housemaid Grace Marks a cold-blooded psychopath or a brutalized innocent? That's just one of the tantalizing, open-ended questions raised in Atwood's superb novel.

2. ***The Colony of Unrequited Dreams*** by Wayne Johnston, 1998 – All but forgotten today, Newfoundland's first premier, Joseph Smallwood, is the protagonist of Johnston's colorful and boisterously entertaining historical novel about an ordinary man scaling the political ladder, albeit with great sacrifice.

excerpt: ***ALIAS GRACE:***
The reason they want to see me is that I am a celebrated murderess. Or that is what has been written down. When I first saw it I was surprised, because they say Celebrated Singer and Celebrated Poetess and Celebrated Spiritualist and Celebrated Actress, but what is there to celebrate about murder? All the same, Murderess is a strong word to have attached to you. It has a smell to it,that word - musky and oppressive, like dead flowers in a vase. Sometimes at night I whisper it over to myself: Murderess, Murderess. It rustles, like a taffeta skirt across the floor.

3. ***Deafening*** by Frances Itani, 2003 – Set in World War I, Itani's luminous debut novel depicts the compelling romance between Grania O'Neill, a deaf nurse, and Jim Lloyd, who's sent to the front right after they wed.

4. ***The Diviners*** by Margaret Laurence, 1974 – The fifth and final book set in Laurence's fictitious town of Manawaka, Manitoba portrays the efforts of Morag Gunn to connect with her estranged teenaged daughter. Living on a farmhouse on the Manitoba prairie, Morag tries to balance her need for solitude against the demands of family in Laurence's insightful, prize winning novel.

5. ***Fifth Business*** by Robertson Davies, 1970 – The first novel in Davies' Deptford Trilogy is a challenging and ingeniously imagined narrative, written in memoir form, about a retired college professor, whose entire life has been shaped by a childhood snowball fight in 1908. Steeped in myth and Jungian archetypes, *Fifth Business* portrays one man's lifelong quest for redemption with wit and originality.

6. ***Joshua Then and Now*** by Mordecai Richler, 1980 – Richler's raucously funny novel finds television writer Joshua Shapiro in the midst of a full-blown mid-life crisis, exacerbated by the disappearance of his wife and the unwanted attention of the press, due to a headline-grabbing sex scandal. As his world seemingly blows up around him, Shapiro reflects on his rough-and-tumble life, to see exactly where it all went wrong.

7. ***Rockbound*** by Frank Parker Day, 1928 – Day's beloved classic is a ripping good historical yarn about a young man's rise from poverty to wealth on Nova Scotia's Rockbound Island, where he gets sucked into the bitter feud between the island clans.

8. ***The Stone Diaries*** by Carol Shields, 1993 – Shields' warmth and compassion for her heroine informs every page of this beautiful and intensely moving fictionalized autobiography, which won the Pulitzer Prize. Her death imminent, elderly Daisy Goodwill Flet reflects on the happiness and heartbreak of her long life, which began inauspiciously in rural Manitoba, circa 1905.

Cartoon Collections

The Far Side of Funny

Turning to your favorite comic strip in the Sunday paper is a pleasant ritual, but when you're a really committed fan, sometimes you want a little more—or a lot more. Luckily, there are some fabulous cartoon collections out there. Whether your tastes run to the warm and poignant or to trenchant satire, you'll find something to tickle your funny bone in these cartoon collections, listed in no particular order.

1. ***The Prehistory of the Far Side: A 10th Anniversary Exhibit*** by Gary Larson, 1989 – This book lets us watch Larson's drawings become simpler and his jokes more honed as he developed the hallmark style of *The Far Side*. More than just a collection of previously published cartoons, we get the creator's commentary on everything from his obsession with cows (whether residing in barns, lifeboats, or suburban houses) to hilarious mix-ups in the funny pages (such as a pair of switched captions that made Dennis the Menace and a pal appear to be eating hamster sandwiches).

2. ***Mad Art: A Visual Celebration of the Art of Mad Magazine and the Idiots Who Create It*** by Mark Evanier, 2002 – The house style of *Mad* magazine illustration is vigorous, vulgar, and even creepy, yet it has a strange kitschy charm. This fiftieth-anniversary collection offers a huge dose of the magazine's peculiar brand of madness.

3. ***The Indispensable Calvin and Hobbes: A Calvin and Hobbes Treasury*** by Bill Watterson, 1992 – The intelligent, beloved cartoon about a little boy and his toy tiger depicts the joys and frustrations of childhood and the need for companionship in full-color and black-and-white drawings.

4. ***The World of Charles Addams*** by Charles Addams, 1991 – With his

dreadful situations and spooky wash drawings, Charles Addams defines black humor. The Addams family in its creaky Victorian house is here, along with some delightfully horrible surprises.

5. ***The Complete Cartoons of the New Yorker*** edited by Robert Mankoff, 2004 – Nearly as famous for its cartoons as for as its prose, the *New Yorker* magazine has published thousands upon thousands of them since the 1920s. This enormous book includes many of the best, from James Thurber to George Booth to Roz Chast, proving that a good laugh can defuse some of the anxieties of modern life. Even better, it comes with two CDs that let you view all the cartoons from the magazine's history on your computer.

6. ***Art Out of Time: Unknown Comics Visionaries 1900–1969*** by Dan Nadel, 2006 – Twenty-nine little-known creators of comics get their due here. If you're interested in the history of comics and stylistic experimentation, these artists will pique your interest and even change some of your ideas about the genre's march of progress.

Cat Lovers' Books

Purr-fect Fiction and Nonfiction

Cats are fascinating animals with many different sides to them—hilariously playful kittens, aloof loners, devoted companions, expert predators, lazy hedonists, skillful acrobats who get stuck in trees—they seem to have no end of contradictory qualities.

And they evoke all kinds of responses in humans—from worship (cats were considered sacred in ancient Egypt) to demonization (medieval Europeans believed Satan took the form of a black cat). In modern times we're not quite so extreme in our reactions, but there are still those who adore cats and those who find them too peculiar or standoffish. If you fall into the former group, you're sure to love these books, listed alphabetically, that explore and celebrate the many aspects of this elegant creature. If you're decidedly not a cat person, be aware that conversions have happened before—and sometimes a good story is the "catalyst."

1. ***250 Things You Can Do to Make Your Cat Adore You*** by Ingrid Newkirk, 1998 – The author, one of the founders of People for the Ethical Treatment of Animals, offers practical advice on how to make

your home more cat-friendly, natural remedies for your cat, and the finer points of feline communication.

2. ***Asleep in the Sun*** by Hans Silvester, 1997 – Napping is an important part of every cat's life. This book is filled with exquisite photographs of what appear to be some of the most idyllic catnaps on earth, in the Greek Cycladic Islands.

3. ***The Cat Who... Series*** by Lilian Jackson Braun – Here's a fictional journalist-and-cat saga that mystery lovers will enjoy. Beginning with *The Cat Who Could Read Backwards* (1966), Braun's series of mysteries follows reporter Jim Qwilleran in his hunts for truth, aided by his Siamese companions Yum Yum and, in later books, Koko.

4. ***The Cat Who Covered the World: The Adventures Of Henrietta and Her Foreign Correspondent*** by Christopher S. Wren, 2000 – This is the true story of a cosmopolitan tabby named Henrietta who accompanied her owners—a foreign correspondent and his family—to Russia, China, South Africa, Egypt, and other distant lands. She brought the author a certain amount of trouble along the way but also humor and much-needed comfort.

5. ***The Cat Who Went to Paris*** by Peter Gethers, 1991 – Before he met Norton, a Scottish Fold cat, the author was a cat-hater. But this alert and refined creature ended up changing his life for the better. Gethers published two more books about Norton—*A Cat Abroad* (1993), and *The Cat Who'll Live Forever* (2001).

6. ***The Character of Cats: The Origins, Intelligence, Behavior, and Stratagems of Felis silvestris catus*** by Stephen Budiansky, 2002 – A rigorous but entertaining survey of the domestic cat and our relationship with it. From feline evolution to our superstitions about cats, you'll learn the fascinating history and science of these animals. Cat owners are likely to punctuate their reading with exclamations of "So that's why they do that!"

7. ***James Herriot's Cat Stories*** by James Herriot, 1994 – Herriot was a dedicated veterinarian and a wonderful storyteller. Here is a delightful collection of his encounters with cats in rural Yorkshire: Alfred, the cat who keeps watch over the counter of his owner's candy shop; Moses, a half-frozen kitten who takes up the life of a piglet; Oscar the socialite; and several other furry patients and friends.

8. ***The Mammoth Book of Cats: A Collection of Stories, Prose and Verse*** edited by Mark Bryant, 1999 – Over the centuries, cats have inspired a great deal of fiction, poetry, and wit. *The Mammoth Book of Cats* offers hundreds of pages of this literature, created by everyone from the anonymous inventors of nursery rhymes to Ralph Waldo Emerson. It's organized by theme; chapters include "The Fireside Sphinx," "Catlings and Kittens," and "Demonic Cats."

Chick Lit

Looking for Mr. Right—or Mr. Right Now

Need a break from the search for Prince Charming—or Mr. Right Now? Then kick off those stilettos, fix yourself a big, fat martini, and curl up with one of these books before heading back into the dating trenches. It's time for a little vicarious *Sex and the Single Girl,* to quote the how-to book written by *Cosmopolitan* editor Helen Gurley Brown, way back in the early 1960s, before the sexual revolution made it okay for "nice girls" to take the occasional walk on the wild side.

Running the gamut from contemporary classics to juicy page-turners, the following books, listed alphabetically, open a window on the world of the single girl in the big city, where these heroines cross paths with sexy cads, jet-setting zillionaires, and the random decent guy.

1. ***Bergdorf Blondes*** by Plum Sykes, 2004 – London-born socialite/fashionista Sykes gives a breezy tour of the designer-clad, Botoxed, and back-stabbing world of Park Avenue heiresses, whose lives center around shopping, men, and still more shopping.

2. ***The Best of Everything*** by Rona Jaffe, 1958 – Incredibly chaste by today's standards, Jaffe's well-crafted page-turner raised eyebrows in the 1950s. Friends and co-workers in a swank New York publishing company, Jaffe's heroines navigate the tricky shoals of romance and career, not altogether successfully.

3. ***Breakfast at Tiffany's*** by Truman Capote, 1958 – Has there ever been a more captivating heroine than Holly Golightly? Capote's beloved free spirit, immortalized on film by Audrey Hepburn, wafts her way through the pages of Capote's novella, looking for a rich husband and setting hearts aflutter—including the reader's.

4. ***Bridget Jones' Diary*** by Helen Fielding, 1996 – A lovable overweight bundle of neuroses, Fielding's zaftig heroine muddles her way through life and love in this pricelessly funny novel, written in diary form, that pays sexy homage to Jane Austen.

5. ***Fear of Flying*** by Erica Jong, 1973 – A 1970s-era pop culture phenomenon, Jong's funny and unabashedly raunchy novel tracks the sexual misadventures of Isadora Wing, an erotic poet who prizes her freedom above all else—including her marriage. Praised by the *Wall Street Journal* as a "latter-day *Ulysses*," *Fear of Flying* spawned two sequels, *How to Save Your Own Life* and *Parachutes & Kisses*.

6. ***The Girls' Guide to Hunting and Fishing*** by Melissa Bank, 1999 – A critical and popular hit, Bank's short story collection is an intelligent and wryly funny alternative to the "chick lit" dreck littering bookstore shelves.

7. ***Lipstick Jungle*** by Candace Bushnell, 2005 – The *Sex and the City* novelist has become the sexy "chick lit" equivalent of a brand name. With *Lipstick Jungle,* Bushnell serves up "more of the same" in this nonetheless satisfying book about three high-flying Manhattan socialites running amok in their Manolo Blahniks.

excerpt: *LIPSTICK JUNGLE:*

"How ya doin, pretty lady?" Kirby asked casually, as if it were perfectly normal for an older woman to come to his apartment in the middle of the afternoon for sex. Nico suddenly felt shy. How was she supposed to behave? How did Kirby expect her to behave? How did he see her—and them? Having no other reference points by which to categorize the situation, she hoped he envisioned them as Richard Gere and Lauren Hutton in American Gigolo. Maybe if she pretended to be Lauren Hutton, she'd be able to get through this scene.

And what was up with that phrase, "pretty lady"?

8. ***Valley of the Dolls*** by Jacqueline Susann, 1966 – *The* bestselling novel of the 1960s, Susann's randy roman a clef is a glossy page-turner about three beautiful young women caught up in the nasty, cutthroat world of showbiz, where "dolls," i.e., sleeping pills, provide irresistible escape from feckless men and predatory divas.

Children's Books

America' Best, 1776-1976

Thirty years ago, the librarians, teachers, authors and publishers who comprise the Children's Literature Association celebrated America's 200th birthday by ranking the eleven best American children's books in the nation's history. Their picks will instantly warm the heart of many a bookworm baby boomer, who read—and reread—some of these perennial favorites in the low-tech days before gaming and instant text messaging.

Although the list rounds up many of the usual literary suspects, the presence of Mark Twain's *The Adventures of Huckleberry Finn* may strike some as odd, given its more recent history, or notoriety, as the American Library Association's fifth most "challenged" book, 1990-2000. That the Children's Literature Association suggests Twain's novel for readers ages ten and up is equally bewildering, since it's doubtful many ten year-olds could fully grasp why Twain uses a certain racial epithet so liberally throughout the text. That said, here are the association's eleven picks, per their Bicentennial era ranking.

1. ***Charlotte's Web*** by E.B. White, 1952 – White's classic barnyard parable has prompted tears from generations of young readers, and quite a few adults, with its heartwarming story of a friendship between the piglet Wilbur and Charlotte, the spider who saves his life. Suggested for all ages.

excerpt: CHARLOTTE'S WEB:
The children ran out to the road and climbed into the bus. Fern took no notice of the others in the bus. She just sat and stared out of the window, thinking what a blissful world it was and how lucky she was to have entire charge of a pig. By the time the bus reached school, Fern had named her pet, selecting the most beautiful name she could think of.
"Its name is Wilbur," she whispered to herself.

2. ***Where the Wild Things Are*** by Maurice Sendak, 1963 – Going to bed without supper turns into the adventure of a lifetime for young Max, who embarks on a fantastic journey to the land of the Wild Things, right in his own bedroom. Sendak's beloved picture book has since been adapted into a ballet and an opera. Suggested for ages four to eight.

3. ***The Adventures of Tom Sawyer*** by Mark Twain, 1876 – Ranked 84th on the ALA's list of most "challenged" books, 1990-2000, Twain's self-described "hymn to boyhood" is a marvelous, picaresque yarn bursting with jaunty good humor and adventure. Suggested for ages ten and up.

4. ***Little Women*** by Louisa May Alcott, 1868 – Alcott's tomboy alter ego, Josephine "Jo" March, remains one of the most appealing heroines in all literature. Whether writing plays or striking out on her own, Jo supplies the passionate heart to Alcott's enthralling saga of the four March sisters in Civil War-era New England. Suggested for ages ten and up.

5. ***The Adventures of Huckleberry Finn*** by Mark Twain, 1885 – Twain's account of the title character's raft journey down the Mississippi River with a runaway slave is a magnificent, multi-layered achievement. Through their encounters with unsavory and colorful characters, all white, Huck comes to regard his companion Jim as the one honorable and trustworthy man he knows. Suggested for ages ten and up, but high schoolers will probably get more out of it.

6. ***Little House in the Big Woods*** by Laura Ingalls Wilder, 1932 – The first book in Wilder's classic Little House series, *Little House in the Big Woods* introduces the spunky, tomboy heroine Laura "Half Pint" Wilder, whose close-knit family endures freezing cold, panther attacks, and marauding bears over the course of a year in the forests of Wisconsin. Suggested for ages six to ten.

7. ***Johnny Tremain*** by Esther Forbes, 1943 – The Revolutionary War provides the dramatic setting for Forbes' stirring and thoughtful novel about a gravely injured apprentice silversmith playing a vital role in the fight against the British in Boston. Suggested for ages ten and up.

8. ***The Wonderful Wizard of Oz*** by L. Frank Baum, 1900 – Join Dorothy Gale and her little dog too, as a Kansas twister whisks them away to the yellow-brick paved land of Oz in Baum's landmark fantasy. Suggested for ages six to ten.

9. ***Little House on the Prairie*** by Laura Ingalls Wilder, 1935 – The best known (and some say the best) of Wilder's Little House books, *Little House on the Prairie* depicts the family's arduous, covered wagon jour-

ney from Wisconsin to the wide open prairies of Kansas. Suggested for ages six to ten.

10. ***Island of the Blue Dolphins*** by Scott O'Dell, 1960 – Based on a true story, O'Dell's powerful novel tells the incredible story of Karana, a Native American girl, who survives alone on an island for nearly twenty years. Suggested for ages twelve and up.

11. ***Julie of the Wolves*** by Jean Craighead George, 1972 – A Newberry Medal winner, George's exciting survival story follows the title character, an orphaned Eskimo girl, as she gets hopelessly lost in the frozen Alaskan tundra. Fortunatcly, a wolf pack accepts her into their fold. Suggested for ages twelve and up.

Children's Books

Beautiful Picture Books

Never underrate the artistic power of a children's book—or the ability of a child to appreciate it! Just because they're young doesn't mean they don't have sensibility. On the contrary, there is an element of childlike wonder in grown-ups' love of grown-up art. This alphabetical list offers some of the loveliest books for children—guaranteed to send both the little ones and the adults into a waking dreamland.

1. ***The Maggie B.*** by Irene Haas, 1975 – For children who love the sea, it's easy to get lost in the rich watercolors of this book. Maggie's wish to sail for a day "with someone nice for company" (who turns out to be her little brother James) is granted—a cheerful and ultra-cozy adventure.

2. ***Outside Over There*** by Maurice Sendak, 1981 – Sendak's masterpiece *Where the Wild Things Are* (1963) is perhaps the perfect children's book, but his other works are well worth looking at and sharing with youngsters. This one is illustrated in a more realistic (though haunting and dreamy) style. It shows young Ida's brave efforts to rescue a baby sibling who has been stolen by goblins.

3. ***The Polar Express*** by Chris Van Allsburg, 1985 – Putting a twist on the legend of Santa Claus, this captivating book sends a little boy to the North Pole on a train that stops in front of his house on Christmas Eve. The illustrations are sumptuous and sweet.

4. ***The Rainbow Goblins*** by Ul De Rico, 1978 – Vivid oil paintings depict the lush primeval landscape where a band of goblins stalk and lasso rainbows in order to drink their colors. One of the most imaginative and beautiful children's books in existence!

5. ***The Runaway Bunny*** by Margaret Wise Brown, illustrated by Clement Hurd, 1942 – A lovely and comforting book for the very young by the author and the illustrator of another classic, *Goodnight Moon*. A little rabbit envisions running away, but in every scenario his mother appears—in the form of a gust of wind, a tree, or some other disguise—to take care of him. The pictures are surreal and gently colorful.

6. ***The Story of Ferdinand*** by Munro Leaf, illustrated by Robert Lawson, 1936 – Ferdinand is a peaceable Spanish bull who loves to rest and smell the flowers, but when he sits down on a bee one day he earns a reputation for ferocity that lands him in the bullring. The illustrations are in sharp black-and-white, earthy and elegant at the same time.

7. ***A Tale of Fairyland (the Princess Nobody)*** written by Andrew Lang, illustrated by Richard Doyle, 1884 – One of the most charming products of the Victorian imagination is this book of troubled royalty and exquisite fairies. The story is engaging, but even more so are the ethereal illustrations, which actually predate the tale of Princess Niente and her suitor, Prince Comic.

8. ***The Tale of Peter Rabbit*** by Beatrix Potter, 1902 – This book about a disobedient little rabbit, like the rest of Potter's books about animals, is extremely charming. For all the grace of the watercolor illustrations, and for all the civilized and humanlike qualities of the protagonists of her books—be they rabbits, hedgehogs, or frogs—Potter's characters remain delightfully animal.

Civil War Nonfiction

True Stories of the Blue and the Gray

Approached by Random House editor Bennett Cerf to write a short, one-volume history of the Civil War, Shelby Foote initially agreed to produce a 200,000-word manuscript. Twenty years later, when the Mississippi-born novelist finally completed his landmark, three-volume history in 1974, *The*

Civil War: A Narrative numbered 1,650,000 words and ran to 3,000 pages. Yet despite glowing reviews, Foote's masterpiece didn't catch on with the general public until 1990, when the courtly Southerner became a surprise television star, thanks to his appearance in Ken Burns' eleven-hour, PBS documentary about the Civil War.

Named the fifteenth best nonfiction book of the twentieth century by Modern Library, Foote's *The Civil War: A Narrative* joins Ulysses S. Grant's memoirs on this alphabetical list of eight nonfiction books about the war between the states.

1. ***April 1965: The Month That Saved America*** by Jay Winik, 2001 – Winik's panoramic and briskly paced look at the last month of the war from a variety of perspectives was praised by *Publishers Weekly* as "popular history at its best."

2. ***Battle Cry of Freedom: The Civil War Era*** by James T. McPherson, 1988 – McPherson's Pulitzer Prize winner is, hands-down, the best, one-volume history of the Civil War.

3. ***Bruce Catton's Civil War*** by Bruce Catton, 1984 – A compendium of three books – *Mr. Lincoln's Army, Glory Road,* and the Pulitzer Prize winning *A Stillness at Appomattox* – from one of America's most revered Civil War historians.

4. ***Chancellorsville*** by Stephen W. Sears, 1996 – Was Lee's victory at Chancellorsville due to his military strategy or just plain luck? That's the provocative question Sears considers in his skillfully written and researched account of this pivotal battle.

5. ***The Civil War: A Narrative*** by Shelby Foote, 1958-1974 – If you read only one book about the Civil War, go with Foote's masterpiece, written with novelistic flair.

6. ***The Negro's Civil War: How American Blacks Felt and Acted During the War for the Union*** by James T. McPherson, 1965 – A necessary and eye-opening book, vigorously written, that smashes racist preconceptions about African-Americans during the Civil War.

7. ***Personal Memoirs of Ulysses S. Grant,*** 1885 – Completed one week prior to his death from throat cancer, Grant's two-volume memoir was hailed by no less than Mark Twain as "the most remarkable work of its kind since the *Commentaries of Julius Caesar.*"

excerpt: ***PERSONAL MEMOIRS OF ULYSSES S. GRANT:***
I always admired the South, as bad as I thought their cause, for the boldness with which they silenced all opposition and all croaking, by press or by individuals, within their control. War at all times, whether a civil war between sections of a common country or between nations, ought to be avoided, if possible with honor. But, once entered into, it is too much for human nature to tolerate an enemy within their ranks to give aid and comfort to the armies of the opposing section or nation.

8. ***Robert E. Lee: A Biography*** by Emory M. Thomas, 1995 – Both lionized and demonized in other biographies, Lee emerges as an admirable, life-sized figure with his share of foibles in this terrific biography.

Civil War Novels

"Look Away, Dixie Land"

Every year, the bloodied but unbowed South rises phoenix-like from the ashes of the Confederacy—at least in the pages of Civil War-era novels, which continue to captivate readers on both sides of the Mason-Dixon Line. In 2005 alone, three novels— Geraldine Brooks' *March,* E.L. Doctorow's *The March,* and Robert Hicks' *The Widow of the South*—made the best-seller list and earned near-universal praise from critics.

The War of Northern Aggression, as die-hard Rebels call it, has provided the sweeping backdrop for the following novels, listed alphabetically, which run the literary gamut from passionate romance to graphically authentic recreations of the battles that tore the country apart.

1. ***Andersonville*** by Mackinlay Kantor, 1955 – Real and fictitious characters intermingle in Kantor's absorbing, Pulitzer Prize winning novel, set in the notorious Confederate prisoner-of-war camp in southwest Georgia. A longtime Civil War buff, Kantor drew extensively upon prisoners' memoirs to depict the inhumane conditions at the prison, overseen by the ineffectual Confederate general John Winder.

2. ***Cold Mountain*** by Charles Frazier, 1997 – For his first novel, North Carolina native Frazier looked to the wartime experiences of his great-great-uncle, a Confederate soldier, for inspiration. The astonishing result is a gripping narrative that transposes Homer's *The Odyssey* to the

Blue Ridge Mountains, which the hero Inman must cross to reunite with the beautiful Ada. A critical and commercial blockbuster, *Cold Mountain* won the rookie author the 1997 National Book Award.

3. ***Enemy Women*** by Paulette Jiles, 2002 – Wrongfully accused of being an "enemy collaborator" by Union soldiers, an eighteen year-old girl from the Missouri Ozarks escapes from prison to embark on a long, dangerous journey home. Favorably compared to *Cold Mountain, Enemy Women* is the auspicious first novel by Jiles, a Missouri-born poet.

4. ***The Killer Angels*** by Michael Shaara, 1974 – A monumental achievement, Shaara's Pulitzer Prize winning novel tells the story of the decisive Battle of Gettysburg from the points of view of the Union and Confederate commanding officers. Stirringly written and historically authentic, *The Killer Angels* inspired filmmaker Ken Burns to make his brilliant documentary, *The Civil War.*

5. ***March*** by Geraldine Brooks, 2005 – A peripheral figure in Louisa May Alcott's *Little Women,* Mr. March takes center stage in Brooks' Pulitzer Prize winning novel, which depicts his life-changing experiences as a Union Army chaplain. What might have been just a clever literary conceit in a lesser writer's hands becomes an enthralling and emotionally potent work of literature from the author of *The Year of Wonders.*

6. ***The March*** by E.L. Doctorow, 2005 – While he reportedly chafes at being labeled a "historical novelist," Doctorow remains best known for *Ragtime,* his brilliant, kaleidoscopic evocation of turn-of-the century America. In *The March,* Doctorow spins a richly detailed literary tapestry about General Sherman's epic march from Atlanta to the Carolinas in the waning days of the Civil War.

excerpt: THE MARCH:

Several prisoners were brought forward. They were given picks and spades and commanded to march in close order down the road. You will find every mine planted there, Sherman said, or be blown up in the process. Jesus! General, have mercy, one of them said, it wasn't us did this. Forward march! Sherman said, and gave the man a kick. He then raised his arms and pushed the air to indicate that everyone was to move back.

Whimpering and trembling with fear, the prisoners after a few stumbling steps abandoned their tools, dropped to their knees, and with their fingers began to search for the land mines. They crawled forward, feeling with their outstretched hands like blind men.

7. ***The Red Badge of Courage*** by Stephen Crane, 1895 – An idealistic Union recruit confronts the hellish reality of war in Crane's iconic Civil War novel, first published in serial form. Drawing heavily upon the real-life experiences of Civil War veterans, Crane evokes the psychological and physical torment of battle with stunning authenticity.

8. ***The Widow of the South*** by Robert Hicks, 2005 – In his ambitious first novel, Hicks turns to a real-life Confederate heroine for inspiration: Carrie McGavock, who turned her Tennessee home into a makeshift hospital/cemetery for the casualties of the 1864 Battle of Franklin. Although some critics faulted Hicks for emphasizing research to the detriment of narrative momentum, most hailed *The Widow of the South* as a sweeping, action-packed yarn.

Coming-of-Age Novels

Innocence Lost

What we know as the coming-of-age novel is technically a bildungsroman, or "novel of formation," in literal translation from German. Typically, the hero or heroine undergoes an emotional, intellectual, and/or spiritual awakening over the course of the narrative that's often bittersweet in tone, even when their stories end on a happy note. Their hard-won epiphanies can strike a deeply personal chord for readers, who often reread their favorite coming-of-age novels over and over again.

Most reading lists of essential coming-of-age novels invariably include J.D. Salinger's *The Catcher in the Rye*, Harper Lee's *To Kill a Mockingbird*, and Mark Twain's *The Adventures of Huckleberry Finn*. Rather than go the usual route, this alphabetical list of coming-of-age novels departs from the standard recommendations to focus on worthwhile, contemporary entries in the genre.

1. ***Annie John*** by Jamaica Kincaid, 1985 – Kincaid's slender but emotionally rich novel is set in her native Antigua, where a young girl's idyllic childhood ends with the onset of a unusually painful adolescence.

2. ***Bastard Out of Carolina*** by Dorothy Allison, 1992 – Allison's searing debut novel, a National Book Award finalist, is the loosely autobiographical story of Ruth Anne "Bone" Boatwright, the dirt-poor, illegitimate daughter of a waitress in rural South Carolina. When her

mother marries a local man, "Bone's" initial joy turns to despair after her alcoholic stepfather begins sexually abusing her.

3. ***The Buddha of Suburbia*** by Hanif Kureishi, 1990 – Languishing in the suburbs of 1970s-era London, a bisexual Anglo-Indian teenager escapes to the city, where he throws himself headlong into sex, drugs, and rock and roll. An acerbic, lively satirical novel from the screenwriter of *My Beautiful Laundrette*.

4. ***The Fortress of Solitude*** by Jonathan Lethem, 2003 – The author of *Motherless Brooklyn* returns to the New York borough with this wonderfully evocative, decades-spanning portrait of two men, black and white, who meet as teenagers and bond over their shared love of music and comic books.

5. ***GraceLand*** by Chris Abani, 2004 – Intense, stunningly rendered first novel about a Nigerian boy desperate to escape the nightmarish squalor of a Lagos ghetto, where he lives with his stern taskmaster of a father.

6. ***Jim the Boy: A Novel*** by Tony Earley, 2000 – A simple, unaffected and deeply moving story of a ten year-old boy growing up in fatherless in Depression-era North Carolina.

7. ***The Miracle Life of Edgar Mint*** by Brady Udall, 2001 – "If I could tell you only one thing about my life it would be this: when I was seven years old the mailman ran over my head." Thus begins Udall's Dickensian story of Mint, the half-white, half-Apache hero, who later embarks on a mission to find and forgive the mailman who inadvertently changed Mint's life forever.

8. ***The Perks of Being a Wallflower*** by Stephen Chbosky, 1999 – Frequently banned, due to its frank portrayal of teenaged homosexuality and drug use, Chbosky's novel about an introverted teenager finding his voice has become a favorite of many teens, who feel a deep affinity for the misfit hero.

Community Life in Fiction

It Takes a Village

They say it takes a village to raise a child—and, let's not forget, it takes all kinds to make a village. Here are five books, listed alphabetically, that

weave tapestries of characters, showing how our individual lives are shaped by the collective life of the places where we live.

1. *Cannery Row* by John Steinbeck, 1945 – This novel describes the lives of various men and women living in a poor neighborhood in Monterey, California. Their attempts to live and find joy in their unconventional lifestyles—canning sardines, shopping at Lee Chong's grocery, and throwing parties—are touching and sad.

2. *Drop City* by T.C. Boyle, 2003 – A National Book Award finalist, Boyle's ninth novel depicts the ill-fated attempt by a group of California hippies, circa 1970, to establish a commune in the Alaskan interior, where they receive a chilly welcome from locals. The *New York Times Book Review* hailed *Drop City* as "one of the funniest, and at the same time, most subtle, novels we've had about the hippie era's slow fade to black."

excerpt: ***DROP CITY:***
It was a bus. A school bus. And Norm, sleepless Norm, fueled on amphetamine and black coffee, was at the wheel, the suede cowboy hat pulled down to the level of the black broken frames of his glasses and Premstar perched in his lap like a ventriloquist's dummy. The gears ground with a shriek, the massive face of the thing swung into the yard and beat the mud into submission and the rain sculpted the two long streaming banks of windows in a smooth wrap. There was the wheeze of the air brakes, a heavy dependable sloshing, and then the bus was idling there before them, as if all they had to do was pick up their schoolbags and lunchboxes and climb aboard.

3. ***Dubliners*** by James Joyce, 1914 – The residents of Dublin are the subjects of this classic collection of short stories. Joyce uses his uncanny ability to get into the heads of all kinds of people and describe the incidents, whether tiny or stunning, that define and reveal their lives.

4. ***Main Street*** by Sinclair Lewis, 1920 – A lovely, idealistic young woman marries a doctor who lives in a small, Minnesota town, which she hopes to transform into a haven for high culture. Her neighbors refuse to cooperate, however, in this satirical gem from the author of *Elmer Gantry*.

5. ***Midaq Alley*** by Naguib Mahfouz, 1947 – The alley is a street in a poor section of Cairo; its inhabitants struggle to find contentment despite difficult circumstances and their own weaknesses and passions. You

will meet Radwan Hussainy, a respected wise man who is gentle and philosophical in his dealings with his neighbors but tyrannizes his wife; Zaita, a sadist who helps beggars improve their prospects by crippling them; and Hamida, an ambitious and beautiful girl who is seduced into prostitution.

Couples Who Write

Dynamic Duos of Literature

Romantic passion is one of the great driving forces of literature. When both partners are gifted writers, their intensity and eloquence only seem to grow, even if love isn't their subject matter. Brief affairs between writers are innumerable, of course, but here are some couples of longer standing, listed in chronological order, who have made great contributions to literary culture. Their relationships ranged from idyllic to tortured and everything in between, but all were highly productive. Note that the tradition of writers marrying continues among today's young writers, such as Nicole Krauss (*The History of Love,* 2005) and Jonathan Safran Foer (*Everything Is Illuminated,* 2002).

1. **Percy Bysshe Shelley** (1792–1822) & **Mary Wollstonecraft Shelley** (1797–1851) – Mary Wollstonecraft Shelley was herself the product of a literary couple: her parents were William Godwin, a novelist and political radical, and the early feminist Mary Wollstonecraft, who died a year after her daughter was born. Percy Bysshe Shelley was an English nobleman whose rebellious streak went against his conservative background. As a teenager he eloped with his first wife; when she committed suicide, he married Mary. He is the author of such poems as "To a Skylark," and she wrote *Frankenstein* (1818) as part of a friendly contest with Percy, Lord Byron, and another friend. Their union was cut off when Percy drowned in 1822.

2. **Robert Browning** (1812–1889) & **Elizabeth Barrett Browning** (1806–1861) – The two poets met after Elizabeth Barrett, who lived as a cloistered invalid, referred to Browning's work in one of her poems. Against her father's wishes, they fell in love and eloped to Italy. Their romance produced a number of beautiful letters and verses, including the famous line "How do I love thee? Let me count the ways" from one of Elizabeth's sonnets to her husband.

3. **Jean-Paul Sartre** (1905–1980) & **Simone de Beauvoir** (1908–1986) – This French pair first met as students in 1929. Pioneers of the existentialist movement in philosophy, they became famous for books such as Sartre's *Being and Nothingness* (1943) and de Beauvoir's *The Second Sex* (1949). They spent most of their lives together as friends and lovers, although their relationship was not exclusive and they never married. They are now buried in the same grave.

4. **Sylvia Plath** (1932–1963) & **Ted Hughes** (1930–1998) – The American Sylvia Plath met the handsome British poet at a party in 1956, and they were soon married. They had two children and both of them began to gain recognition for their work, but they were separated by the time Plath committed suicide in 1963. Hughes edited Plath's Pulitzer-prizewinning *Collected Poems* after her death, and decades later, shortly before his own death, published a book of poems addressed to her called *Birthday Letters* (1998).

5. **Louise Erdrich** (born 1954) & **Michael Dorris** (1945–1997) – Erdrich, the author of *The Beet Queen* (1986), and Dorris, the author of *A Yellow Raft in Blue Water* (1987), shared a love of literature, as well as their mixed Native American and European heritage. The married couple raised three adopted children and three children of their own, and collaborated extremely closely on much of their work. They separated in 1995. Plagued by family troubles, Dorris committed suicide in 1997.

Courtroom Novels

Crackerjack Legal Thrillers

Taking "write what you know" as their literary credo, lawyers-turned-novelists John Grisham, Steve Martini, and Scott Turow bring all their legal expertise to engrossing courtroom novels emphasizing gritty realism over implausible contrivances—until the denouement, when justice is almost always served. In that respect, Grisham, Martini, and Turow are following the example of the prolific attorney/author Erle Stanley Gardner, whose defense attorney hero Perry Mason never lost a case in eighty pulp yarns, bearing such kitschy titles as *The Case of the Terrified Typist* and *The Case of the Grinning Gorilla.*

Of all the Perry Mason novels Gardner cranked out from 1933 until his death in 1970, his 1942 entry, *The Case of the Careless Kitten*, is generally conceded to be his finest effort. It may not boast the literary pedigree of the seven other courtroom novels, listed below alphabetically, but it's not every day you read a courtroom thriller in which a cat helps a lawyer crack a case.

1. ***Anatomy of a Murder*** by Robert Traver, 1958 – Quite possibly, the finest courtroom novel in twentieth century American literature. A former prosecutor in Michigan's Upper Peninsula takes up the defense of a U.S. Army officer accused of murdering a man who may have raped the officer's promiscuous wife.

2. ***The Case of the Careless Kitten*** by Erle Stanley Gardner, 1942 – A treat for mystery fans and cat-lovers alike, *The Case of the Careless Kitten* finds Perry Mason at the top of his game, as always, in this pulp yarn that's literally the cat's meow.

3. ***Compulsion*** by Meyer Levin, 1956 – Levin's retelling of the infamous, 1920s-era Leopold and Loeb murder case is a fascinating blend of fact and speculative fiction.

4. ***The Lincoln Lawyer*** by Michael Connelly, 2005 – Connelly's first foray into the legal thriller genre marks a triumphant change of pace for the author of the best-selling Harry Bosch mystery novels. A cynical, borderline amoral Los Angeles criminal lawyer has an unexpected crisis of conscience while representing a realtor accused of beating a prostitute.

5. ***Primal Fear*** by William Diehl, 1993 – A knockout legal thriller with a whammy of surprise ending. A high-powered Chicago defense attorney has his work cut out for him defending a disturbed young man accused of murdering a Roman Catholic archbishop.

6. ***Reversible Errors*** by Scott Turow, 2002 – With startling efficiency, Turow churns out one crackerjack legal thriller after another. His sixth novel, *Reversible Errors,* finds a corporate attorney in the throes of a full-on mid-life crisis. Swallowing a lifetime of disappointments and regrets, he finds unexpected solace in his court-appointed role as the lawyer for a death row inmate.

7. ***Snow Falling on Cedars*** by David Guterson, 1994 – A character-driven and unusually vivid novel about a Japanese-American farmer on

trial for murder on an island in Puget Sound, circa 1954. Seamlessly jumping back and forth in time, Guterson examines World-War-II-driven racism in his haunting first novel.

8. ***Undue Influence*** by Steve Martini, 1994 – Martini's third novel featuring defense attorney Paul Madriani is a rattling good page-turner that ranks among the author's very best. Representing his sister-in-law in a nasty custody battle, Madriani suddenly finds himself defending her in a murder trial, when her ex-husband's trophy wife is brutally slain.

Creative Nonfiction

Blurring the Line Between Fact and Fiction

Creative nonfiction makes strange literary bedfellows: both the dapper, old school Southern gentleman Tom Wolfe and "gonzo journalist" Hunter S. Thompson excel at this hybrid of literary fiction techniques and reportage that encompasses such disparate genres as travel writing, personal essay, and nonfiction novels like Truman Capote's *In Cold Blood*. Although they use dialogue and write scenes to give their work the emotional depth and narrative momentum of fiction, practitioners of this form must be scrupulous in their attention to facts—or suffer the consequences. Case in point: James Frey, whose bruising, allegedly true account of his stint in rehab for alcohol and drug abuse, *A Million Little Pieces,* was revealed to be largely fabricated.

Ranging far and wide over such subjects as the AIDS crisis, the 1960s-era anti-war movement, and third world healthcare, the following books, listed alphabetically, are some of the most compelling works of creative nonfiction published since the 1960s.

1. ***And the Band Played On*** by Randy Shilts, 1987 – Chilling, infuriating and heartbreaking, Shilts' exhaustive account of the early days of the AIDS crisis weaves disparate storylines into a masterly narrative. Tragically, Shilts would die of AIDS in 1994.

2. ***Armies of the Night*** by Norman Mailer, 1968 – Mailer scored a one-two punch, winning both the National Book Award and the Pulitzer Prize for his nonfiction novel about the anti-Vietnam War movement. Such real-life figures as Abbie Hoffman, Dr. Benjamin Spock, and Mailer himself play prominent roles in *Armies of the Night*.

excerpt: ***AND THE BAND PLAYED ON:***
The gay man arrived at Dr. Willy Rozenbaum's examining room, complaining of a severe weight loss and a shortness of breath. Again, Rozenbaum made the diagnosis of Pneumocystis, as baffled about the cause as he had been for the Portuguese cab driver, the Zairian airline employee, and the French woman who had spent time in Central Africa. That afternoon's mail brought from the United States the MMWR [Morbidity and Mortality Weekly Report] describing the pneumonia outbreak in Los Angeles. This was related to the man he had seen this morning, Rozenbaum knew, and there was only one explanation. It couldn't be anything in the environment; Los Angeles was virtually on the other side of the world. It had to be a new infectious agent.

3. ***Black Hawk Down: A Story of Modern War*** by Mark Bowden, 1999 – Grueling and unforgettable, Bowden's pulse-pounding chronicle of the U.S. Army's disastrous, 1993 mission into the streets of Mogadishu, Somalia thrusts you headlong into the eighteen-hour firefight between U.S. soldiers and Somalis.

4. ***The Children*** by David Halberstam, 1998 – A giant of post-war American journalism, Halberstam has written classic books on the Vietnam war, media tycoons, and baseball. With *The Children,* Halberstam immerses readers in the early days of the civil rights movement in the Jim Crow-era South. An exceptional achievement from the Pulitzer Prize winning journalist.

5. ***The Electric Kool-Aid Acid Test*** by Tom Wolfe, 1968 – Wolfe's indelible record of his psychedelic bus ride with Ken Kesey and his LSD-swilling Merry Pranksters into hippiedom is a superlative example of creative nonfiction.

6. ***Fear and Loathing in Las Vegas*** by Hunter S. Thompson, 1971 – Fueled by alcohol and copious amounts of drugs, Thompson and his lawyer zoomed off to Las Vegas to attend a narcotic officers' convention. The father of "gonzo journalism" later transformed their experiences into the freewheeling acid trip of book that's a surreal meditation on the American dream.

7. ***Mountains Beyond Mountains: The Quest of Dr. Paul Farmer, A Man Who Would Cure the World*** by Tracy Kidder, 2003 – The Pulitzer Prize winning author of *The Soul of a New Machine* and *House* chronicles the astonishing story of Farmer, a idiosyncratic, fiercely dedicated physician who's been compared to Albert Schweitzer and

Mother Teresa for his treatment of the poor in Haiti, Peru, and Russia. The *New York Times* pronounced *Mountain Beyond Mountains* "inspiring, disturbing, daring and completely absorbing."

8. ***Random Family: Love, Drugs, Trouble and Coming of Age in the Bronx*** by Adrien Nicole LeBlanc, 2003 – For ten years, LeBlanc followed the lives of two, working-class Latina women and their extended families in the Bronx. The result is a stunning and empathetic chronicle of resilience in the midst of squalor, rampant crime, and lives gone to drugs. A finalist for the National Book Critics Circle Award.

Crime Fiction

Hard-Boiled Classics

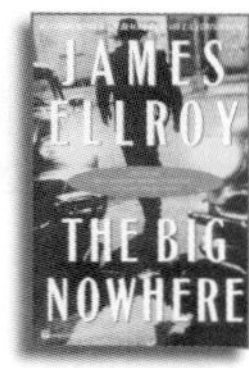

Duplicitous femme fatales, corrupt cops on the take, sadistic criminals who delight in torturing their victims to death—these are the denizens of the shadowy underworld of hard-boiled crime fiction, that peculiarly American literary genre. Born in the pages of the 1920s-era pulp magazine *Black Mask* (founded by H.L. Mencken and George Jean Nathan), the genre was honed and refined by the legendary Dashiell Hammett, the author of *The Maltese Falcon* and *Red Harvest*. His stories about cynical, world-weary detectives unraveling mysteries of Byzantine complexity basically set the template for the genre, which continued to flourish in the novels of Raymond Chandler, Mickey Spillane, and more recently, James Ellroy.

Although most readers associate hard-boiled crime fiction with detective yarns, the genre is not the sole province of Sam Spade, Philip Marlowe, and other private eyes. The novels of James M. Cain (*The Postman Always Rings Twice*) and Jim Thompson (*The Grifters*) aren't mysteries, but lurid, sex-soaked narratives of amoral characters whose crimes eventually catch up with them. Dubbed "literary noir," these novels are still classified as hard-boiled crime fiction. Here are eight classics of the genre, listed alphabetically, from masters of hard-boiled crime fiction past and present.

1. ***The Big Nowhere*** by James Ellroy, 1988 – Exceptionally dark, grimly compelling novel about two Los Angeles police detectives searching for a serial killer targeting gay men while simultaneously rooting out suspected "Commies" in Hollwood, circa 1950.

2. ***The Dain Curse*** by Dashiell Hammett, 1929 – Looking for clues in

a diamond heist, a detective uncovers a wealthy family's disturbing involvement with the occult in this vintage Hammett novel.

3. ***The Deep Blue Goodbye*** by John D. MacDonald, 1964 – MacDonald introduces his Florida-based "salvage consultant" Travis McGee, an ex-football player with a knack for finding missing persons and property, in *The Deep Blue Goodbye.*

4. ***Double Indemnity*** by James M. Cain, 1936 – The source for Billy Wilder's classic film noir is a marvel of narrative economy about a two-bit insurance salesman seduced into committing murder by a calculating femme fatale.

5. ***Farewell, My Lovely*** by Raymond Chandler, 1940 – According to Ross MacDonald, "Chandler wrote like a slumming angel and invested the sun-blinded streets of Los Angeles with a romantic presence." In *Farewell, My Lovely,* Chandler's legendary detective, Philip Marlowe, goes in search of an ex-convict's missing girlfriend and gets ensnarled in a murder linked to a jewel thief ring.

6. ***The Killer Inside Me*** by Jim Thompson, 1952 – Overlooked during his lifetime, Thompson has been posthumously embraced as one of the all-time great pulp writers. *The Killer Inside Me* is arguably his best, and most disturbing work. Outwardly placid, a small town Texas deputy is fighting a losing battle to suppress his urge to commit acts of savage violence.

excerpt: ***THE KILLER INSIDE ME:***
I'd been trying to place him, and finally it had come to me. It s been several years since I'd seen that big ugly mug in one of the out-of-town papers, and the picture hadn't been so good a resemblance. But I remembered it, now, and some of the story I'd read about him. He'd taken his degree at the University of Edinburgh at a time when we were admitting their graduates to practice. He'd killed half a dozen people before he picked up a jerkwater Ph.D., and edged into psychiatry.

7. ***Point Blank*** by Richard Stark, 1962 – "Richard Stark" is one of several pseudonyms used by Donald E. Westlake, the author of over one hundred books (and counting). Originally titled *The Hunter, Point Blank* is a tough, in-your-face crime drama about a criminal, shot and left for dead by his former partner, out for vengeance.

8. ***Solomon's Vineyard*** by Jonathan Latimer, 1941 – A textbook exam-

ple of hard-boiled crime fiction at its best. A tough St. Louis private detective's got his work cut out for him when he must save a beautiful heiress from a lunatic religious cult. Oozing sleaze and kinky sex, *Solomon's Vineyard* was initially banned in the United States.

Diarists

From Private to Public

For centuries, men and women have used diaries and journals to record the events in their lives, relieve pent-up feelings, and sort things out for themselves. Though they usually begin as very private papers, published diaries by someone who has lived through remarkable times or simply is a remarkable writer can make very compelling reading for strangers many years later. Here are some of history's best-known diarists, listed in no particular order. If any of these strike a chord with you, you might want to get a special notebook (or set up an Internet blog if that's more your style) and take the time to reflect on your own unique thoughts and experiences.

1. **"Alice,"** anonymous author of *Go Ask Alice,* 1971 – "Alice" begins her diary with the concerns of an ordinary, rather insecure teenage girl. After she begins experimenting with drugs and the freewheeling hippie lifestyle, she enters a nightmare of addiction. There have been questions about the authenticity of the diary, but for many, it is a convincing portrayal of the helplessness of being young and addicted.

2. **Matsuo Basho,** author of five "travel sketches," seventeenth century – Basho, one of Japan's great poets, spent much of his life wandering through his country. He recorded his travels in a charming combination of verse and prose, bringing to life the people and the natural environment of feudal Japan.

3. **Mary Chesnut,** author of *A Diary from Dixie,* 1905, republished as *Mary Chesnut's Civil War,* 1981 – A woman in the peculiar position of being an abolitionist and the wife of a Confederate general, Chesnut kept a detailed and vivid diary of life in the years during the Civil War.

4. **Anne Frank,** author of *The Diary of a Young Girl,* 1952 – When the Nazis stepped up their persecution of Jews during World War II, the thirteen year-old girl, along with her parents and sister, another Jewish family, and a dentist, went into hiding in a "secret an-

nex" in a building in Amsterdam. For two years they lived in this cramped space, making as little noise as possible and subsisting on the food, sometimes rotten, that their helpers were able to sneak to them. Frank's diary describes the ordeal, along with her first love with a fellow young hideaway. Days after the last entry, the Nazis discovered the families and she was sent to the Bergen-Belsen concentration camp, where she died of typhus.

excerpt: ***THE DIARY OF A YOUNG GIRL:***
The sun is shining, the sky is a deep blue, there is a lovely breeze and I'm longing—so longing—for everything. To talk, for freedom, for friends, to be alone. And I do so long ... to cry! I feel as if I'm going to burst; and I know that it would get better with crying; but I can't, I'm restless, I go from one room to the other, breathe through the crack of a closed window, feel my heart beating, as if it is saying, "Can't you satisfy my longings at last?"

5. **Samuel Pepys,** author of a diary written in the seventeenth century, first deciphered and published in part in 1825 – History books can tell you a lot about Restoration England, but there is nothing like experiencing it firsthand through the eyes of Samuel Pepys, a tailor's son who rose to political office. He gives an honest account of his times and himself, warts and all—we read about him visiting the theater, arguing with his wife, beating his servants, discussing the latest fashions, criticizing himself and vowing to reform, and so on. He also describes the Plague and the Great Fire in London.

Espionage Novels

Cloak and Dagger Classics

Stirred, but rarely shaken, Ian Fleming's Agent 007, James Bond, is one of the most enduring characters in popular culture, due largely to the long-running film series (twenty-two films and counting) that began with 1962's *Doctor No.* For the most part, however, these splashy, spectacle-driven films bear only the slightest resemblance to Fleming's original novels, which are darker and comparatively more realistic in tone. The gimmickry and gadgets that drive the Bond films are MIA from the twelve novels and two short story collections Fleming wrote between 1953 and his death in 1964. Today, most critics name Fleming's fifth book, *From Russia With Love,* as the best of the series—it was also the only novel that made President John F. Kennedy's list of ten favorite books for the March 17, 1961 issue of *Life* magazine.

From Russia With Love is one of ten, crackling good espionage yarns, listed alphabetically, that plunge readers into the shadowy world of conspiracies, cover-ups, and covert operations that's all in a day's work for master spies.

1. ***A Coffin for Dimitrios*** by Eric Ambler, 1939 – Looking for artistic inspiration, a British mystery writer in 1930s-era Istanbul gets embroiled in a deadly web of intrigue while investigating the murder of the enigmatic Dimitrios—who may not be dead after all. A rattling good thriller from one of the acknowledged masters of the espionage genre.

2. ***From Russia With Love*** by Ian Fleming, 1957 – A gorgeous Soviet siren, Tatiana Romanova, lures the unflappable Bond into a trap set up by 007's chief, cold war nemesis, the SMERSH organization, in Fleming's gripping espionage yarn.

3. ***The Ipcress File*** by Len Deighton, 1962 – The antithesis of 007, Deighton's middle-aged, cynical anti-hero is more of a paper-pusher whose dogged research into the mysterious disappearance of British scientists thrusts him into a bizarre plot involving mind control. Convoluted, sometimes to the point of confusion, *The Ipcress File* is nonetheless an ingenious and sardonically funny thriller—the first in what became known as Deighton's Harry Palmer series.

4. ***The Kill Artist*** by Daniel Silva, 2000 – Ranked the equal of John Le Carre and Graham Greene by *The Washingtonian,* CNN correspondent-turned novelist Silva is at his relentless, pulse-pounding best in *The Kill Artist,* which depicts a former Israeli intelligence operative's hunt for a deadly Palestinian terrorist.

5. ***The Moscow Club*** by Joseph Finder, 1991 – Finder's 1991 ambitious debut novel is a densely plotted, post-cold war era thriller about a CIA analyst investigating a mysterious document reportedly dictated by Lenin on his deathbed. Thus begins a hair-raising, globe-trotting thriller that places Finder's hero in perpetual harm's way— from both the KGB and the CIA.

6. ***Night Soldiers*** by Alan Furst, 1988 – Furst's literary career took off with this riveting, atmospheric thriller, set in 1934, about a young

Bulgarian recruited by Soviet intelligence. Doubled-crossed while on assignment during the Spanish Civil War, Furst's traumatized hero takes refuge in Paris, where he eventually joins the French resistance in World War II.

7. ***Our Man in Havana*** by Graham Greene, 1958 – A giant of twentieth century English literature, Green excelled at writing novels, plays, short stories, travel books, screenplays, and criticism. One of his best and most diverting "entertainments"—as Green called his mysteries/espionage thrillers—is this witty, razor sharp novel about a vacuum cleaner salesman turned unlikely spy in pre-Castro era Cuba. Greene himself served in Great Britain's Secret Intelligence Service from 1941 to 1944.

excerpt: OUR MAN IN HAVANA:
Suddenly, without warning, one of the policemen slapped his face. He felt shock rather than anger. He belonged to the law-abiding class: the police were his natural protectors. He put his hand to his cheek and said, "What in God's name do you think . . . ?" The other policeman with a blow in the back sent him stumbling along the pavement. His hat fell off into the filth of the gutter. He said, "Give me my hat," and felt himself pushed again. He began to say something about the British Consul and they swung him sideways across the road and sent him reeling.

8. ***Tinker, Tailor, Soldier, Spy*** by John Le Carre, 1974 – Arguably the greatest living writer of espionage thrillers, Le Carre launched his brilliant Karla Trilogy with this 1974 best-seller, that finds middle-aged and embittered British agent George Smiley on the hunt for a Soviet "mole," who may have penetrated British Intelligence decades earlier. *The Honourable Schoolboy* and *Smiley's People* are the other novels in Le Carre's Karla Trilogy.

Expatriate Nonfiction

Dispatches from Abroad

Living in a place for an extended period of time yields a different kind of knowledge than just visiting it as a tourist. Not all of us are lucky enough to be offered a position as a correspondent in Paris, or to be able to buy a villa in Tuscany. But we can still learn about far-off countries from expatriates living there—an intimate perspective, yet with the foreigner's sense of

curiosity and appreciation—and, sometimes, crankiness. The following books, listed alphabetically, take you to some of the world's most beautiful, fabled, and dynamic locales.

1. ***Bad Times in Buenos Aires*** by Miranda France, 1999 – The author, a young British journalist, brings a keen sense of history to her descriptions of Buenos Aires. As the title suggests, she doesn't wear rose-tinted glasses: there are rats, bad phone lines, and other urban ills a-plenty. But there is also the glamour of the tango, and unexpected aspects of the culture to ponder—everyone seems to be in psychoanalysis, for example.

2. ***City of Djinns: A Year in Delhi*** by William Dalrymple, 1993 – Dalrymple shares his fascinating time living in the capital of India, a city of destruction, renewal, and remarkable people and traditions. Daily life, popular pastimes, festivals, and the multifarious past all come to life in his account.

3. ***Foreign Babes in Beijing: Behind the Scenes of a New China*** by Rachel DeWoskin, 2005 – In this perceptive and funny book, a young American public-relations specialist literally has a starring role in China's rapidly changing culture. DeWoskin plays what she really is—a foreign babe in Beijing—in a popular Chinese soap opera. Her unusual tale makes for a great read and will teach you a lot about modern China, too.

4. ***The Japan Journals: 1947–2004*** by Donald Richie, edited by Leza Lowitz, 2004 – A writer and film director, Richie moved to Japan to work as a typist just after the end of World War II. His journals and diaries reflect his own active life there—social and sexual—and the changes in Japanese culture over the course of a half century.

5. ***Paris to the Moon*** by Adam Gopnik, 2000 – the *New Yorker* magazine sent Gopnik to Paris for five years, with his wife and young son, to write about his experiences there. The result is an engaging, precisely observed series of adventures in the beautiful but complicated city. Gopnik enjoys the traditional charms of Paris, even as he and the city deal with strikes, a formidable bureaucracy, and the pressures of globalization.

6. ***A Street in Marrakech*** by Elizabeth Warnock Fernea, 1975 – This book focuses on the relationships between the American author and

the women of the street where she lives in the historic city of Marrakech. We may think of Marrakech as exotic, but to Fernea's Morrocan neighbors she was the strange one, at least at first.

7. ***Under the Tuscan Sun*** by Francis Mayes, 1996 – Vicariously savor the rich, relaxed lifestyle of Cortona, Italy as you read this memoir. The work of restoring an old villa in the hills proves as much a pleasure for the author as the beautiful landscape and culture of Tuscany.

8. ***A Year in Provence*** by Peter Mayle, 1989 – Month by month, Mayle details his and his wife's first year in their new home in the south of France—replete with eccentric neighbors, gifted workmen, quaint customs, and enormous, vividly described meals. Prepare to be charmed—and hungry.

Families of Writers

Chips Off the Old (Writer's) Block

What combination of genes and environment goes to make a great writer? We don't know for sure, but in spite of all the cases of lone geniuses who have to battle philistine relatives in order to get their work done, literary ability does sometimes run in families. Here are some of the most notable examples, listed alphabetically by the family name.

1. **The Brontë Sisters: Charlotte** (1816–1855), **Emily** (1818–1848), and **Anne** (1820–1849) – The Reverend Patrick Brontë, an Irishman who moved to England, was a published poet and kept his home well stocked with books. Brontë's family was unlucky: his wife died when Anne, the youngest, was less than two, and two of his daughters died from the conditions at an awful boarding school (later immortalized in *Jane Eyre*). Like the passionate children in *Wuthering Heights*, the Brontë sisters and their brother Branwell spent much of their youth playing on the Yorkshire moors. They also passed the time reading and making up stories. In 1847, the three surviving sisters all published novels—*Jane Eyre* by Charlotte, *Wuthering Heights* by Emily, and *Agnes Grey* by Anne. Female writers were severely frowned on in that day, so they used the pen names Currer, Ellis, and Acton Bell, respectively—although "Currer Bell" received correspondence from his publisher care of a Miss Brontë.

2. **A.S. Byatt** (born 1936) and **Margaret Drabble** (born 1939) – Byatt and Drabble are also sisters from Yorkshire who grew up in a family that loved to read. Their relationship has been more troubled and competitive than the Brontës', but sibling tensions haven't prevented them from both becoming prolific and successful writers. Byatt published a novel called *The Game* (1967), which depicts a rivalry between two sisters, and Drabble published *The Pepper Moth* (2001), which is largely based on their mother. Byatt is also the author of *Possession: A Romance* (1990) and *Angels and Insects* (1992), among many other books. Drabble is the author of *A Summer Bird-cage* (1963), *The Needle's Eye* (1972), and *The Witch of Exmoor* (1996), among many others.

3. **The Brothers Grimm: Jacob** (1785–1863) and **Wilhelm** (1786–1859) – Jacob and Wilhelm Grimm were scholars who helped develop the study of German linguistics. But we know them for their marvelous collections of fairy tales, first published in the early nineteenth century. It may seem incongruous that the men who familiarized the world with "Hansel and Gretel," "Cinderella," and "Little Red Riding Hood"—magical tales, but containing plenty of hardship and some gruesome scenes—had wonderful childhoods, at least until they were around ten and eleven years-old, respectively. When their father died, life became much harder, but, as resourceful as any of their fairy tale heroes, they worked hard in school and ended up achieving success and renown.

4. **The Huxley family: Thomas Henry** (1825–1895), **Julian** (1887–1975), and **Aldous** (1894–1963) – This family possessed a dual genius for science and literature. T.H. Huxley, the author of *Evidence as to Man's Place in Nature* (1863) and *Evolution and Ethics* (1893), was known as "Darwin's bulldog" for his role in defending, explaining, and popularizing the theory of evolution by natural selection. One of his sons married a niece of the Victorian poet and philosopher Matthew Arnold; Julian and Aldous Huxley were among their children. Julian became a biologist and popularizer of science, and Aldous became a novelist and essayist who also shared an interest in science—probably his best-remembered work today is *Brave New World* (1932), a fantasy about the dark side of technology.

5. **William James** (1842–1910) and **Henry James** (1843–1916) – These

American brothers, whose father was a journalist and theologian, traveled all over Europe with their family as they grew up. William became a psychologist and philosopher, producing such groundbreaking works as *The Principles of Psychology* (1890) and *The Varieties of Religious Experience* (1902). Henry became a novelist, penning such masterpieces as *The Portrait of a Lady* (1881) and *The Turn of the Screw* (1898). An anonymous writer commented on the relationship between the brothers' styles and concerns: "Mr. James, I mean Mr. William James, the humorist who writes on psychology, not his brother, the psychologist who writes novels." Their sister Alice, an invalid, is also remembered for her diary.

Female Sleuths in Fiction

From Miss Marple to V.I. Warshawski

In her tweeds and sensible shoes, Miss Jane Marple of the quaint village of St. Mary Mead initially seems to be like any other elderly British spinster—the type of sweet old lady who lives for cucumber sandwiches at tea time and natters on about her rose garden.

But as the saying goes, first impressions can be deceiving—and none more so than in the case of Miss Marple, the shrewd and methodical amateur sleuth heroine of thirteen Agatha Christie mysteries. The most famous female sleuth in all literature, Miss Marple cracked her last case in 1976's *Sleeping Murder*. Thirty years later, there are scores of female sleuths—private detectives, forensic anthropologists, bounty hunters—solving crimes in the pages of best-selling mysteries. Here are eight notable mysteries featuring female sleuths, written by women, listed alphabetically.

1. ***B is for Burglar*** by Sue Grafton, 1985 – The second entry in Grafton's Kinsey Milhone Alphabet Mystery Series and arguably the best. Santa Barbara private investigator Kinsey Milhone encounters a veritable rogue's gallery of suspects in this winner of the Shamus Award from the Private Eye Writers of America organization.

2. ***A Bitter Feast*** by S.J. Rozan, 1998 – What first appears to be a missing persons case gradually turns into something far more complex and deadly for Chinese-American private investigator Lydia Chin and her partner in Rozan's gripping mystery, the fifth in the series.

3. ***Blacklist: V.I. Warshawski*** by Sara Paretsky, 2003 – Set in the aftermath of 9/11, Paretsky's eleventh V.I. Warshawski mystery finds the leggy, wisecracking Chicago private investigator looking into a possible link between a murdered journalist and a suspected Arab terrorist.

4. ***Body of Evidence*** by Patricia Cornwell, 1991 – The second of Cornwell's mysteries featuring Dr. Kay Scarpetta, the chief medical examiner of Virginia. In this solidly plotted novel, teeming with twists and turns, Scarpetta investigates the murder of a local romance novelist.

5. ***Both Ends of the Night*** by Marcia Muller, 1997 – Tracking down the killer of her flight instructor, hard-boiled private investigator Sharon McCone must leave her native San Francisco for the frozen Minnesota wilderness. A *Publishers Weekly* "Best Book" of 1997.

6. ***Eleven On Top*** by Janet Evanovich, 2005 – Juicily entertaining entry in Evanovich's Stephanie Plum series, about a New Jersey lingerie buyer-turned bounty hunter.

7. ***A Murder is Announced*** by Agatha Christie, 1950 – Most critics and fans regard *A Murder is Announced* as the best of the Miss Marple mysteries. Responding to a newspaper advertisement, townspeople arrive to play what they think is a murder game—until a stranger is shot dead before them.

8. ***An Unsuitable Job for a Woman*** by P.D. James, 1972 – Chilling mystery introduces novice sleuth Cordelia Gray, who just inherited a detective agency and now must solve her first crime: the bizarre murder of a wealthy man's son, found hanging by the neck. *People* magazine calls James "the greatest living mystery writer."

Food Books

Histories of Culinary Staples

We take great delight in our favorite foods, but often take their presence in our lives for granted. In fact, many of them—from staples like bread and salt to the most decadent treats—have fascinating and surprising histories. Did you know that the Aztecs drank chocolate as a bitter tonic, mixed with hot chilies rather than sugar? Or that the consumption of tea, beer, and wine may have saved lives in past

centuries by disinfecting water? Tea because water was boiled for its preparation, beer and wine because their alcohol killed bacteria. Or that caramel was used as a depilatory before it was eaten as candy?

In recent years, historians and food experts have produced a smorgasbord of books about the stories behind our foods, which are also the stories of evolving cultures, daring voyages, and international trade wars. Whether you're a cook, a connoisseur, a history buff, or simply someone who loves a good meal, these books, listed alphabetically, are certain to entertain you and to change the way you look at your food.

1. ***Beer: A History of Suds and Civilization from Mesopotamia to Microbreweries*** by Gregg Smith, 1995.
2. ***Bittersweet: The Story of Sugar*** by Peter MacInnis, 2002.
3. ***The Empire of Tea*** by Alan and Iris MacFarlane, 2004.
4. ***The History of Bread*** by Bernard Dupaigne, 1999.
5. ***Olives: The Life and Lore of a Noble Fruit*** by Mort Rosenblum, 1996.
6. ***Robbing the Bees: A Biography of Honey—The Sweet Liquid Gold that Seduced the World*** by Holley Bishop, 2005.
7. ***Salt: A World History*** by Mark Kurlansky, 2002.
8. ***Spice: The History of a Temptation*** by Jack Turner, 2004.
9. ***The Story of Wine*** by Hugh Johnson 1989.
10. ***Sweets: The History of Candy*** by Tim Richardson, 2002.
11. ***The True History of Chocolate*** by Sophie D. Coe and Michael D. Coe, 1996.
12. ***Uncommon Grounds: The History of Coffee and How It Transformed Our World*** by Mark Pendergrast, 1999.

French Literature

Helena Frith Powell's Sexy Favorites

Ah, l'amour—the French may not have invented it, but they've sung its virtues, lamented its sorrows, and sampled its delights with passionate abandon since time immemorial in literature, poetry and sometimes graphically frank memoir. Taking "Je ne regrette rien!" as their motto, French writers have burnished their country's image as a veritable hothouse of torrid, and frequently tortured romance, as well as steamy, envelope-pushing sex that raises more than prudes' eyebrows.

So what if you'd like to cultivate your own certain "je ne sais quo," but can't swing the pricey airfare to France? There's always the vicarious pleasures offered by the following books, according to English journalist Helena Frith Powell. An unabashed Francophile whose book *Two Lipsticks and a Lover* celebrates the effortless chic and mystique of French women, Powell ranked these titles the ten sexiest French books for *The Guardian*.

Vive la France!

1. ***Cheri*** by Colette, 1920 – A May-December romance that Frith Powell calls "every woman's fantasy," *Cheri* depicts the all-consuming romance between a worldly courtesan on the brink of fifty and her much younger, aristocratic lover. For Colette, the scandal-magnet novelist who carried on very public affairs with both men and women, *Cheri* mirrors her own relationship with her stepson.

2. ***Madame de*** by Louise de Vilmorin, 1951 – A pair of heart-shaped diamond earrings brings ruin for debt-ridden aristocrat Madame de in this novel of adultery by de Vilmorin, the one-time fiancé of writer/aviator Antoine de Saint-Exupery. Per Frith Powell, *Madame de* is "the book that French girls love to take seriously."

3. ***The Ravishing of Lol Stein*** by Marguerite Duras, 1964 – Ditched by her fiancé for another woman in a crowded ballroom, Duras' heroine finds an unusual outlet for her pain: voyeurism. Nothing, not even marriage and motherhood, provides the same measure of solace to the sexually obsessed heroine of Duras' novel, which Frith Powell dubs "possibly the maddest book ever written."

4. ***Bonjour Tristesse*** by Francoise Sagan, 1954 – Written when Sagan was just eighteen years-old, *Bonjour Tristesse* charts the sexual awakening of Cecily, a carefree teenager spending the summer at her father's villa on the French Rivera. According to Frith Powell, Sagan's prodigious first novel is "sexy, poignant, moving ... a must."

5. ***Madame Bovary*** by Gustave Flaubert, 1857 – Flaubert's classic novel of a bored provincial woman's self-destructive plunge into adultery and gambling contains "some of literature's sexiest moments," per Frith Powell. In fact, when *Madame Bovary* was published, shocked French legal authorities attempted to prosecute Flaubert for "immorality." He was later acquitted.

6. ***Emmanuelle*** by Emmanuelle Arsan, 1957 – Published on the sly in 1957, this supposedly autobiographical novel details a woman's erotic

education in prose that leaves little or nothing to the imagination. According to Frith Powell, the heroine's sexual adventures have "entertained French boys since publication."

7. ***Les Liaisons Dangereuses*** by Choderlos de Laclos, 1782 – Brilliantly adapted for the stage and screen by English playwright Christopher Hampton, this epistolary novel immerses the reader in the cruel sexual games of the decadent French aristocracy. Through the ruthless scheming of the characters Marquise de Merteuil and the Vicomte de Valmont, Frith Powell feels that *Les Liaisons Dangereuses* "turns seduction into a game and an art form."

8. ***I Wish Someone Were Waiting for Me Somewhere*** by Anna Gavalda, 1999 – A collection of short stories by a writer who's been likened to a Gallic version of American humorist Dorothy Parker. Frith Powell singles out the first story, "The Courting Rituals of the Saint-Germain-des-Pres," for its "sexual tension."

9. ***Cyrano de Bergerac*** by Edmond de Rostand, 1897 – True love eventually conquers all, including a large schnozz, in this beloved, oft-told story of the seventeenth-century swordsman that Frith Powell cites as "proof of the enduring attraction of words."

10. ***The Delta of Venus*** by Anais Nin, 1969 – Frith Powell calls novelist/diarist Nin the "quintessential female player." This provocative collection of erotica reveals Nin to be a sensual, uninhibited writer with a poet's gift for imagery.

excerpt: THE DELTA OF VENUS:

She could have lived for nothing else. In fact, she lived for nothing else. The rest of the time—when she was not with him—she felt and heard nothing clearly. She was absent. She only came to life fully in his room. All day, as she did other things, her thoughts circled around him. Alone in bed, she remembered his expressions, the laughter at the corner of his eyes, the willfulness of his chin, the glittering of his teeth, the shape of his lips as he uttered words of desire.

Futuristic Fiction
Utopias and Dystopias

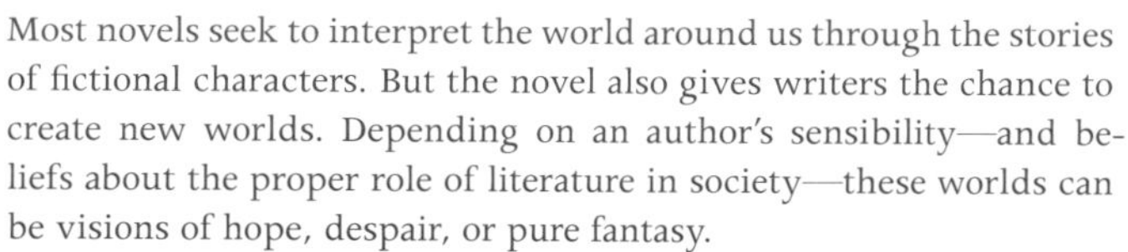

Most novels seek to interpret the world around us through the stories of fictional characters. But the novel also gives writers the chance to create new worlds. Depending on an author's sensibility—and beliefs about the proper role of literature in society—these worlds can be visions of hope, despair, or pure fantasy.

Sir Thomas More coined the term "utopia," based on the Greek words for "no" and "place," in the sixteenth century. He used it as the title of his narrative about an imaginary land where a humanistic government had succeeded in eliminating crime, poverty, and other social ills. Since then, many writers have dreamed up their own ideal systems, as well as the reverse—nightmarish societies, often made possible by misuses of science. The term "dystopia" was coined around fifty years ago to describe such worlds.

The following alphabetical list of novels offers some of literature's most indelible visions of heavens and hells. Some imagine what might happen if the darker sides of human nature, technology, and power politics took over; others envision well-ordered societies that could come into being if only we could start all over.

1. ***1984*** by George Orwell, 1949 – In the totalitarian state run by "Big Brother," individuality, love, privacy, and truth itself are forbidden.

2. ***Atlas Shrugged*** by Ayn Rand, 1957 – In a socialized United States where the strong must sacrifice themselves to the weak, the intelligent and able go on strike in the hope of bringing back capitalism.

3. ***Brave New World*** by Aldous Huxley, 1932 – In the world of the future, embryos are raised in bottles, a wonder drug takes the place of genuine happiness, and individuality and moral choice are considered obsolete.

4. ***Fahrenheit 451*** by Ray Bradbury, 1953 – In the twenty-fourth century, books are outlawed and television is used to control the masses. A "fireman" whose job it is to burn books meets a young woman who has defied the law, inspiring him to steal one of the books he is commanded to burn.

excerpt: ***FAHRENHEIT 451:***
The woman knelt among the books, touching the drenched leather and cardboard, reading the gilt titles with her fingers while her eyes accused Montag.
"You can't ever have my books," she said.
"You know the law," said Beatty. "Where's your common sense? None of those books agree with each other. You've been locked up here for years with a regular damned Tower of Babel. Snap out of it! The people in those books never lived. Come on now!"
She shook her head.

5. ***The Handmaid's Tale*** by Margaret Atwood, 1984 – A theocracy has taken over the United States and deprived women of the right to hold property or jobs. Instead, they become property whose sole value is child-bearing.

6. ***Herland*** by Charlotte Perkins Gilman, 1915 – Three men venture into a land populated entirely by women, an ideal society guided by the maternal instinct.

7. ***The Time Machine*** by H.G. Wells, 1895 – A time-traveler visits the future, where humankind has evolved into two classes—predators (the Morlocks, descended from industrial workers) and prey (the Eloi, descended from aristocrats).

8. ***We*** by Eugene Zamyatin, 1920 – A thousand years in the future, the United States government has reduced all life to mathematics. People are identified by numbers instead of names, and even love is turned into a formula in an attempt to render it powerless.

Gay & Lesbian Novels

The Publishing Triangle's Top Ten

In this era of *Will & Grace, Queer Eye for the Straight Guy* and *The L Word,* it seems the "love that dare not speak its name" is loudly present and relatively accepted in mainstream culture. Yet not so very long ago, such matter-of-fact, non-stereotypical depictions of gay and lesbian life were rare, if not downright impossible to see in films and television. Only in the pages of novels could people find honest and emotionally complex representations of gay and lesbian life, but many writers paid the price for tackling such a controversial subject.

When twenty-three year-old Gore Vidal published his groundbreaking gay novel *The City and the Pillar* in 1948, the staid *New York Times* excoriated Vidal and refused to review his next five novels. And closeted British novelist E.M. Forster scribbled the note "Publishable, but worth it?" on the manuscript for *Maurice,* which would only be published posthumously in 1971—nearly sixty years after Forster wrote it.

In 2004, the Publishing Triangle, an association of gays and lesbians in publishing, asked a panel of thirteen judges to rank the hundred best lesbian and gay-themed novels of all time. Here are the panel's top-ten choices, per their ranking.

1. ***Death in Venice*** by Thomas Mann, 1912 – The exquisite agonies of romantic obsession consume an older novelist, whose unrequited love for a beautiful Italian youth spells his downfall in Mann's classic novella, reportedly inspired by Austrian composer Gustav Mahler.

2. ***Giovanni's Room*** by James Baldwin, 1956 – The author of *Go Tell It on the Mountain* courted controversy with his second novel, a ruminative and deeply melancholy first-person account of a closeted American man's furtive love affair with an Italian bartender in post-World War II Paris.

3. ***Our Lady of the Flowers*** by Jean Genet, 1942 – Written during one of Genet's many prison stints, *Our Lady of the Flowers* is an explicit, unabashedly autobiographical novel that immerses the reader in the decadent Parisian underworld of male prostitutes, drag queens, and career criminals. Despite its sordid topic, *Our Lady of the Flowers* is a remarkable mixture of harsh realism and poetic imagery.

4. ***Remembrance of Things Past*** by Marcel Proust, 1913–1927 – Along with James Joyce's *Ulysses,* Proust's seven volume magnum opus is regularly hailed as the crowning achievement in twentieth century literature. Over 2,000 characters, many of them gay and lesbian, inhabit the pages of Proust's epic roman a clef.

5. ***The Immoralist*** by Andre Gide, 1902 – While recovering from tuberculosis, a Parisian scholar experiences a profound sexual awakening and devotes himself to the pursuit of pleasure, albeit with grave consequences, in this novel from the Nobel Prize winning novelist.

6. ***Orlando*** by Virginia Woolf, 1928 – According to British politician Nigel Nicholson, Woolf's *Orlando* was the author's love letter to his

mother, Vita Sackville-West. Blurring the lines between fiction and nonfiction, *Orlando* chronicles the gender-bending experiences of the title character, an ageless young man in Elizabethan England who becomes a woman centuries later.

7. ***The Well of Loneliness*** by Radclyffe Hall, 1928 – Initially banned in Great Britain, Hall's sorrowful tale of a masculine "invert," i.e., lesbian, who endures heartbreak remains a classic of the genre, even though Hall's prose style is a bit unwieldy at times.

excerpt: ***THE WELL OF LONELINESS:***
That evening she and Mary walked over the fields to a little town not very far from their billets. They paused for a moment to watch the sunset, and Mary stroked the new Croix de Guerre; *then she looked s traight up into Stephen's eyes, her mouth shook, and Stephen saw that she was crying. After this they must walk hand in hand for a while. Why not? There was no one just then to see them.*

8. ***Kiss of the Spider Woman*** by Manuel Puig, 1976 – Later adapted for the screen and stage, Puig's novel primarily consists of an extended conversation between two prisoners in an Argentine jail cell: a movie-loving drag queen and a socialist revolutionary. Over time, these two radically different men develop a friendship that ripens into a sexual bond.

9. ***The Memoirs of Hadrian*** by Marguerite Yourcenar, 1951 – Recently named one of the hundred best novels published since 1923 by *Time* magazine, Yourcenar's tour de force takes the form of a letter, written by the Roman Emperor Hadrian to his successor, Marcus Aurelius. Some of the novel's most memorable passages address Hadrian's love for the Greek youth Antonius, whose death plunged his older lover into deep despair.

10. ***Zami*** by Audre Lorde, 1983 – Lorde called *Zami* her "biomythography," since it blends autobiography and fiction to spellbinding effect. The daughter of West Indian immigrants, Lorde was a self-described "black feminist lesbian poet warrior" whose poetry celebrates the spiritual and erotic connection between women.

Graphic Novels

Time *Magazine's Top Ten*

Not so long ago, the literati would have dismissed the term "graphic novel" as an oxymoron—with the emphasis on "moron." At the most, the graphic novel was seen as nothing more than a glorified comic book, a pulpy diversion for kids, who should be reading the classics, rather than wasting their minds on junk about superheroes, friendly ghosts, and teenagers named Jughead.

Today, however, even the most discerning (translation: snobby) members of the literary establishment have revised their lowly opinion of the graphic novel. Thanks to such acclaimed works as *Watchmen* and *Jimmy Corrigan: The Smartest Kid on Earth,* the graphic novel is no longer viewed as the bastard stepchild of serious fiction. It is serious fiction, tackling such weighty themes as racism and politics and religion in vividly illustrated, full-color or black-and-white panels.

In 2005, *Time* magazine columnist Andrew D. Arnold named his picks for the ten best graphic novels to date. Here are his choices, listed alphabetically.

1. ***Berlin: City of Stones*** by Jason Lutes, 2000 – Hailed by Arnold as "one of premier works of historical fiction in the medium," Lute's first volume in a projected trilogy of graphic novels spans eight months in the waning years of Germany's Weimar Republic, circa 1928-1929. Reminiscent of Christopher Isherwood's *Berlin Stories* (the inspiration for *Cabaret*), Lutes' graphic novel is an epic flight of imagination that evokes the era in all its wanton decadence and political turmoil.

2. ***Blankets*** by Craig Thompson, 2003 – Growing up in a fundamentalist Christian family in rural Wisconsin, an aspiring artist is torn between love and family in Thompson's autobiographical work that "magically recreates the high emotional stakes of adolescence," according to Arnold.

3. ***Bone*** by Jeff Smith, 2004 – A compendium of Smith's fifty-five-issue fantasy adventure, *Bone* appeals to readers of all ages, thanks to its goofy wit and exciting, roller-coaster ride of a yarn. Cast out of their home, the three Bone cousins—Fone, Smiley, and Phoney—eventually get caught up in an epic battle with the evil forces of the dread Lord of the Locusts. Arnold praises Smith for "infusing every panel with dynamic energy."

4. ***The Boulevard of Broken Dreams*** by Kim Deitch, 2002 – The veteran underground comic artist depicts the mental disintegration of a 1930s-era animator, whose psychic tormentor is a menacing cat named Waldo, who may just be a hallucination. In this retro-style graphic novel, Deitch "explores the nature of reality… and the redemptive power of art," per Arnold.

5. ***The Dark Knight Returns*** by Frank Miller, 1986 – Stripping away any trace of the campiness that marked the Caped Crusader's television series, Miller turned Batman into a brooding loner who returns after a ten-year absence to find Gotham City a crime-ridden, urban wasteland. The template for Tim Burton's Gothic *Batman* films, Miller's *The Dark Knight Returns* makes Arnold's list since it "masterfully combines satire with superhero antics."

6. ***David Boring*** by Daniel Clowes, 2000 – Praised by Arnold for his "ability to create offbeat characters and write sardonic humor," Clowes does just that with his graphic novel about a rootless young man looking for love in a big city.

7. ***Ed the Happy Clown*** by Chester Brown, 1989 – Brown's "fantastically funny, violent and absurd debut novel" earns Arnold's raves for its surreal story of a malcontent clown beset by cannibals, Martians, and Ronald Reagan. Hugely influential, *Ed the Happy Clown* is truly a one-of-a-kind graphic novel.

8. ***Jimmy Corrigan: The Smartest Kid on Earth*** by Chris Ware, 2000 – Praised by Arnold as "the most perfect novel yet seen in this format," Ware's ambitious, melancholy story centers on the title character, a middle-aged sad sack. Like all the Corrigan men before him, Jimmy has lived a life of "quiet desperation." His only relief comes in fantasies in which he's "the smartest kid on Earth."

9. ***Palomar: The Heartbreak Soup Stories*** by Gilbert Hernandez, 2003 – Best known for the *Love and Rockets* comic book series, Hernandez follows generations of a family in a community south of the U.S. border in this deeply compelling "uber graphic novel" that Arnold compares to William Faulkner for its "richness of character."

10. ***Watchmen*** by Alan Moore, 1986 – Arguably the greatest graphic novelist, Moore has written such classics as *V for Vendetta* and *From Hell*. He first made a splash with this cult favorite, stunningly illustrated

by Dave Gibbons, that Arnold calls "a complex murder mystery, with intense unforgettable characters."

Ghosts in Literature

Visitors from the Great Beyond

From *The Odyssey* to the Harry Potter books, the shades of people who used to live on the earth have haunted our stories. Sometimes these filmy creatures are quite real in the stories; other times they are figments of the imagination; and other times it's never quite clear. But in this alphabetical list of books enlivened, so to speak, by visitations from the dead, we won't say which is which.

1. ***The Castle of Otranto*** by Horace Walpole, 1764 – This early Gothic novel concerns the power struggles of the realm of Otranto. The scheming Manfred acts selfishly despite plain signs (well, supernatural signs) that fate is set against his domination of Otranto. Eventually, his plans come crashing down because of an enormous ghost.

2. ***A Christmas Carol*** by Charles Dickens, 1843 – This may be Dickens' best-loved work. A deceased business associate and three more ghosts appear to the dour and miserly Ebenezer Scrooge to show him Christmas past, present, and future—sights that change him forever.

3. ***Hamlet*** by William Shakespeare, circa 1600–1601 – Would you kill someone at the prompting of a ghost? The dead father of Hamlet, the prince of Denmark, appears to his son and accuses Hamlet's uncle Claudius (now on the throne) of having murdered him. Hamlet declines into a state of paralysis as he tries to decide whether or not to avenge his father.

4. ***The Legend of Sleepy Hollow*** by Washington Irving, 1819 – A schoolmaster in love with a local girl finds his plans interrupted by the appearance of the ghost of a Hessian trooper, who rides around in search of his own head.

5. ***The Turn of the Screw*** by Henry James, 1898 – This is the nightmarish story of a governess at an English country estate trying to rescue the children under her care from the influence of their former governess and the steward—both dead.

Golf Novels

Comic Hijinks on the Links

Golf has long inspired writers to wax poetic about the glories of the game. Then there's Dan Jenkins, the sportswriter/novelist who gleefully skewers the PGA in his hilarious satire, *Dead Solid Perfect*. Published in 1974, the book depicts the raucous and raunchy misadventures of good ol' boy Kenny Lee Puckett on the PGA Tour. Following Jenkins' lead, other writers have mined comic gold from the colorful personalities, botched shots, and petty rivalries that are part of the game's lore. The following novels, in alphabetical order, capture golf in all its wonder and absurdity.

1. ***Dead Solid Perfect*** by Dan Jenkins, 1974 – Sexy, rude, and laugh-out-loud funny, Jenkins' wild and woolly comic send-up of the PGA Tour is not for the easily offended or politically correct.

2. ***The Foursome*** by Troon McAllister, 2000 – The adage "A fool and his money shall soon part" comes true for four incredibly rich and arrogant golfers in this darkly comic novel. Arriving at the luxurious golf resort Swithen Bairn, they meet their undoing in the form of Eddie Caminetti, who's both the resort's proprietor and resident hustler.

3. ***The Green*** by Troon McAllister, 1999 – Two-bit Florida golf hustler Eddie Caminetti hits the jackpot when desperate pro Al Bellamy drafts him for the United States Ryder Cup team. The proverbial odd man out, the fast-talking con artist ultimately proves invaluable to the team in this good-natured send-up of the biennial competition.

4. ***Missing Links*** by Rick Reilly, 1996 – Sick and tired of playing on a course littered with abandoned cars and shopping carts, four working class golfers scheme to crash the nearby Mayflower Club, Boston's most exclusive golf course. What begins as a friendly bet, however, soon spirals into comic disaster once they get a look at how the other half golfs.

5. ***The Money-Whipped Steer-Job Three-Jack Give-Up Artist*** by Dan Jenkins, 2001 – Near the very bottom of the PGA money list, Bobby Joe "Spin" Grooves has never won a major tournament in his sixteen-year career. In a final bid for credibility, he sets his sights on making the U.S. Ryder team, a goal that will probably be a lot easier than keeping his ex-wives and a jealous girlfriend at bay.

Harlem Renaissance Classics

Afro-Americana

The 1920s saw the dawn of what African-American philosopher/ Rhodes scholar Alain Locke famously dubbed the era of the "New Negro"—a period of unprecedented artistic growth in literature, art, and music by African-Americans, many of whom called New York's Harlem home. As WASP blue bloods and Greenwich village bohemians trekked uptown to hear Duke Ellington and his orchestra perform at the Cotton Club, poets and writers like Countee Cullen, Langston Hughes, and Zora Neale Hurston explored the questions of racial identity and African-American culture in their self-published magazine, *Fire! Devoted to Younger Negro Artists.*

Although the "Harlem Renaissance" would more or less end with the onset of the Depression in the 1930s, its legacy endures in the unusually high number of classic novels published by Hughes, Hurston and other, lesser-known writers. Here are eight of the most celebrated novels by "Harlem Renaissance" authors, listed alphabetically.

1. ***Cane*** by Jean Toomer, 1923 – A commercial disappointment upon publication, Toomer's extraordinary novel is an amalgam of poetry, short fiction, and character sketches that was truly ahead of its time. Adeptly mixing these literary forms, Toomer illuminates the plight of the African-American in the American South.

2. ***Fire in the Flint*** by Walter White, 1924 – Light-skinned, with blonde hair and blue eyes, White nonetheless identified himself as black and served as the executive director of the NAACP from 1931 to 1955. In this overlooked classic, White tackles racism head-on in his taut narrative about a Harvard-educated black doctor running afoul of the Klu Klux Klan in rural Georgia.

3. ***Home to Harlem*** by Claude McKay, 1927 – A black, World War I U.S. Army deserter returns from Europe to live the high life in 1920s-era Harlem, where he encounters a veritable rogue's gallery of dreamers, schemers, and hustlers in McKay's boldly realized, atmospheric novel.

4. ***Infants of the Spring*** by Wallace Thurman, 1932 – Thurman fires off satirical barbs at Langston Hughes, Zora Neale Hurston, and other

leading figures of the "Harlem Renaissance" in this witty and daring (for its time) roman a clef, about the artists, writers and entertainers living in a rooming house nicknamed "Niggeratti Manor."

5. ***Jonah's Gourd Wine*** by Zora Neale Hurston, 1934 – Praised as "one of the greatest writers of our time" by Nobelist Toni Morrison, the novelist, folklorist, and anthropologist depicts the rise and fall of a womanizing preacher in her challenging but rewarding first novel, written in black Southern dialect.

6. ***Not Without Laughter*** by Langston Hughes, 1930 – Renowned as a poet, Hughes tried his hand at fiction with this sensitively written coming-of-age story about a poor young black boy, dreaming of a life beyond the suffocating confines of rural Kansas.

7. ***Quicksand*** by Nella Larsen, 1928 – Born to a black father and a Danish mother, Helga Crane feels inexorably caught between two worlds. She embarks on a journey to find her niche, but as time passes, becomes increasingly disillusioned, in Larsen's tragic, largely autobiographical novel.

8. ***Plum Bun*** by Jessie Redmon Fauset, 1928 – Able to "pass," a beautiful, light-skinned black woman deludes herself into thinking that being taken for white will bring her everlasting happiness, only to grapple with other issues, in Fauset's insightful novel.

Historical Fiction

Dreaming Up the Past

Even in the "olden days" of ancient Greece, writers were looking back nostalgically at past times that seemed more heroic, more romantic, and more picturesque than their own contemporary societies. Historical fiction is a genre whose possibilities are all the richer for its strange combination of verisimilitude and pure, unfettered imagination. If we could read an attempt by a twenty-fifth century author to write historical fiction about our times, would it seem like an authentic picture of them? Impossible to know, but we can tell when we've got hold of a good historical novel—feeling swept away into a distant time and place is a good indicator. Here are eight acclaimed novels, listed alphabetically, set as far back as the biblical era. Most of them do take liberties with the facts, but they succeed in making the characters, social milieus, and events feel convincing in their own way.

1. ***Ivanhoe*** by Sir Walter Scott, 1819 – The adventures of a dishonored knight redeeming himself in medieval England's struggle between the Normans and the Saxons. Robin Hood and Friar Tuck make appearances here, plus some unforgettable ladies.

2. ***Les Misérables*** by Victor Hugo, 1862 – The story of Valjean, a decent peasant who becomes a criminal and later a mayor, serves as the basis for a passionate exploration of the nature of morality, crime, innocence, and even the sewers of Paris. The upheavals of early nineteenth century France comes to life in this long and winding tale.

3. ***The Other Boleyn Girl*** by Philippa Gregory, 2001 – There's more drama in the true history of Henry VIII's court than most soap opera writers could ever make up—conflicting loyalties, devious power plays, illicit sex, and executions. Experience all this through the eyes of Mary Boleyn, Anne's less ambitious—and ultimately more fortunate—sister.

4. ***Ragtime*** by E.L. Doctorow, 1975 – Playing much more loosely with historical characters (Harry Houdini, Sigmund Freud, and the Archduke Franz Ferdinand all show up in this somewhat zany book), Doctorow evokes the vitality and tensions of early, twentieth century America.

5. ***The Red Tent*** by Anita Diamant, 1997 – Dinah is the daughter of Jacob, briefly mentioned in the *Old Testament*. She becomes the central character here, a vehicle for the author to imagine the world of biblical women in rich, poetic detail.

6. ***The Scarlet Letter*** by Nathaniel Hawthorne, 1850 – In seventeenth century Salem, Massachusetts (the town of witchcraft-trial infamy), a woman named Hester Prynne refuses to identify the father of her illegitimate child and is forced to wear a scarlet "A," indicating that she is guilty of adultery. But this is only the beginning of a story that questions the nature of sin and purity.

7. ***Shogun*** by James Clavell, 1975 – The saga of an English ship pilot in Japan in the year 1600, when the nation is on the brink of great

change. John Blackthorne gradually learns the ways of the country, falls in love with a Catholic Japanese woman, and is drawn into the samurais' violent political struggles.

excerpt: ***THE SCARLET LETTER:***
The young woman was tall, with a figure of perfect elegance on a large scale. She had dark and abundant hair, so glossy that it threw off the sunshine with a gleam; and a face which, besides being beautiful from regularity of feature and richness of complexion, had the impressiveness belonging to a marked brow and deep black eyes. She was ladylike, too, after the manner of the feminine gentility of those days; characterised by a certain state and dignity, rather than by the delicate, evanescent, and indescribable grace which is now recognised as its indication. And never had Hester Prynne appeared more ladylike, in the antique interpretation of the term, than as she issued from the prison.

8. ***A Tale of Two Cities*** by Charles Dickens, 1859 – In the years leading up to the French Revolution, tensions simmer between oppressive aristocrats and bitter common folk. A man wrongly imprisoned in Paris for nearly two decades is reunited with his long-lost daughter and escapes to London, but their family is still not immune from the violence of the times in this affecting tale of love and sacrifice.

Historical Overviews

The Family of Man

For all our flaws, we humans have got to hand it to ourselves for at least one thing—we're a fascinating species. The variety of languages, cultures, discoveries, and experiences that form our shared history is pretty amazing. There are lots of wonderful books that look at small slices of history—what it was like to live through a certain war, or why that war took place; how a new religion evolved after its founding; how great political experiments were tried; the struggles and joys of a single extraordinary person in a particular time and place. But in order to appreciate all that, sometimes we need to step back and get a broad view of ourselves and our history. The following books, listed alphabetically, do just that in vivid detail.

1. ***The Discoverers: A History of Man's Search to Know His World and Himself*** by Daniel J. Boorstin, 1983 – This is actually a history of science, but it provides insight into many of the most important breakthroughs in history, from the development of solar timekeeping

to the birth of the modern world. As sweeping as the scope of the book is, it depicts individuals and societies with a wonderful vividness, explaining the hindrances to innovation and the ways people have overcome them.

2. ***Guns, Germs, and Steel: The Fates of Human Societies*** by Jared Diamond. 1997 – Why did Westerners, rather than New Guineans, Africans, or Native Americans, come to dominate much of the rest of the world? Diamond aims to answer this question by examining the geographical and environmental circumstances that allowed people of the West to domesticate plants and animals and become immune to devastating diseases. The book offers an important angle on the development of civilizations, although it has been criticized for implying that explanations are either environmental or racist, while ignoring cultural factors that change over time and have nothing to do with skin color.

3. ***Heroes of History: A Brief History of Civilization from Ancient Times to the Dawn of the Modern Age*** by Will Durant, 2001 – Durant is most famous for the multi-volume *Story of Civilization,* which he wrote with his wife, Ariel Durant. This single volume, published after his death, is a more compact exploration of thinkers and leaders, from Buddha to Leonardo da Vinci. It's an engrossing overview of changing philosophies, religions, and world views.

4. ***The Journey of Man: A Genetic Odyssey*** by Spencer Wells, 2002 – Historians are not the only people who can tell us about our pasts, and we have more than written documents to teach us about our common history. Both the fossil record and the genetic record that lives on in all of us have much to reveal about our common history. Wells explains what studying the relatively stable male Y chromosome has taught us about our origins and migrations, confirming that we all developed in Africa and that our racial differences are superficial.

5. ***The New History of the World*** by John M. Roberts, 2002 – This revision of an earlier work covers the history of mankind from its earliest civilizations to the fall of the Berlin Wall and 9/11. Remarkably thorough, it can be considered a one-book survey course.

Hoaxes and Forgeries in Literature

Don't Believe Everything You Read...

Forgers have all kinds of different purposes and motivations. They see a creative challenge; they want to show up the other nonsense that gets into print; they want to bolster their country's history or make someone else look bad; and some of them just want to get famous by any means. Editors, historians, and fact checkers have their work cut out for them—and so do readers. Whether it's an obscure web page on the Internet or a respectable academic journal, don't abandon your skepticism! Here are just a few notable cases of forgeries and hoaxes in the last two and a half centuries, listed in no particular order.

1. **Ossian** – In 1760, at a time when the literary world seemed to be looking for refreshment from overcivilized poetry, a Scottish tutor (and poet of limited success) named James Macpherson won fame by publishing a volume called *Fragments of Ancient Poetry Collected in the Highlands of Scotland*. He claimed to have translated the verses from Scottish Gaelic and that they dated from the third century. A group of his countrymen raised a hundred pounds to fund Macpherson in a search for the epic that they hoped was the source of the fragments, and within a few years he had published two sections of the epic supposedly written by the bard Ossian. Macpherson was accused of forgery in his own time, and modern scholarship has confirmed that the "ancient" poetry was more invention than translation. It did, however, influence the romantic poetry of the following century.

2. **Thomas Chatterton's Rowley** – Even more beloved by the romantic poets was the "marvelous boy" Thomas Chatterton, who produced his own poetic forgeries just a few years after the Macpherson controversy—and whom John Keats called "the purest writer in the English Language." His invention was a fifteenth century monk named Rowley, who wrote such lovely lyrics as "Mie love ys dedde, / Gon to hys death-bedde, / Al under the wyllowe-tree." Chatterton, the son of a widowed seamstress, wrote his "medieval" poems on scraps of old parchment. He had limited success in attracting interest in them during his short lifetime and remained desperately poor. At the age of seventeen, half-starved, he committed suicide in his garret in London.

3. **Mark Twain's Sensational Journalism** – Mark Twain was a newpaperman as well as a fiction writer and humorist, and he didn't always keep these roles separate. When he lived in Nevada and wrote for the *Territorial Enterprise,* he wrote two satirical articles that were taken seriously and picked up by other Western newspapers. The first, published in 1862, concerned the supposed discovery of a fossilized man who had died of exposure long ago and was preserved with his hand in a peculiar position—thumbing his nose. The next hoax, which he published the following year, told of a speculator who had lost his mind and massacred his family, then cut his own throat and ridden into town holding his wife's bloody scalp in one hand. Neither had the slightest basis in fact.

4. **The Protocols of the Elders of Zion** – In contrast to many hoaxes that are relatively harmless, this forged document has been used off and on for over a century to justify discrimination and violence against an ethnic group. It details the plans of a group of Jewish financiers in the late nineteenth century to destroy Christian society and dominate the world. The Russian secret police may have been responsible for the forgery; in any case, whoever the real authors were, they didn't even have the virtue of originality. Much of the contents of "the Protocols" was drawn from two earlier works of fiction, Maurice Joly's satire *Dialogues aux enfers entre Machiavel et Montesquieu* (1864) and Hermann Goedsche's novel *Biarritz* (1868, published under the pen name Sir John Retcliffe).

5. **The Ern Malley Affair** – Now, back to the relatively harmless. In 1944, the Australian avant-garde literary magazine *Angry Penguins* devoted its June issue to a recently discovered poet named Ern Malley, whom the editor praised for the "perfection and integrity of his verse." His sister Ethel, it seemed, had discovered sixteen of the garage mechanic's poems after his death and submitted them. In fact, they were the work of two living poets, James Phillip McAuley and Harold Stewart, who were disgruntled with the course of modern poetry and invented Ern Malley to expose its absurdity. They composed the works in a single day, dreaming up such portentous lines as "When the hysterical vision strikes / The facade of an era it manifests / Its insidious relations." It's still a controversial question whether the editor had awful standards or the poets were so talented that their "bad" poetry was unintentionally good.

Hollywood Nonfiction

Tinsel Town Laid Bare

Described by Hollywood producer Joe Roth as "the most observant, knowledgeable and intuitive screenwriter in the business today," two-time Academy Award winner William Goldman has written such classic films as *All the President's Men, Butch Cassidy and the Sundance Kid,* and *Marathon Man*. After forty-plus years of swimming with the showbiz sharks—and living to tell about it—Goldman wittily summed up his impressions of Hollywood in three words: "Nobody knows anything." So begins his 1983 memoir *Adventures in the Screen Trade,* which has become essential reading for wannabe scribes or anyone trying to make sense of the fear, arrogance, and confusion endemic to Tinsel Town, where sure-fire properties often tank at the box office, and Teflon-coated executives fail upwards while others crash and burn.

Here are eight must-reads, listed alphabetically, that give readers the insider scoop on life and work in the Dream Factory, where as the saying goes, "You're only as good as your last picture."

1. ***Adventures in the Screen Trade: A Personal View of Hollywood and Screenwriting*** by William Goldman, 1983 – Goldman's collection of essays, reminiscences, and screenwriting tips is a bracingly funny and whip-smart book that spawned an equally good sequel, *Which Lie Did I Tell? More Adventures in the Screen Trade.*

2. ***City of Nets: A Portrait of Hollywood in the 1940s*** by Otto Friedrich, 1986 – A monumental social history of Hollywood that reads like a vivid, epic novel. Although the film industry is covered extensively in Friedrich's book, he widens his gaze to write about everything from the zoot suit riots to mobster Bugsy Siegel.

excerpt: CITY OF NETS:

[Errol] Flynn's search for enjoyment consisted of endless drinking and fornicating, plus a certain indulgence in drugs. On the crest of a hill on Mulholland Drive, he designed and built a $125,000 house that embodied all the sensual fantasies of that time and place, from glass cases filled with guns to a cockfighting arena in the stable to bedrooms outfitted with black silk hangings, sable bed coverings, and two-way mirrors in the walls and ceilings, so that guests could watch the other guests at play.

3. ***The Devil's Candy: The Anatomy of a Hollywood Fiasco*** by Julie

Salamon, 1991 – No doubt filmmaker Brian De Palma still rues the day he agreed to let *Wall Street Journal* reporter Julie Salamon shadow him 24/7 during the making of *The Bonfire of the Vanities*. What was supposed to be De Palma's masterpiece turned out to be a colossal bomb. In Salamon's lively and fascinating account of how not to make a hit film, only Tom Hanks emerges unscathed from the wreckage of *The Bonfire of the Vanities*.

4. ***Easy Riders, Raging Bulls: How the Sex, Drugs and Rock'n' Roll Generation Changed Hollywood*** by Peter Biskind, 1998 – Truth is far stranger than fiction in Biskind's jaw-dropping overview of Hollywood in the 1970s, when wunderkinds Francis Ford Coppola, Martin Scorsese, and Steven Spielberg forever transformed the movie business. While it's packed with juicy, often embarrassing anecdotes about stars and filmmakers running wild, *Easy Riders, Raging Bulls* is an informative and insightful analysis of an industry in crisis.

5. ***An Empire of Their Own: How the Jews Invented Hollywood*** by Neal Gabler, 1988 – In his vigorously written and thorougly researched book about the early movie moguls, Gabler examines the cultural and political forces that inspired Harry Cohn, Louis B. Mayer, and Samuel Goldwyn, among others, to find their niche in Hollywood.

6. ***Final Cut: Art, Money and Ego in the Making of Heaven's Gate, the Film That Sank United Artists*** by Stephen Bach, 1985 – Given creative and financial carte blanche after the success of *The Deer Hunter,* director Michael Cimino let his bloated ego get the better of him—and everyone involved in the making of his dream project, *Heaven's Gate*. One of the biggest disasters in Hollywood history, *Heaven's Gate* effectively rendered Cimino persona non grata in Hollywood and forced United Artists to close. A United Artists executive at the time, Bach chronicles the film's ill-fated production in this book that veteran producer David Brown called "compulsively readable."

7. ***Picture*** by Lillian Ross, 1952 – A regular contributor to the *New Yorker*, Ross got permission from director John Huston to watch him direct *The Red Badge of Courage* in 1950. First published in serial form in the *New Yorker, Picture* is widely considered the best book ever written about Hollywood—a revealing, warts-and-all portrait of movie studio politics, hubris, and Machiavellian intrigue.

8. ***The Studio*** by John Gregory Dunne, 1969 – Granted unlimited access to observe the corporate and production divisions of Twentieth Century Fox for one year, i.e., 1967, Dunne wrote this meticulously detailed and wonderfully engaging account of glitzy excess, bad behavior, and ego-driven studio politics that's a classic of Hollywood journalism.

Hollywood Novels

Dream Factory Fiction

A likable scoundrel who co-owned and managed The Brown Derby during Hollywood's golden heyday, Wilson Mizner memorably described Tinsel Town as "a trip through a sewer in a glass-bottomed boat." Most writers would tend to agree with Mizner's scathing assessment of the Dream Factory, where crass commercialism invariably trumps art. Of course, that didn't stop such literary heavyweights as F. Scott Fitzgerald, William Faulkner, and Dorothy Parker, to name just three, from toiling in the lucrative Hollywood trenches as screenwriters. But while most novelists regard working in Hollywood as nothing more than a glorified form of indentured servitude, they certainly come away with a wealth of juicy material. Exploring the often grim reality beneath the glamour, the following novels, listed alphabetically, depict the surreal mixture of fantasy, desperation, ego, and ruthlessness that is Hollywood.

1. ***The Day of the Locust*** by Nathanael West, 1939 – A critical and commercial disappointment when it was published in 1939, West's haunting portrait of the has-beens and hopefuls relegated to the Hollywood "fringe" is now regarded as a classic of twentieth century American literature.

2. ***Force Majeure*** by Bruce Wagner, 1991 – Loosely autobiographical, Wagner's bleak, scathingly funny novel chronicles the emotional and creative meltdown of a struggling screenwriter, forced to work as a chauffeur. Sparing no one, least of all his literary alter ego, Wagner gleefully satirizes all the usual Hollywood suspects, as well as some real-life celebrities.

3. ***Get Shorty*** by Elmore Leonard, 1990 – The inimitable pulp stylist Elmore Leonard hits the comic bulls-eye with this laugh-out-loud funny

page turner about a small-time loan shark diving into the Hollywood cesspool, where he's neck deep in colorful lowlifes. Breathlessly paced and full of Leonard's zingy one-liners, *Get Shorty* was followed by a sequel, *Be Cool*.

4. ***Inside Daisy Clover*** by Gavin Lambert, 1963 – Written in journal form, Lambert's overlooked novel offers a fresh, insightful take on the familiar rags-to-riches saga of the title character, a teenaged movie star deemed "washed-up" at the age of eighteen. Funny, self-aware and vulnerable, Daisy Clover is one of the most appealing heroines in all of the novels written about Hollywood.

5. ***The Last Tycoon*** by F. Scott Fitzgerald, 1940 – Tragically, Fitzgerald died before he completed *The Last Tycoon,* his thinly veiled portrait of the legendary MGM wunderkind, Irving Thalberg. Yet even in its truncated form, Fitzgerald's final novel is a dazzling achievement that had the potential to become another masterpiece, on par with *The Great Gatsby*, in its depiction of the power struggle between idealistic producer Monroe Stahr and his arch-rival Pat Brady.

6. ***The Loved One*** by Evelyn Waugh, 1947 – The English novelist satirizes Tinsel Town in his perversely funny jab of a novel, set in the ultra-exclusive Whispering Glades funeral home, where the chief embalmer and the crematorium cosmetician fall in love while preparing dead movie stars for their final close-up.

7. ***Play it as it Lays*** by Joan Didion, 1970 – Her career and personal life in tatters, a despondent actress/model fights a losing battle to hold onto her humanity in this dark and troubling look at life in the Hollywood fast lane.

8. ***What Makes Sammy Run?*** by Budd Schulberg, 1941 – Sammy Glick, the conniving, amoral opportunist at the center of Schulberg's grandly entertaining debut novel, is one of the all-time great heels in American literature. Sammy's rise from a Lower East Side tenement to Hollywood palace is strewn with casualties, but he's "running" too fast, forever in pursuit of his next triumph, to notice the damage in his wake.

Holocaust Literature

Never Forget

"Never forget." It's both a lament and a vow regarding the estimated six million victims of the Holocaust. More than sixty years after the end of World War II, the unspeakable atrocities perpetrated by Nazi Germany under the aegis of Hitler's "Final Solution" defy rationality. How could this happen? It's a question that's obsessed writers since the full magnitude of the horrific genocide became public knowledge.

With piercing insight, harrowing detail, and occasional mordant wit, the following titles, listed alphabetically, represent some of the most unforgettable books written about the Holocaust.

1. ***Fateless*** by Imre Kertész, 1975 – Masterful, shattering novel from Kertész, the 2002 Nobel Prize winner. Reportedly autobiographical, *Fateless* immerses the reader in the grueling concentration camp experiences of the narrator, a fourteen year-old Hungarian Jewish boy.

2. ***If Not Now, When?*** by Primo Levi, 1982 – Levi's only novel is a stunner about a group of Jewish Soviet partisans fighting their way across war-torn Eastern Europe in hopes of reaching Palestine.

3. ***King of the Jews*** by Leslie Epstein, 1979 – Appointed the head of the *Judenrat* in the Jewish ghetto of Lodz, Poland, an unscrupulous, charismatic doctor treats the ghetto like his personal fiefdom in Epstein's marvelous and complex novel.

4. ***The Painted Bird*** by Jerzy Kosinski, 1965 – Not for the faint-hearted, Kosinski's graphically violent novel about a war orphan suffering undue cruelty at the hands of Eastern European peasants is nonetheless a remarkable achievement.

5. ***Schindler's List*** by Thomas Keneally, 1982 – Winner of the Booker Prize, Keneally's seamless blend of fact and fiction tells the incredible story of an unlikely savior: womanizing, boozing playboy businessman Oscar Schindler, who saved the lives of a thousand Polish Jews in World War II.

6. ***The Shawl*** by Cynthia Ozick, 1989 – Comprised of a short story and a novella, *The Shawl* is a brilliant character study about an elderly Holocaust survivor, living in embittered retirement in Florida, who lost her sense of self in the camps.

7. ***Sophie's Choice*** by William Styron, 1979 – Styron's masterpiece unfolds through the eyes of Southern born-writer "Stingo," whose life is forever changed by his relationship with the beautiful, tormented concentration camp survivor, Sophie Zawistowski.

excerpt: SOPHIE'S CHOICE:
Sophie paused for a few moments and locked her eyelids shut as if in savage meditation, then gazed once more out onto the baffling distances. "So there is one thing that is still a mystery to me. And that is why, since I know all this and I know the Nazis turned me into a sick animal like all the rest, I should feel so much guilt over all the things I done there. And over just being alive. This guilt is something I cannot get rid of and I think I never will."

8. ***This Way for the Gas, Ladies and Gentlemen*** by Tadeusz Borowski, 1947 – Unflinching, matter-of-fact stories of concentration camp life narrated by the author's fictional alter ego, Tadeusz. A major influence on Imre Kertész, Borowski committed suicide in 1951, reportedly bereft over the brutality of the Communist regime in Poland.

Immortal Lines

Most Quoted Books in Barlett's Familiar Quotations

What books are richest in memorable lines? To find out, we hunted through the most recent incarnation of *Bartlett's Familiar Quotations,* the seventeenth edition (2002, edited by Justin Kaplan). *Bartlett's* is surely one of the world's most delightful and instructive reference works. Here are the books that can boast fifty or more entries in it, listed in descending order, along with some of their most compelling lines. *Paradise Lost's* respectable 136 quotations would certainly seem to disprove Alexander Pope's quip that the book offers readers "One simile that solitary shines / In the dry desert of a thousand lines"!

While Shakespeare emerges as the single most quotable author, and we give him his own list here, the *Bible* has more than seven times the quotations of *Hamlet*. In the first edition of *Bartlett's,* published by a Massachusetts bookseller in 1855, the *Bible* and the Bard were the best-represented sources—which just goes to show that "the more things change, the more they remain the same" (a saying coined, as *Bartlett's* tells us, by Alphonse Karr in *Les Guêpes,* 1849).

TITLE	*ENTRIES IN BARTLETT'S*

1. ***The Holy Bible*** (various authors) — 1,610

   "And God said, Let there be light: and there was light" (Genesis 1:3); "Let my people go" (Exodus 5:1); "The meek shall inherit the earth" (Psalms 37:11); "The truth shall make you free." (John 8:32)

2. ***Paradise Lost*** (John Milton) — 136

   "No light, but rather darkness visible"; "All hell broke loose"

3. ***Don Quixote de la Mancha*** (Miguel de Cervantes) — 112

   "To give the devil his due"; "There's no sauce in the world like hunger"; "Honesty's the best policy."

4. ***The Canterbury Tales*** (Geoffrey Chaucer) — 93

   "Whan that Aprill with his shoures soote / The droghte of March hath perced to the roote"; "If gold ruste, what shal iren do?"

5. ***Life of Johnson*** (James Boswell) — 83

   "A decent provision for the poor is the true test of civilization"; "Depend upon it, sir, when a man knows he is to be hanged in a fortnight, it concentrates his mind wonderfully"; "Clear your mind of cant."

6. ***Proverbs*** (John Heywood) — 79

   "Haste maketh waste"; "Two heads are better than one"; "Would ye both eat your cake and have your cake?"; "Enough is as good as a feast."

7. ***The Iliad*** (Homer) — 72

   "Rosy-fingered dawn appeared, the early-born"; "Smiling through tears"; "There is a fullness of all things, even of sleep and of love."

8. ***Complete Poems*** (Emily Dickinson) — 69

   "'Hope' is the thing with feathers— / That perches in the soul"; "There's a certain Slant of light, / Winter afternoons— / That oppresses, like the Heft / Of Cathedral tunes"; "Much Madness is divinest sense— / To a discerning Eye."

9. ***Maxims*** (Publilius Syrus) — 63

   "Treat your friend as if he might become an enemy"; "A rolling stone gathers no moss"; "No one knows what he can do till he tries"; "Prosperity makes friends, adversity tries them."

10. ***The Divine Comedy*** (Dante Alighieri) 61

"All hope abandon, ye who enter here!"; "And thence we came forth, to see again the stars"; "A great flame follows a little spark."

11. ***Childe Harold's Pilgrimage*** 56
(George Noel Gordon, Lord Byron)

"I stood in Venice on the Bridge of Sighs."

12. ***Aeneid*** (Virgil) 55

"Of arms and the man I sing"; "Each of us bears his own Hell"; "Fortune favors the brave."

13. ***The Anatomy of Melancholy*** (Robert Burton) 53

"A dwarf standing on the shoulders of a giant may see farther than a giant himself"; "All our geese are swans."

14. ***Lamia, Isabella, The Eve of St. Agnes, and Other Poems***
(John Keats) 50

"A thing of beauty is a joy forever"; "What leaf-fring'd legend haunts about thy shape?" "'Beauty is truth, truth beauty'—that is all / Ye know on earth, and all ye need to know."

Indian Novels

Noteworthy Fiction from the Subcontinent

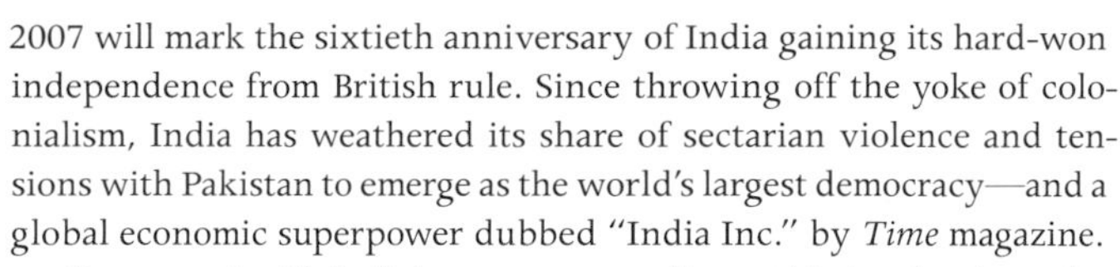

2007 will mark the sixtieth anniversary of India gaining its hard-won independence from British rule. Since throwing off the yoke of colonialism, India has weathered its share of sectarian violence and tensions with Pakistan to emerge as the world's largest democracy—and a global economic superpower dubbed "India Inc." by *Time* magazine.

Concurrent with India's emergence on the world stage has been the flowering of Indian literature, thanks to the internationally acclaimed work of Nobelist V.S. Naipaul, cultural provocateur Salman Rushdie, and political firebrand Arundhati Roy, to name three. Although life under the British Raj is a recurrent theme in many novels by contemporary Indian writers, the following books, listed alphabetically, explore everything from family dynamics to India's caste system in prose evoking the luxuriant colors and breathtaking diversity that is India.

1. ***The Death of Vishnu*** by Manil Suri, 2001 – Set in contemporary Bombay, Suri's luminous and finely wrought novel uses the death of the ti-

tle character, a vagrant who lives in the stairs of an apartment building, as the narrative catalyst for this seriocomic portrait of Indian society.

2. ***The God of Small Things*** by Arundhati Roy, 1997 – Roy's 1997 Booker Prize winner prompted comparisons to Dickens, Faulkner, and Garcia Marquez, yet it has its own, highly original voice. Through the life-changing experiences of seven year-old fraternal twins in Kerala, India, circa 1969, Roy illuminates the impact of the caste system and the oppression of women on contemporary Indian society.

excerpt: THE GOD OF SMALL THINGS:
Mammachi held a gleaming violin under her chin. Her opaque fifties sunglasses were black and slanty-eyed, with rhinestones on the corners of the frames. Her sari was starched and perfumed. Off-white and gold. Her diamond earrings shone in her ears like tiny chandeliers. Her ruby rings were loose. Her pale, fine skin was creased like cream on cooling milk and dusted with tiny red moles. She was beautiful. Old, unusual, regal. Blind Mother Widow with a violin.

3. ***A House for Mr. Biswas*** by V.S. Naipaul, 1961 – The Indo-Trinidadian novelist established himself with this darkly comic novel about downtrodden Mohun Biswas, whose dreams of owning a home in Trinidad are frustrated at every turn. Reportedly inspired by Naipaul's father, *A House for Mr. Biswas* made *Time* magazine's list of hundred best English-language novels published since 1923.

4. ***Hullabaloo in the Guava Orchard*** by Kiran Desai, 1998 – Tired of being nagged by his parents, a n'er-do-well takes refuge in a guava orchard, where he becomes the unlikeliest holy man the villagers have ever seen. A zany, light-hearted farce that's often laugh-out-loud funny.

5. ***Midnight's Children*** by Salman Rushdie, 1980 – It may not be Rushdie's most famous (or infamous) book—that would be *The Satanic Verses*—but *Midnight's Children* is arguably his best. It's a brilliantly conceived and written epic in the magic realist tradition about two boys born at the stroke of midnight, August 15, 1947: the exact moment of India's independence from British rule.

6. ***The Point of No Return*** by Siddharta Deb, 2002 – In a remote corner of India in the 1980s, a young Bengali man reminisces about his aged father's life, which had been forever altered by the partitioning of India in 1947. Told in reverse chronological order, Deb's first novel is

an impeccably crafted meditation on the often strained relationship between fathers and sons.

7. ***Raj*** by Gita Mehta, 1991 – Covering more than fifty years in India's tumultuous history, Mehta's sweeping panorama of a novel depicts the former British colony's move towards independence through the eyes of Princess Jaya of Balmer.

8. ***A Suitable Boy*** by Vikram Seth, 1993 – Don't be put off by the sheer bulk of Seth's second novel. It's an engaging and immensely readable story—an old-fashioned yarn with a huge cast of memorable characters—set in 1950s-era India, where an overbearing mother attempts to find the title character for her daughter.

Irish Novels

Noteworthy Fiction from the Emerald Isle

Legend has it that if you kiss the famous Blarney Stone just outside Cork in southwest Ireland, you'll be rewarded with the gift of eloquence. Whether any of Ireland's illustrious literary figures have bent over backwards to plant their lips on this stone is not known, but the Emerald Isle has certainly produced some of the most dazzling and inventive wordsmiths of all time. In the eighteenth century, Jonathan Swift and Laurence Sterne put Ireland on the world's literary map with *Gulliver's Travels* and *Tristram Shandy,* respectively. And in the 1920s, Dublin-born James Joyce revolutionized fiction with his colossal, modernist, stream-of-consciousness epic *Ulysses*. Spanning one day in the life of Leopold Bloom, this protean, densely allusive and often bawdy book was named the twentieth century's greatest English-language novel by Modern Library in 1999.

Taking up the mantle from Joyce, Flann O'Brien, and Samuel Beckett, among others, contemporary Irish writers like John Banville, Roddy Doyle, and Edna O'Brien continue to explore life in Eire in fiction blessed with Blarney Stone eloquence. Here are eight notable books, listed alphabetically, by Irish writers past and present.

1. ***At Swim, Two Boys*** by Jamie O'Neill, 2002 – Written over the course of ten years, O'Neill's stream-of-consciousness novel about two teenaged boys falling in love against the backdrop of the impending 1916 Easter Rebellion is a literary tour de force.

2. ***The Country Girls*** by Edna O'Brien, 1960 – Leaving behind their strict convent upbringing to revel in their newfound freedom in London, O'Brien's naïve heroines Kate and Baba try to maintain their friendship amid numerous distractions—namely men. Controversial when published, *The Country Girls* is the first novel in O'Brien's trilogy charting the roller coaster friendships of her heroines.

3. ***Fools of Fortune*** by William Trevor, 1983 – Hailed by Irish novelist Frank Delaney as one of the "great books that deals with the Irish question," Trevor's Whitbread Prize winner depicts the psychological fallout of the Anglo-Irish War on a wealthy man and his mother, the sole survivors of a brutal attack on their estate.

4. ***The Ginger Man*** by J. P. Donleavy, 1955 – One of the Modern Library's hundred best novels of the twentieth century, Donleavy's jaunty and ribald comic novel chronicles an Irish-American academic's drunken, womanizing exploits through the pubs of Dublin.

5. ***The Last September*** by Elizabeth Bowen, 1929 – In the midst of the bloody tumult of the IRA's war against the British government in Ireland, an idealistic young woman of privilege rejects her aristocratic family's values to find her identity, in Bowen's most famous novel.

6. ***Paddy Clarke Ha Ha Ha*** by Roddy Doyle, 1993 – The author of *The Commitments* won England's Booker Prize for this rollicking coming-of-age yarn about a working class ten year-old on the hunt for adventure in the streets of Barrytown. Doyle's feel for the colorful vernacular of his street urchin title character lends *Paddy Clarke Ha Ha Ha* a bracing immediacy.

excerpt: THE SEA*:*

We seemed to spend, Chloe and Myles and I, the most part of our days in the sea. We swam in sunshine and in rain; we swam in the morning, when the sea was sluggish as soup, we swam at night, the water flowing over our arms like undulations of black satin; one afternoon we stayed in the water during a thunderstorm, and a fork of lightning struck the surface of the sea so close to us we heard the crackle of it and smelt the burnt air.

7. ***The Sea*** by John Banville, 2005 – Grieving the recent death of his wife, a middle-aged man retreats to the Irish seaside village where he spent his summers during childhood. Flashing back and forth be-

tween the past and present, Banville's Booker Prize winning character study is an elegiac, beautifully written gem.

8. ***Ulysses*** by James Joyce, 1922 – Rightly hailed as a work of genius, *Ulysses* is one of the most challenging and infinitely rewarding novels you'll ever tackle.

Jazz Age Books

Linda Wagner-Martin's Favorites

The reckless bravado and extravagant excesses of the Jazz Age come vividly to life in the novels of F. Scott Fitzgerald, the hard-drinking, high-living writer whose stormy personal life informs his fiction. With his beautiful but unstable "flapper" muse Zelda at his side, Fitzgerald "burned the candle at both ends," to paraphrase poet Edna St. Vincent Millay, both at home and abroad as a charter member of the 1920s-era "Lost Generation." In between parties, Fitzgerald sobered up long enough to write two of biographer Linda Wagner-Martin's picks for the top ten Jazz Age books. The author of *Zelda Sayre Fitzgerald: An American Woman's Story,* Wagner-Martin includes both fiction and nonfiction titles in her list, which she contributed to *The Guardian* newspaper.

1. ***The Beautiful and the Damned*** by F. Scott Fitzgerald, 1922 – Fitzgerald once said, "'Sometimes I don't know whether Zelda and I are real or whether we are characters in one of my novels." The fun-loving couple in *The Beautiful and the Damned* certainly bears more than a passing resemblance to the Fitzgeralds. According to Wagner-Martin, Fitzgerald's second novel "helped create the term 'Jazz Age.'"

2. ***The Green Hat*** by Michael Arlen, 1924 – Born Dikran Kouyomdjian in Bulgaria, the Armenian immigrant transformed himself into the very English Michael Arlen when he embarked on his literary career in London, circa 1920. With *The Green Hat,* which became a long-running play starring Talullah Bankhead, Arlen "set the stage for 'the new woman' characters," per Wagner-Martin.

3. ***The Great Gatsby*** by F. Scott Fitzgerald, 1925 – Fitzgerald's masterpiece, *The Great Gatsby* exposes the underside of the American dream in this haunting story of an enigmatic millionaire's attempts to rekindle a past love with a society belle. Wagner-Martin states that *The*

Great Gatsby "showed the futility of monetary success ... not backed up by moral conviction."

4. ***The Sun Also Rises*** by Ernest Hemingway, 1926 – Reportedly written in just six weeks, *The Sun Also Rises* established Hemingway as one of the key writers of the "Lost Generation." His loosely autobiographical novel about expatriates drinking their way across post-World War I Europe reaches its memorable conclusion in Pamplona, Spain, the site of the running of the bulls. According to Wagner-Martin, *The Sun Also Rises* "captures the mood of the hard-drinking and hard-loving 'Jazz Age.'"

5. ***Save Me a Waltz*** by Zelda Sayre Fitzgerald, 1932 – A talented writer in her own right, Zelda Sayre Fitzgerald completed her only novel while hospitalized for schizophrenia. A thinly veiled autobiography, *Save Me A Waltz* is "the best treatment of the agony, and the satisfaction, of art," per Wagner-Martin.

6. ***Sanctuary*** by William Faulkner, 1932 – Lurid, sex-soaked Southern Gothic shocker, supposedly written to make a fast buck, about a party girl kidnapped and raped by bootleggers in Prohibition-era Mississippi. Steeped in atmosphere, *Sanctuary* "provides the best early treatment of Stockholm Syndrome," raves Wagner-Martin.

7. ***The Autobiography of Alice B. Toklas*** by Gertrude Stein, 1933 – The gnome-like experimental writer/modern art patron writes in an idiosyncratic, repetitious style that leaves many readers cold. This "spoof of the memoir genre," per Wagner-Martin, may be Stein's most accessible book: a lively account of her Parisian years with life partner, Alice B. Toklas.

8. ***A Moveable Feast*** by Ernest Hemingway, 1964 – Hemingway's memoir provides an engaging, albeit romanticized tour of 1920s-era Paris. "Rightly famous," says Wagner-Martin, *A Moveable Feast* recounts Hemingway's unforgettable encounters with such notables as James Joyce, Ezra Pound, and F. Scott Fitzgerald.

9. ***Ernest Hemingway: The Paris Years*** by Michael Reynolds, 1989 – In the second volume of his five-book biography of Hemingway, ace biographer Reynolds turns his attention to the novelist's formative experiences and relationships in the "City of Lights." Wagner-Martin calls this exhaustively researched book "the standard work" about Hemingway's time abroad.

10. ***Favored Strangers: Gertrude Stein and Her Family*** by Linda Wagner-Martin, 1995 – Wagner-Martin's own contribution to the list examines Stein's life and times vis-à-vis her relationships with Toklas and her older brothers, who shared her passion for modern art.

Jewish-American Novels

From Sholem Aleichem to Michael Chabon

He was known as the "Jewish Mark Twain." An estimated 100,000 mourners attended his Brooklyn funeral in 1916. And his tragicomic stories about Tevye the milkman in Czarist Russia inspired one of Broadway's longest-running musicals. Yet while the great Yiddish humorist/writer Sholem Aleichem may not be as widely read today, he certainly helped pave the way for Saul Bellow, Philip Roth, and other Jewish-American novelists too numerous to list who've flourished in twentieth century American literature.

Although Jewish-American writers have achieved preeminence in all literary genres— from science fiction (Isaac Asimov) to poetry (Stanley Kunitz) to children's literature (Maurice Sendak), to name three—the following novels, listed alphabetically, specifically address the Jewish-American experience in its many permutations, past and present.

1. ***The Adventures of Augie March*** by Saul Bellow, 1953 – Eulogized by Roth as part of the "backbone of twentieth century American literature," Bellow won the first of his three National Book Awards for this superb picaresque about the title character's rough-and-tumble coming-of-age in Depression-era Chicago. Both Martin Amis and Salman Rushdie regard *The Adventures of Augie March* as "the great American novel."

2. ***Adventures of Mottel: The Cantor's Son*** by Sholem Aleichem, 1953 – Unfinished at the time of Aleichem's death in 1916, this boisterously funny novel about a poor Russian Jewish immigrant in turn-of-the-century America was published sans ending in English in 1953.

3. ***The Amazing Adventures of Kavalier and Clay*** by Michael Chabon, 2000 – Chabon's Pulitzer Prize winning novel is a dazzling narrative about two Jewish cousins/comic book innovators in World War II-era America.

4. ***Call it Sleep*** by Henry Roth, 1934 – Overlooked when first published, Roth's stream-of-consciousness novel about a Jewish immigrant growing up in New York's Lower East Side is now considered one of the greatest books of twentieth century American literature.

5. ***The Chosen*** by Chaim Potok, 1967 – A heartwarming story of two boys, a Modern Orthodox Jew and the son of a Hasidic rebe, and their struggles with their fathers in 1940s-era Brooklyn.

6. ***Enemies: A Love Story*** by Isaac Bashevis Singer, 1972 – Winner of the 1978 Nobel Prize for Literature, Singer wrote short stories, children's books, memoirs, and novels in a career spanning sixty-odd years. In this tragicomic novel, a Holocaust survivor living in New York City, circa 1949, finds himself torn between three very different women.

7. ***Goodbye, Columbus and Five Short Stories*** by Philip Roth, 1959 – Roth first scored with his blisteringly funny satirical novella *Goodbye, Columbus*, about a graduate student from a working class background who falls for the pampered daughter of a wealthy Jewish businessman. Winner of the 1960 National Book Award.

8. ***The Puttermesser Papers*** by Cynthia Ozick, 1997 – Ozick's National Book Award finalist is a witty and shrewdly observed blend of mysticism and character study about Ruth Puttermesser, a middle-aged Jewish lawyer in New York City.

excerpt: THE PUTTERMESSER PAPERS:

At the unsatisfying age of fifty-plus, Ruth Puttermesser, lawyer, rationalist, ex-public official, took a year off to live on her savings and think through her fate. In the second week of her freedom—no slavery of paperwork, no office to go to (a wide tract of her life already bled out in the corridors of the Municipal Building, enough!)—it came to her that what she ought to do was marry. This was not a new idea: it had been her mother's refrain as far back as three decades ago or more, ever since Puttermesser's first year in law school.

Latino Novels

Viva Hispania!

In 1990, Cuban-American Oscar Hijuelos became the first Latino writer to win the Pulitzer Prize for his second novel, *The Mambo Kings Play Songs of Love*. This elegiac, jazzily atmospheric story of two Cuban brothers/musi-

cians fleeing Havana for 1950s-era New York effectively jump-started the boom in Latino literature. Although several, notable works of Latino-themed fiction had preceded *The Mambo Kings,* none of them had ever caught on with the general public quite like Hijuelos' acclaimed best-seller, which was later turned into a popular film starring Antonio Banderas.

Today, with the Latino population in the United States estimated at forty million and growing, the market for Latino fiction will only continue to expand. Spanning genres from historical fiction to salsa-flavored "chick lit" to coming-of-age stories, here are eight of the more notable Latino-themed novels listed alphabetically.

1. ***Bless Me, Ultima*** by Rudolfo Anaya, 1973 – In New Mexico, circa 1940s, a seven year-old Chicano boy finds an unlikely mentor in his aged aunt, a mystical healer, who comes to live with the family. Under her benevolent influence, he gradually comes to terms with his parents' divergent expectations and his cultural identity. Anaya's coming-of-age novel won the Premio Quinto Sol, the national Chicano literary award.

2. ***Bodega Dreams*** by Ernesto Quinonez, 2000 – Steeped in the vernacular and street customs of Spanish Harlem, Quinonez's debut novel practically boils over with raw energy and ebullient wit. Chino, the streetwise hero, is torn between his love for an ultra-religious classmate and the lure of quick money offered by Willie Bodega, a local gangster.

3. ***The Dirty Girls' Social Club*** by Alisa Valdes-Rodriguez, 2003 – Often called the Latina answer to *Waiting to Exhale,* Valdes-Rodriguez's tangy, breezily paced first novel follows the professional and romantic lives of six Latinas, who met as Boston University undergraduates.

4. ***Dreaming in Cuban*** by Cristina Garcia, 1992 – A 1992 National Book Award finalist, Garcia's arresting family saga blends otherworldly imagery and political upheaval as it portrays the lives of three generations of Cuban women.

5. ***The House on Mango Street*** by Sandra Cisneros, 1984 – Growing up in a rough, inner city Latino neighborhood in Chicago, sensitive, bookish Esperanza Cordero finds solace in writing poetry and short stories. A captivating and moving debut novel from Mexican-American poet/novelist Cisneros, the author of *Caramelo.*

excerpt: ***THE HOUSE ON MANGO STREET:***
Your abuelito is dead, Papa says early one morning in my room. Esta muerto, and then as if he just heard the news himself, crumples like a coat and cries, my brave Papa cries. I have never seen my Papa cry and don't know what to do.

I know he will have to go away, that he will take a plane to Mexico, all the uncles and aunts will be there, and they will have a black-and-white photo taken in front of the tomb with flowers shaped like spears in a white vase because this is how they send the dead away in that country.

6. ***The Hummingbird's Daughter*** by Luis Alberto Urrea, 2005 – Urrea reportedly spent twenty years researching and writing this marvelous historical epic based on the life of his Great Aunt Teresita, the "Saint of Cabora" a political lightning rod denounced by the Catholic Church and embraced by Mexico's indigenous people.

7. ***The Mambo Kings Play Songs of Love*** by Oscar Hijuelos, 1989 – Visions of music stardom in their eyes, brothers Nestor and Cesar Castillo leave Cuba in 1949 for New York, where they encounter triumph and tragedy as the "Mambo Kings."

8. ***The Ordinary Seaman*** by Francisco Goldman, 1997 – Goldman's second novel couldn't be more timely—or wrenching. Promised work on a freighter, fifteen Central American illegal immigrants find themselves trapped on a derelict ship moored at a Brooklyn pier. Based on a true story, *The Ordinary Seaman* is another triumph from the acclaimed Guatemalan author of *The Long Night of White Chickens.*

Letters

Great Collections from the Past

One of the most entertaining and surprising ways to get to know the people of the past is to read the letters they sent one another. There are a wealth of collections of the letters of great writers from Jane Austen to J.R.R. Tolkien—see if you can find any by your favorite author the next time you're at the bookstore or library. Some novels are even written completely in the form of letters, like Montesquieu's eighteenth-century *Persian Letters,* in which Persian travelers visit the exotic land of Europe. What follows is an alphabetical list of collections of real-life letters that let you peek into the lives of some of the world's greatest observers, lovers, and wits. Reading them just might make you decide, in this age of e-mail, to pen some spirited snail mail yourself!

1. ***Lawrence of Arabia: The Selected Letters*** edited by Malcolm Brown, 1988 – A glimpse into the private world of the legendary T.E. Lawrence, soldier, leader, archaeologist, and writer.

2. ***The Letters of Abelard and Héloise*** by Peter Abelard, Héloise, translated by Betty Radice, 1974 – The passionate correspondence between the tragic medieval lovers, a Parisian scholar and his student, who continued to write to each other even after they became a monk and an abbess.

3. ***Letters to a Young Poet*** by Rainer Maria Rilke, 1929 – A classic volume of meditations on love, art, and life from one poet to another.

excerpt: LETTERS TO A YOUNG POET:
And about emotions: all emotions are pure which gather you and lift you up; that emotion is impure which seizes only one side of your being and so distorts you. Everything that you can think in the face of your childhood, is right. Everything that makes more of you than you have heretofore been in your best hours, is right. Every heightening is good if it is in your whole blood, if it is not intoxication, not turbidity, but joy which one can see clear to the bottom. Do you understand what I mean?

4. ***The Poems of Exile: Tristia and the Black Sea Letters*** by Ovid, translated by Peter Green, 1994 – Late in his life, the author of *Metamorphoses* was banished by the Roman emperor Augustus to a distant fishing village on the Black Sea. We don't know why he was exiled, but we do have these letters in verse, some of them quite beautiful, pleading—unsuccessfully, alas—to be allowed back to Rome.

5. ***Selected Letters*** by Madame de Sévigné, edited by Leonard Tancock, 1982 – Politics, culture, and everyday concerns in Louis XIV's France come to life in the letters of this court lady, mother, and friend to the likes of the great aphorist La Rochefoucauld.

Magical Realist Literature

Latin America's Literary Wizards

A doomed young beauty with yellow eyes and green hair; a child with a curly pig's tail who's eaten by ants; time stopping for a condemned prisoner facing a firing squad— such fantastic events abound in the worlds conjured by the Latin American magical realists. Although this peculiar hybrid of extravagant fantasy and gritty, socially conscious realism is not the exclusive province of Latin American novelists—both England's John Fowles and Germany's Gunter Grass are considered magical realists—the genre's best known writers hail from Latin America. Along with Argentine novelist/poet/short story writer Jorge Luis Borges, Colombian Nobel Prize winner Gabriel Garcia Marquez is a literary wizard of magical realism, whose masterpiece, *100 Years of Solitude* has sold over ten million copies worldwide.

Here are eight of the most acclaimed works of Latin American magical realism, listed alphabetically.

1. ***100 Years of Solitude*** by Gabriel Garcia Marquez, 1967 – A gorgeous, intricately woven narrative tapestry that demands your complete attention, Garcia Marquez's family saga envelopes you in the rising and sinking fortunes of the Buendia family, over the course of a century in the mythical Colombian village of Macondo.

2. ***Collected Fictions*** by Jorge Luis Borges, 1998 – Heady, metaphysical short stories that defy categorization from Borges, whose preoccupations with time and memory figure prominently in this compendium of his dazzling, otherworldly *ficciones.*

3. ***Dona Flor and Her Two Husbands*** by Jorge Amado, 1966 – A beautiful young widow's second marriage is nearly derailed by the meddling ghost of her first husband in this bawdy, ebullient romp from Brazilian modernist Amado.

4. ***Hopscotch*** by Julio Cortazar, 1963 – Experimental novel, written in 155 chapters that can either be read consecutively or randomly—hence the title—from Argentine novelist/short story writer Cortazar. After his Parisian mistress disappears, an Argentine expatriate returns home to Buenos Aires, where he takes a series of jobs ranging from circus trainer to insane asylum attendant.

5. ***The House of the Spirits*** by Isabel Allende, 1985 – What began as Allende's letter to her dying grandfather eventually became the manuscript for this Chilean journalist's first novel: a family saga that some critics initially dismissed for its similarity to *100 Years of Solitude*. Over time, however, *The House of the Spirits* has emerged from the considerable shadow of Garcia Marquez's novel to stand on its own merits as a soaring work of imagination.

6. ***Inez*** by Carlos Fuentes, 2000 – In shimmering prose, the Mexican novelist weaves together two parallel love stories that take place in London, circa 1940, and in prehistoric times, respectively.

excerpt: INEZ:
It was a crystal seal. Opaque but luminous. That was its greatest marvel. In its place on the tripod by the window, light could shine through it, and then the crystal scintillated. It shot delicate sparks, and illegible letters appeared, revealed by the light: letters of a language unknown to the aged orchestra conductor, a score in a mysterious alphabet, perhaps the language of a lost people, maybe a voiceless clamor that came from a long-ago time...

7. ***The Lost Steps*** by Alejo Carpentier, 1953 – A composer flees civilization to immerse himself in the primitive world of an Amazonian tribe, in this stunning adventure novel from the Cuban novelist/journalist.

8. ***Love in the Time of Cholera*** by Gabriel Garcia Marquez, 1988 – In Garcia Marquez's magisterial novel of unrequited love, a man woos the object of his affection in a highly unorthodox courtship that spans a half-century.

Maugham's Picks

W. Somerset Maugham's Ten Best Novels in Western Literature

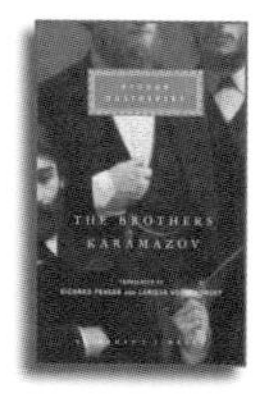

Over the course of a prolific, genre-hopping literary career that spanned more than sixty years, English novelist/playwright/essayist and short story writer W. Somerset Maugham (1874-1965) established himself as one of the twentieth century's great men of letters. Revered for such classic novels as *The Razor's Edge* (1944) and the semi-autobiographical *Of Human Bondage* (1915), the latter widely considered his masterpiece, Maugham defied the starving artist stereotype to lead a wildly glamorous life in a sumptuous French Riviera villa, until World War II turned him into a jet-setting refugee.

During the 1920s and 1930s, however, Maugham's wealth and celebrity provoked the scorn of many critics and fellow writers, who unfairly—perhaps jealously—dismissed him as a literary dandy. Yet Maugham was intensely passionate about literature, which should "be read with enjoyment. If it does not give that it is worthless." Or so he writes in the introduction to his 1948 collection of essays, *Great Novelists and Their Novels.* With that criterion in mind, Maugham chose the following ten novels as the all-time best, which are listed per his ranking.

1. ***War and Peace*** by Leo Tolstoy, 1869 – A perennial fixture on critics' lists of the world's great novels, Tolstoy's massive yet intimate epic depicts the interwoven lives of three aristocratic families during Napoleon's invasion of Russia, circa 1805-1813. Both a sweeping epic and a polemic—Tolstoy interrupts the narrative to discourse on politics and history—*War and Peace* is a demanding yet utterly enthralling novel.

2. ***Pere Goriot*** by Honore de Balzac, 1834 – Balzac casts a jaundiced eye on nineteenth century Paris in this realistic, coming-of-age novel about a poor but rabidly ambitious young man determined to make his mark in high society. Remarkable for its vivid evocation of nineteenth century Paris, which registers as strongly as any of the flesh and blood characters, *Pere Goriot* has been cited as a major influence on such writers as Emile Zola and Marcel Proust.

3. ***Tom Jones*** by Henry Fielding, 1749 – A rollicking comic picaresque teeming with bawdy good humor, *Tom Jones* chronicles the misadventures of the title character, a cheerfully unrepentant womanizer looking for his parents in eigthteenth century England.

4. ***Pride and Prejudice*** by Jane Austen, 1813 – Austen's brilliant comedy of manners is one of the most beloved novels of all time. Nearly 200 years after its publication, the tempestuous love story of Elizabeth Bennett and Fitzwilliam Darcy continues to enchant readers with its sparkling mixture of droll wit, heartfelt romance, and astute class observations in Regency-era England.

5. ***The Red and the Black*** by Stendal, 1831 – Along with Balzac, nineteenth century French novelist Stendhal is regarded as one of the

founders of realistic literature. *The Red and the Black* is undeniably his masterwork: a dense, psychologically acute rendering of an amoral, self-deluding young man whose hunger for society's approval ultimately seals his downfall. Laden with allusions to the work of Shakespeare and Voltaire, among many others, *The Red and the Black* is unsparing in its criticism of French high society.

6. ***Wuthering Heights*** by Emily Brontë, 1847 – Has there ever been a more swoon-worthy love story than *Wuthering Heights?* Brontë's only novel, published the year of her death from tuberculosis, is a brooding, mood-drenched tale of the volatile romance of Heathcliff and Cathy, set in the dreary Yorkshire moors where Brontë grew up, the younger sister of *Jane Eyre* novelist Charlotte Brontë.

7. ***Madame Bovary*** by Gustave Flaubert, 1857 – Considered quite le scandale when published, *Madame Bovary* depicts the gradual downward spiral of the title character, a vain and restless bourgeois woman who deserts her husband and child to embark on a brazen love affair. A bold and frankly realistic novel, *Madame Bovary* sent a shock wave through nineteenth century literary circles.

excerpt: ***MADAME BOVARY:***
Then the lusts of the flesh, the longing for money, and the melancholy of passion all blended themselves into one suffering, and instead of turning her thoughts from it, she clave to it the more, urging herself to pain, and seeking everywhere occasion for it. She was irritated by an ill-served dish or by a half-open door; bewailed the velvets she had not, the happiness she had missed, her too exalted dreams, her narrow home.

8. ***David Copperfield*** by Charles Dickens, 1850 – Reportedly the most autobiographical of Dickens' novels, this wonderfully engaging character study follows the title character through triumph and tragedy from birth to middle age. Filled with some of the memorable characters in all of English literature—Micawber, Uriah Heep, and the title character/narrator—*David Copperfield* was the author's "favorite child" of all his novels.

9. ***The Brothers Karamazov*** by Fyodor Dostoevsky, 1880 – Hailed by Sigmund Freud as "the most magnificent novel ever written," Dostoevsky's final novel is a towering achievement of psychological depth and philosophical complexity. The murder of the drunken, n'er-do-

well Karamazov patriarch draws us into the lives of the title characters, who struggle with the moral and spiritual repercussions of parricide in nineteenth century Russia.

10. ***Moby Dick*** by Herman Melville, 1851 – The sole American novel on Maugham's list, *Moby Dick* is much more than simply a seagoing yarn about Captain Ahab's obsessive pursuit of the legendary white whale. While contemporary readers may find Melville's huge, sprawling allegorical novel a bit unwieldy, due to Melville's tendency to go off on nonfiction tangents, *Moby Dick* is nonetheless a stunning, one-of-a kind novel that occupies an almost mythic stature in American literature.

Meditative Literature

Writings on Solitude

Our means of communication are amazing—cell phones, e-mail, televisions set into the walls of elevators, and who knows what will be next—but they can make it hard to get a moment's peace. Sometimes we can use a little time completely alone to balance all that interconnectedness. Silence, solitude, and reflection, especially in a natural setting, can teach us valuable lessons about our lives and provide a wordless peace. For inspiration, here are some books, listed alphabetically, by writers who committed to making time for reflection.

1. ***Fifty Days of Solitude*** by Doris Grumbach, 1994 – With her companion away for over a month, the author, in her seventies, spends the time alone in their home in coastal Maine, occasionally visiting town but avoiding speaking to anyone. "A strong wind had disconnected the antenna to the television set," she writes; at home, she focuses on her books, her mail, and her thoughts. It is a hushed but not always easy time.

2. ***Gift from the Sea*** by Anne Morrow Lindbergh, 1955 – During a brief sojourn by the ocean, Lindbergh meditates on the rhythms of nature and the lovely shells that wash up on the beach, using the peaceful interlude to restore her spirit and gain insight into her busy life. "The sea does not reward those who are too anxious, too greedy, or too impatient," she writes. "Patience, patience, patience is what the sea teaches."

3. ***Journal of a Solitude*** by May Sarton, 1973 – Sarton ponders on the question of how to balance connection with others and solitude for a life that is both emotionally rich and creatively productive. Judging by her many beloved books, she was remarkably successful in striking this balance.

4. ***Society and Solitude*** by Ralph Waldo Emerson, 1870 – The title essay (originally lecture) in this collection discusses the necessity and difficulty of being alone in order to create works of genius. Emerson, one of America's greatest philosophers, believes that it is possible for us to fulfill our highest potentials "if we keep our independence, yet do not lose our sympathy."

5. ***Thoughts in Solitude*** by Thomas Merton, 1956 – The author was a Trappist monk, but his thoughts on the importance of solitude to our spiritual and ethical lives have at least as much relevance—perhaps more—for those of us who live in the secular world.

Memoirs

Celebrity Kiss & Tell-Alls

Dropping names and her drawers with tireless frequency, the late, blowsy character actress Shelley Winters dished the dirt with gossipy relish about her sexual exploits with Hollywood stars in her best-selling 1980 autobiography, *Shelley: Also Known as Shirley.* And while few stars have divulged as many "intimate" details about their Tinsel Town affairs as the four-time married Winters, others have written frankly about their struggles with mental illness, alcoholism, and drug abuse. Due in part to the increasing "tabloidization" of the media, where nothing is off-limits and paparazzis launch surprise attacks on celebrities, it's become the norm for stars to 'fess up to scandals, addictions, and other indiscretions in juicy autobiographies. Here are eight celebrity tell-alls, listed alphabetically, that give readers the inside scoop on Hollywood, from its golden age to today.

1. ***Dean and Me (A Love Story)*** by Jerry Lewis with James Kaplan, 2005 – With surprising candor and more than a touch of regret, Lewis probes his volatile, love-hate relationship with former partner, Dean Martin, in this even-handed memoir.

2. ***The Kid Stays in the Picture*** by Robert Evans, 1994 – Discovered by Norma Shearer poolside at the Beverly Hills Hotel, Evans acted in a few films before finding his unlikely niche as a studio mogul. In his funny, warts-and-all chronicle of his roller coaster professional and personal lives, Evans gives readers their money's worth of Hollywood dirt.

3. ***The Million Dollar Mermaid*** by Esther Williams with Digby Diehl, 1999 – Memorably dissed by Fanny Brice, who said of her, "Wet she's a star; dry she ain't," the MGM bathing beauty leaves the pool to share revealing anecdotes about her co-stars, stormy marriage to Fernando Lamas, and affair with cross-dressing he-man Jeff Chandler.

4. ***My Wicked, Wicked Ways*** by Errol Flynn, 1959 – A scandal magnet for much of his film career, the dashingly handsome swashbuckler burned the proverbial candle at both ends, drinking, womanizing, and carousing his way into an early grave at age fifty. Published just months after his death, *My Wicked, Wicked Ways* vividly demonstrates what it meant to be "In like Flynn."

5. ***A Paper Life*** by Tatum O'Neal, 2004 – Although Ryan O'Neal has publicly disputed many of his daughter's most shocking claims in this headline-making book, *A Paper Life* is a Hollywood cautionary tale that tracks the fallen child star's decline into heroin addiction, following a combative marriage to tennis player John McEnroe.

6. ***Shelley: Also Known as Shirley*** by Shelley Winters, 1980 – While she refrains from sharing graphic details about her torrid affairs with Marlon Brando, William Holden, and Burt Lancaster, to name three, Winters otherwise lets it all hang out, in a autobiography that spawned a 1989 sequel, *Shelley II: The Middle of My Century.*

7. ***Tab Hunter Confidential: The Making of a Movie Star*** by Tab Hunter with Eddie Muller, 2005 – Under the predatory sway of notorious Hollywood agent Henry Willson, Arthur Gelien became 1950s-era heartthrob Tab Hunter—a blonde, blue-eyed All-American boy whose homosexuality was a carefully guarded secret. Now in his seventies and happily out of the closet, Hunter writes about his checkered career and long-term affair with Anthony Perkins in his frank autobiography.

8. ***What Falls Away*** by Mia Farrow, 1997 – "Hell hath no fury" like Farrow scorned, as the actress proves in her autobiography, which

spews ample venom at her ex-lover, Woody Allen. A true child of Hollywood privilege, Farrow also paints a starry portrait of her life, career, and marriages to Frank Sinatra and Andre Previn.

Memoirs

Childhoods Interrupted

If you think you had it rough growing up, odds are that Frank McCourt probably had it worse—a lot worse. In his phenomenally popular memoir *Angela's Ashes,* McCourt writes movingly of the extreme hardship he endured as a poverty-stricken Irish Catholic boy in the slums of Limerick, circa 1930s. What little money McCourt's alcoholic wastrel of a father managed to scrap together usually went towards his pub tab, rather than the family, despite the best efforts of McCourt's mother, Angela. Yet there's not a whiff of self-pity in McCourt's lively, colorful memoir of childhood interrupted.

Thanks in large part to *Angela's Ashes,* the memoir has become a staple on the nonfiction best-seller list. While some memoirs of rampant dysfunction and abuse paint dark, nightmarish portraits of family life in explicit, borderline exploitative detail, the following memoirs, listed alphabetically, brook that unfortunate literary trend towards melodramatic freak show tell-alls. With unsparing honesty, rueful humor, and keen insight, these books, listed alphabetically, reveal the joys and sorrows of childhood—and how these authors found the tools to survive, often under extraordinary duress.

1. ***All Over But the Shoutin'*** by Rick Bragg, 1997 – To describe Bragg's childhood in rural northern Alabama as "hardscrabble" would be an understatement. Deserted by her husband, an alcoholic, psychologically traumatized Korean War veteran, Bragg's dirt-poor mother worked 24/7 to provide for him and his two brothers. In this richly evocative memoir, the *New York Times* reporter pays tribute to his remarkable mother.

2. ***Angela's Ashes*** by Frank McCourt, 1996 – The proverbial luck of the Irish did not shine on the embattled, tragedy-prone McCourt clan, who returned to Ireland from New York in search of a better life, only to sink deeper into poverty. Yet in the midst of all this suffering, there is ample wit and warmth in McCourt's Pulitzer Prize winning best-seller.

3. ***Don't Let's Go to the Dogs Tonight: An African Childhood*** by Alexandra Fuller, 2001 – The daughter of white, gun-wielding farmers, Fuller grew up in 1970s-era Rhodesia (now Zimbabwe), when racial tensions regularly exploded into violence. In plain-spoken yet intensely felt prose, Fuller describes a childhood composed of equal parts wonder and anxiety.

4. ***The Glass Castle*** by Jeannette Walls, 2006 – Although she's the very image of the sleek, urban sophisticate, New York gossip columnist Walls still bears the scars of a poor, itinerant childhood that took her from Arizona to West Virginia. Her parents were brilliant, loving eccentrics spectacularly ill-equipped to feed and clothe Walls and her siblings on a regular basis. Utterly devoid of self-pity, *The Glass Castle* is an emotionally powerful memoir that's unforgettable.

5. ***I Know Why the Caged Bird Sings*** by Maya Angelou, 1969 – A landmark autobiography from one of America's most beloved poets, *I Know Why the Caged Bird Sings* is a stunning work, at once lyrical and brutally honest. Spanning Angelou's childhood and adolescence, *I Know Why the Caged Bird Sings* addresses the racism Angelou faced growing up in Depression-era Arkansas.

6. ***The Liar's Club*** by Mary Karr, 1995 – Born into a "terrific family of liars and drunks" in a tiny, East Texas refinery town, Karr mines literary gold in this compelling tragicomic saga that packs an emotional wallop. An equally mesmerizing sequel, *Cherry,* followed in 2001.

7. ***Running With Scissors*** by Augusten Burroughs, 2002 – Given the sheer insanity of Burroughs' childhood, it's a miracle he can still form sentences, much less write such a morbidly hilarious memoir that leaves you shaking—with shocked laughter, that is.

8. ***Them: A Memoir of Parents*** by Francine du Plessix Gray, 2005 – The novelist and Marquis de Sade biographer explores the emotional turmoil lurking beneath the glittering surface of her childhood in 1940s-era Manhattan, where her parents ran in the most exclusive circles. Although Gray's Russian emigre mother displayed all the maternal instincts of a snake, *Them* is no *Mommie Dearest,* but an elegant and surprisingly even-handed memoir.

Memoirs

Curious Careers

Have you ever wondered what it's really like to be a spy? A chef at a fine restaurant? An FBI agent posing as a jewel thief? Or a real jewel thief? Not to worry if these careers are beyond your reach (or beyond your wishes)—you can learn all about them from the safety and peace of a comfortable armchair. Listed alphabetically, these memoirs offer plenty of excitement, little-known facts about mysterious corners of society, and insights into the minds of people in unusual (and often illegal) circumstances.

1. ***Blowing My Cover: My Life as a CIA Spy*** by Lindsay Moran, 2005 – A recent Harvard graduate, the author joined the Central Intelligence Agency in her late twenties. Her career with the CIA (working undercover in Macedonia) was brief but challenging. She writes about the intensive training process, the difficulties of remembering all the details of her fake life, and the strains of being unable to communicate freely with some of the people most important to her.

2. ***Catch Me If You Can: The True Story of a Real Fake*** by Frank W. Abagnale with Stan Redding, 1980 – As a young man, Frank Abagnale was a brazen and frighteningly successful liar. He spent millions of dollars that he didn't have, traveled internationally free of charge by pretending to be a pilot, and conned people into placing him in several other positions of responsibility for which he was unqualified. Now an expert in fraud prevention, Abagnale may not win your admiration, but his story will astonish you (and convince you of the value of thorough background checks).

3. ***Confessions of a Master Jewel Thief*** by Bill Mason and Lee Gruenfeld, 2003 – This is the story of another resourceful but less-than-stellar character, a family man with a secret criminal career. Bill Mason describes his carefully planned thefts of jewels from Phyllis Diller, a mafia boss, and various others.

4. ***Donnie Brasco: My Undercover Life in the Mafia*** by Joseph D. Pistone, 1987 – Pistone, an FBI agent, spent about half a decade working undercover among criminals, pretending to be a jewel thief named Donnie Brasco. Here he shares what he learned about the Mafia life-

style and describes the challenges of his dangerous and ultimately disorienting jobs.

5. ***Jumping Fire: A Smokejumper's Memoir of Fighting Wildfire*** by Murray A. Taylor, 2000 – For over a quarter century, Taylor spent his summers parachuting out of airplanes into remote areas of the rugged, beautiful Alaskan landscape to battle wildfires. This memoir mainly describes 1991, a particularly fiery year. Courage, strength, and a strong sense of humor are all job requirements—and Taylor is also a wonderful storyteller.

6. ***Kitchen Confidential: Adventures in the Culinary Underbelly*** by Anthony Bourdain, 2000 – There is often a wide gulf between the people who consume the food at the world's better restaurants and the people who create that food. Bourdain, an accomplished chef, swings the kitchen doors wide open for curious gourmands. You might not want to see everything he reveals, but you're sure to be a better-informed customer, and it's an entertaining read.

7. ***Memoirs of a Sword Swallower*** by Daniel P. Mannix, 1951 – Mannix explains how he came to be a fire-eater and sword-swallower, some tricks of the trade to keep the entertainment from becoming fatal, and what carnival life is really like, writing with sympathy about his fellow special talents and "freaks."

8. ***Spy Handler: Memoir of a KGB Officer*** by Victor Cherkashin and Gregory Feifer, 2005 – A unique Russian perspective on cold war–era espionage, this is the story of the KGB agent who recruited CIA agent Aldrich Ames and FBI agent Robert Hanssen as double agents for the Soviet Union. It's a thoughtful but frightening exposé of deception, blackmail, and treason.

Memoirs

Political Lives

We see them on TV, holding press conferences and giving speeches. And we read about them in newspapers and history books, but it's often devilishly hard to get a sense of politicians' inner lives. Luckily, many of the most influential political figures have written autobiographies. Given the nature of the beast, we have to read

them skeptically. In many cases, undoubtedly, even a retired leader will keep the impulse for "spinning" the truth that helped him or her rise to prominence. Even so, these are fascinating reads, listed alphabetically, about some of history's most interesting characters, and what really goes on behind the scenes in high places.

1. ***All Too Human*** by George Stephanopoulos, 1999 – The author managed Bill Clinton's bumpy presidential campaign and served as a senior (albeit very young) advisor during Clinton's first term in office. He writes insightfully about Bill, Hillary, the vice president, and the other major players; the administration's internal rivalries; and the extreme stress of his crash course in high and low politics.

2. ***Gandhi, An Autobiography: The Story of My Experiments With Truth*** by Mohandas Karamchand Gandhi, 1927–1929 – Gandhi wrote this book two decades before India won its independence from Britain. It is not an exhaustive account of his political activities, but instead describes the development of the ethical ideas that led him to devote himself to justice by way of satyagraha, nonviolent resistance—the basis for his remarkable political achievements.

3. ***Inside the Third Reich: Memoirs*** by Albert Speer, 1970 – An architect and friend of Adolf Hitler, Speer held important positions in Hitler's government in the 1930s and 1940s. It is still debatable how much he knew about the regime's most heinous crimes (he himself served twenty years in prison after the Nuremberg tribunal), but this is a valuable, firsthand look at the personality of the dictator and the workings of his totalitarian system.

4. ***Long Walk to Freedom: The Autobiography of Nelson Mandela*** by Nelson Mandela, 1994 – Mandela helped form the African National Congress Youth League as a young man and went on to make immense sacrifices for the cause of ending apartheid. Learn about his long struggle against both the brutal and the subtle aspects of South Africa's racist system.

5. ***Memoirs of the Second World War*** by Winston S. Churchill, 1959 – If you don't have time for Churchill's six-volume *The Second World War,* read this abridgement. It describes the most dramatic and, arguably, the most important conflict of the twentieth century from the perspective of the man who warned that it was coming long before

anyone wanted to listen, and rallied his countrymen (along with international allies) for victory.

6. ***My Life*** by Bill Clinton, 2004 – Very little of Clinton's life and presidency seems to be left out of this detailed and energetic account. He describes his troubled but lively youth in Arkansas, the formation of his political ideas, and what it was really like to spend eight years in the Oval Office during an accomplished but scandal-ridden presidency.

7. ***My Life*** by Leon Trotsky, 1930 – One of the early leaders of the Communist movement in Russia, Trotsky was later exiled by Stalin and ultimately murdered. Trotsky's intelligence and the drama of his story (two escapes from banishment in Siberia, negotiating Russia's separate peace at the end of World War I, organizing the Red Army, and so on) make this an extraordinary read.

8. ***Worth the Fighting For: The Education of an American Maverick, and the Heroes Who Inspired Him*** by John McCain and Mark Salter, 2002 – An earlier book, *Faith of My Fathers* (1999), describes the Arizona senator's experiences in Vietnam. This one begins after McCain's release from the POW camps and recounts his eventful political career through his bid for the presidency in 2000. It also explains why McCain admires his heroes—military, political, athletic, and cultural—and what he learned from them.

Memoirs

Political Revolution Chronicles

Some of the most dramatic and harrowing passages in human history have taken place during times of political revolution. The United States owes its democracy to one such revolution, but many of them have not met with such success. In all too many cases, legitimate grievances have led to the overthrow of one oppressive regime, only to replace it with chaos or new forms of oppression. This alphabetical list comprises some firsthand accounts of life in revolutionary times—some by people who were more or less obscure, others by prominent people. By definition, of course, the subject matter of these memoirs is divisive; we can't claim that all the authors are free from bias of one sort or another. But they all offer insight into very unusual times.

1. ***An American Family in the Mexican Revolution*** by Robert Woodmansee Herr and Richard Herr, 1999 – Based on family documents, this is the story of American silver miners in Mexico during a period of tumultuous national politics (beginning during the long-lived presidency of Porfirio Díaz and continuing through several revolts and coups from 1911 into the 1920s) and troubled relations between Mexico and the United States (including resentment of privileged American investors).

2. ***Blessed by Thunder: Memoir of a Cuban Girlhood*** by Flor Fernández Barrios, 1999 – The author was a small child when the Cuban revolution took place, but her memory reaches back far, and its repercussions affected her entire youth. Her father had political troubles—first for being suspected of pro-Castro sympathies, later for considering leaving the country after Castro's takeover—and she herself spent two years harvesting tobacco and sugar at a work camp while still a young girl.

3. ***How We Survived Communism and Even Laughed*** by Slavenka Drakuli, 1991 – A Croatian woman describes daily life before, during, and just after the 1989–90 revolution in Zagreb, prior to the ensuing civil war. It's an intelligent and sensitive look at the legacy of decades of communism.

4. ***Iran Awakening: A Memoir of Revolution and Hope*** by Shirin Ebadi and Azadeh Moaveni, 2006 – A winner of the Nobel Peace Prize, Ebadi was Iran's first female judge. She originally had high hopes for the revolution that overthrew the unpopular shah in 1979, but found herself demoted by the theocratic regime because of her gender. However, she went on to become a prominent human rights attorney. This is a fascinating inside view of the Islamic revolution in Iran and its aftermath.

5. ***Life and Death in Shanghai*** by Nien Cheng, 1986 – When Mao Zedong's Cultural Revolution sent China into upheaval, the author became a target of persecution because she worked for a foreign company and was prosperous. While people all around her were intimidated into making false confessions (and accusations), she stood her ground. She spent several years in jail; after her release, she discovered that her daughter had died in custody. The author continued to be harassed and was even knocked down in front of a bus. Throughout it all she maintained her sense of truth and dignity.

6. ***Memoirs of Madame Roland*** by Jeanne-Marie Roland de la Platière, 1795 – Madame Roland and her husband were prominent members of the Girondin party during the French Revolution—a revolution that destroyed many of its own leaders. She ended up going to the guillotine, famously saying on the way, "O Liberty, what crimes are committed in thy name!" She wrote her memoirs during the months she spent in prison before her execution; they recount both her early life and her revolutionary years.

7. ***Memoirs of a Revolutionary*** by Victor Serge, 1951 – A remarkable writer, Serge shares the equally remarkable story of his political experiences in the first half of the twentieth century in Europe. He was an anarchist who originally supported the Russian Revolution but lived to see it turn into a brutal dictatorship. The book brings this turbulent time to life with great immediacy.

8. ***The Revolutionary War Memoirs of General Henry Lee*** by Henry Lee, 1812 – The father of Robert E. Lee, General Henry "Light-Horse Harry" Lee was an important military leader and politician; he was friends with George Washington and helped win the political battle for Virginia to ratify the Constitution. In 1808 and 1809 he was imprisoned for debts, and made good use of the time by writing this book.

Metamorphosis in Literature

Startling Transformations in Prose and Verse

One of the great delights of the literary arts is their ability to give form to dreams and fantasies. There is no limit to a writer's imagination, and a skillful writer can make the strangest things seem quite natural. A compelling theme in literature is that of transformation, or metamorphosis. One of the most famous tales of metamorphosis is Franz Kafka's story by that name, but there are many others. Why do we like reading about these things, pleasant or unpleasant? Partly because they tickle our fancies, no doubt, and partly because we can identify with them on some level, even if most of the transformations we undergo are less dramatic. Here are some of the most amazing metamorphoses in prose and verse, listed alphabetically.

1. ***Alice's Adventures in Wonderland,*** 1865, and ***Through the Look-***

ing Glass and What Alice Found There, 1872, by Lewis Carroll – A mushroom that makes you grow or shrink, courtiers who turn into a pack of playing cards, a fussy baby who turns into a pig—Carroll's classics are full of alarming transformations. For full immersion in this world where precise logic mingles freely with utter nonsense, try to get editions with the original illustrations by Sir John Tenniel.

2. ***Just So Stories*** by Rudyard Kipling, 1902 – These imaginative tales of origins explain how the world changed from primordial times and became the interesting place it is today, with alphabets and wondrous beasts. For example, find out how a misadventure on the banks of the "great grey-green, greasy Limpopo River" gave the elephant his long trunk.

3. **"Lamia"** by John Keats, 1820 – This is a tragic poem about enchantment and disillusionment. Lamia is a sorceress trapped in the form of a serpent who falls in love with a mortal young man. She regains human form, seduces him, and conjures up a palace where they are to marry, but the young man's mentor, a level-headed philosopher, sees through the illusion and destroys their joy.

4. ***Metamorphoses*** by Ovid, circa 8 AD – This beautiful collection of myths by one of Rome's great poets concerns "bodies changed to various forms." A girl fleeing the embraces of a god turns into a laurel tree; a nymph becomes fused with the boy she is amorously attacking, creating the hermaphrodite; a beloved sculpture, in the tale of Pygmalion, comes to life under its creator's caresses. The strange stories are told with such vividness that they have inspired centuries of artwork and spinoff literature.

5. **"The Metamorphosis"** by Franz Kafka, 1915 – The dehumanization of modern life becomes literal in this story of an earnest fellow named Gregor Samsa. He works hard as a traveling salesman, laboring to pay off a large debt his parents owe his employer, but is forced to miss work for the first time in five years when he wakes up one morning "transformed in his bed into a gigantic insect." He injures himself trying to maneuver his body around, and when he ventures out of his room his family drives him right back in—in all, one of the grimmest and most affecting short stories you'll ever read.

6. ***The Stolen Child*** by Keith Donohue, 2006 – Donohue's wonder-

fully imaginative first novel depicts the experiences of Henry Day, a Pennsylvania farm boy, who's snatched by a band of feral, woodland changelings and replaced by a doppelganger. While Henry tries to adapt to life as a hobgoblin, his replacement takes human form and grows up to become a musical prodigy.

7. ***The Strange Case of Dr. Jekyll and Mr. Hyde*** by Robert Louis Stevenson, 1886 – Dr. Jekyll begins as a good man of sound character, but he performs a reckless experiment on himself that has grisly results. He develops a chemical that changes him into Mr. Hyde, an alternate personality in which all the potential evil in his nature flourishes. He also develops an antidote to change himself back into Dr. Jekyll, but, of course, things go awry.

8. **"The Ugly Duckling"** by Hans Christian Andersen, 1843 – This is the simple, beautifully written story of a "duckling" who, on account of his hideousness, suffers rejection and mockery in his native barnyard and wherever he goes. Finally driven to the point of complete despair, he discovers that he has grown into a swan. The pathos and truth in this tale of unconscious transformation make it a true classic of world literature.

Muckraking Classics

Exposés Past and Present

Never at a loss to turn a colorful phrase, Teddy Roosevelt contributed such choice terms as "lunatic fringe" and "bully pulpit," among many others, to the American vernacular during his two terms as the twenty-sixth president of the United States. One of his most enduring terms—"muckraker," i.e., a man who rakes dung—was originally intended as a put-down of crusading investigative journalists like Ida Tarbell, whose exposé of the Standard Oil Company monopoly eventually led to the break-up of John D. Rockefeller's industrial giant. Over time, however, the term "muckraker" has become a term of honor for investigative journalists, much to the chagrin of the U.S. government and big business. Here are eight classic exposés, listed alphabetically, from muckrakers past and present.

1. ***All the President's Men*** by Bob Woodward and Carl Bernstein, 1974 – Rightly called the political exposé of the twentieth century, *All the*

President's Men is a thrilling account of the two *Washington Post* reporters who broke the Watergate scandal that forced President Nixon's resignation.

2. ***The American Way of Death*** by Jessica Mitford, 1963 – Prior to her death in 1996, Mitford revised and updated her witty exposé of the exploitative and greedy practices driving the United States funeral industry. It's not for the squeamish, since Mitford goes into grisly detail about embalming processes.

3. ***A Century of Dishonor: The Classic Exposé of the Plight of the Native Americans*** by Helen Hunt Jackson, 1881 – Disgusted by the U.S. government's callous mistreatment of Native Americans stretching back to the Revolutionary War, Jackson poured her anger into this book, which she wrote while gravely ill. Initially ignored by Congress, *A Century of Dishonor* later helped spur the creation of the Indian Rights Association.

4. ***Chain of Command: The Road from 9/11 to Abu Ghraib*** by Seymour Hersh, 2004 – A blistering critique of the Bush adminstration's "War on Terror" from the veteran *New Yorker* contributor, who reveals the intelligence failures and foreign policy decisions behind the U.S.-led invasion of Iraq.

5. ***Fast Food Nation*** by Eric Schlosser, 2001 – The insidious grip of the fast food industry on Americans' wallets and waistlines is the all-too-timely subject of Schlosser's powerful and disturbing book that's been compared to *The Jungle*.

excerpt: FAST FOOD NATION:

The teenage fast food workers I met in Colorado Springs, Colorado, told me other horror stories. The safety of the food seemed to be determined more by the personality of the manager on duty than by the written policies of the chain. Many workers would not eat anything at their restaurant unless they'd made it themselves. A Taco Bell employee said that food dropped on the floor was often picked up and served. An Arby's employee told me that one kitchen worker never washed his hands at work after doing engine repairs on his car.

6. ***How the Other Half Lives: Studies Among the Tenements of New York*** by Jacob A. Riis, 1890 – This impassioned plea for social reform captures the squalor and despair of slum life for poverty-stricken immigrants in striking prose and photographs.

7. ***The Jungle*** by Upton Sinclair, 1906 – Sinclair's fictionalized exposé of the meat-packing industry depicts a Lithuanian immigrant's horrific experiences in a turn-of-the-century Chicago stockyard. Sinclair's graphic, stomach-churning novel led to the passage of the Meat Inspection Act and the Pure Food and Drug Act.

8. ***Nickel and Dimed: On (Not) Getting By in America*** by Barbara Ehrenreich, 2001 – Going undercover as one of the "working poor" for a few months, Ehrenreich gets a firsthand look at the struggles of unskilled laborers to survive in today's economy.

Mysteries

Mystery Writers of America, Inc.'s Top Ten

In 1995, fifty years after Mystery Writers of America, Inc. was established, reportedly over a several-martini lunch in New York City, the organization took a break from presenting its prestigious Edgar Awards (named for the association's patron saint, Edgar Allan Poe) to rank the top hundred mystery novels of all time. Although most of their choices neatly fit within the traditional confines of the genre, it appears that the MWA apply the term "mystery" far more broadly than suspected—how else to explain the presence of Bram Stoker's *Dracula* (#70) and Tom Clancy's *The Hunt for Red October* (#84) on their list? Then again, maybe they had a few martinis before casting their votes!

Kidding aside, here are the MWA's top ten choices, ranked in descending order of votes, for the all-time best mysteries.

1. ***The Complete Sherlock Holmes*** by Sir Arthur Conan Doyle, 1887-1927 – Armchair sleuths will revel in this definitive collection of Doyle's four Sherlock Holmes novels and fifty-six short stories.

2. ***The Maltese Falcon*** by Dashiell Hammett, 1930 – Later immortalized onscreen by Humphrey Bogart, San Francisco private eye Sam Spade takes on the strangest case of his career in Hammett's tough, straightforward detective yarn.

3. ***Tales of Mystery and Imagination*** by Edgar Allan Poe, 1852 – Classic compendium of Poe's short stories and poems, including "The Fall of the House of Usher," "Murders in the Rue Morgue," and "The Raven."

4. ***The Daughter of Time*** by Josephine Tey, 1951 – While recuperating from minor injuries, Scotland Yard inspector Alan Grant becomes obsessed with England's infamous fifteenth century king, the hunchback Richard III, who allegedly murdered his nephews in the Tower of London. As he pores over all the available research, Grant begins to think that Richard III was innocent. Absorbing and unusual historical mystery from the Scottish-born Tey.

5. ***Presumed Innocent*** by Scott Turow, 1987 – Turow's first novel is a humdinger of a legal thriller—a tautly written and grittily realistic narrative full of twists and turns. When a beautiful associate is savagely raped and murdered, a county prosecutor becomes the chief suspect after it's discovered that the victim was his mistress.

6. ***The Spy Who Came in from the Cold*** by John Le Carre, 1963 – Gripping, brilliant cold war espionage thriller from Le Carre, the master of that genre. A British agent stationed in Berlin gets the most dangerous assignment in his career, when he must go deep undercover into the Soviet bloc. Graham Greene called *The Spy Who Came in from the Cold* "the finest spy story ever written."

7. ***The Moonstone*** by Wilkie Collins, 1868 – The theft of a rare Indian diamond known as the Moonstone is the inciting incident for Collins' complex, character-driven mystery, which unfolds from multiple points of view in epistolary form.

8. ***The Big Sleep*** by Raymond Chandler, 1939 – Chandler introduces his hard-boiled, Los Angeles private eye, Philip Marlowe, in this complicated noir about a simple blackmail case that rapidly spirals into something far more lethal and lurid.

excerpt: THE BIG SLEEP:
Geiger lay on the bed. The two missing strips of Chinese tapestry made a St. Andrew's Cross over the middle of his body, hiding the blood-smeared front of his Chinese coat. Below the cross his black-pajama'd legs lay stiff and straight. His feet were in the slippers with thick white felt soles. Above the cross his arms were crossed at the wrists and his hands lay flat against his shoulders, palms down, fingers close together and stretched out evenly. His mouth was closed and his Charlie Chan moustache was as unreal as a toupee. His broad nose was pinched and white. His eyes were almost closed, but not entirely. The faint glitter of his glass eye caught the light and winked at me.

9. ***Rebecca*** by Daphne Du Maurier, 1938 – "Last night I dreamt I went to Manderlay again." Thus begins Du Maurier's mesmerizing chiller about a meek young bride, living in the dark shadow cast by her aristocratic husband's deceased first wife, the beautiful, cruel Rebecca.

10. ***And Then There Were None*** by Agatha Christie, 1939 – The grande dame of mystery novels is at her sinister best in this wonderful whodunit about ten strangers, lured to an island home, where they're murdered, one-by-one, according to the nursery rhyme, "Ten Little Indians."

Native-American Novels

Life On and Off the Reservation

According to Choctaw/Cherokee writer/literary scholar Louis Owens, novelists of Native American descent only published nine novels between the years 1854 and 1968—a tragic mirror of their marginalized place in American society. Happily, that 114-year literary drought began to end with the 1968 publication of N. Scott Momaday's *A House Made of Dawn,* the first novel by a Native American writer to win the Pulitzer Prize. Momaday's critical and commercial success opened the proverbial floodgates for other Native American novelists and poets, ranging from Sherman Alexie to Louise Erdrich to James Welch, to launch what critic Kenneth Lincoln called a "Native American Renaissance" in his 1983 book of the same name. Erdrich in particular has established herself as one of America's best novelists, thanks to such acclaimed best-sellers as *Love Medicine, The Beet Queen,* and *The Last Report on the Miracles at Little No H*orse, a 2001 National Book Award finalist.

Here are eight of the most acclaimed and influential novels by Native American novelists, listed alphabetically, that all address questions of identity, cultural traditions, and the pressure to assimiliate, in prose alternately tragic and comic.

1. ***Ceremony*** by Leslie Marmon Silko, 1977 – Shattered by his WWII experiences as a POW in a Japanese camp, a young man of Laguna Indian and white descent turns to a medicine man for help. Through his mentor's teachings, Silko's protagonist achieves catharsis by immersing himself in ancient rituals and connecting to the land, in Silko's gravely beautiful first novel.

2. ***Fools Crow*** by James Welch, 1986 – Set in the aftermath of the Civil War, Welch's coming-of-age-novel follows the title character, a member of the Lone Eaters band of the Pikuni tribe of Montana, as he witnesses the escalating tensions between the Pikunis and the "Napikwans," i.e., white men. A taut narrative laced with dread, *Fools Crow* is an elegiac stunner from the author of the equally acclaimed *The Death of Jim Loney.*

3. ***Green Grass, Running Water*** by Thomas King, 1993 – Wildly imaginative and funny novel about four, elderly Native Americans breaking out of a mental hospital for the umpteenth time, and how they profoundly impact the lives of an oddball Canadian Blackfoot family. Blending mysticism and good-natured satirical humor, *Green Grass, Running Water* is a whip-smart and engaging novel.

4. ***A House Made of Dawn*** by N. Scott Momaday, 1968 – Momaday's landmark novel covers similiar thematic ground to *Ceremony:* a Native American World War II veteran returns home, drunk and disillusioned, to the New Mexico Indian reservation. Sent to prison for killing a man in a drunken rage, the protagonist continues his self-destructive spiral until he reconnects with his dying grandfather. The *Cleveland Plains Dealer* praised *A House Made of Dawn* as "almost unbearably authentic and powerful."

5. ***Love Medicine*** by Louise Erdrich, 1984 – Winner of the National Book Critics Circle Award, Erdrich's virtuoso debut novel spans a half-century in the lives of several Chippewa Indian families in and around a North Dakota reservation. Told from multiple points of view, *Love Medicine* is a sometimes bleak yet completely absorbing novel that many critics still regard as Erdrich's best to date.

6. ***Reservation Blues*** by Sherman Alexie, 1995 – A multihyphenate talent—poet/novelist/filmmaker—Alexie won the American Book Award for his auspicious debut novel *Reservation Blues,* about Coyote Springs, a Native American rock and roll band led by Thomas Builds-the-Fire, who uses a supernatural guitar from the ghost of blues great Robert Johnson to take the band from the Spokane Reservation to New York City. Wryly funny and insightful, *Reservation Blues* is a seriocomic winner.

7. ***The Surrounded*** by D'Arcy McKnickle, 1936 – One of the nine novels

by Native American writers published between 1854 and 1968, McKnickle's 1936 book about the psychological and cultural repercussions of assimilation has been called "the first modern American Indian novel." After his mother kills a game warden for shooting her other son, a Native American violinist becomes a fugitive.

8. ***A Yellow Raft on Blue Water*** by Michael Dorris, 1987 – Best known for *The Broken Cord,* his award-winning, nonfiction account of adopting a Lakota Indian boy with fetal alcohol syndrome, Dorris first won acclaim for this emotionally potent story of three generations of women in a Native American family torn apart by alcoholism and long-buried family secrets.

excerpt: ***A YELLOW RAFT ON BLUE WATER:***
You don't live on a reservation without learning respect for the red, white, and blue. Every powwow, every graduation, every grade-school basketball game in the school gym, out come the Honor Guard dressed in their fancy-dance costumes, with the man in the middle carrying the flag. When they appear, everybody gets quiet so that the only sound is the cowbells and jingles on the bearers' outfits. They do a circuit around the place and then park in the front while one of them offers a prayer in Indian, then they parade off slow and solemn. You stand at attention with your hand over your heart. It isn't till they leave, out of the light or the room or the gym, that you hear a kind of sigh pass through the crowd.

Nature Writing

At Home in the World

Save for the ongoing strife in the Middle East, no issue generates more ink, or controversy, than the threat of global warming. If temperatures continue to rise unchecked, the environmental consequences could be very dire. Although there is considerable, often vehement disagreement in both the scientific and political communities as to the climate change worst-case scenarios, few, if any, would argue against the need to protect the environment and conserve resources.

In light of skyrocketing energy prices, plummeting clean air standards and other ecological woes, perhaps it's time to return to the writings of naturalist/philosopher Henry David Thoreau, whose memoir *Walden; or*

Life in the Woods stresses the utmost importance of living in harmony with nature. An early classic of American nature writing, *Walden* has lost none of its relevance for contemporary readers. In a 2001 poll of readers conducted by The World at Home, a website devoted to promoting "ecological literacy," *Walden* came in second on the list of the ten best books about nature writing.

1. ***Desert Solitaire*** by Edward Abbey, 1968 – Reviled and revered by environmentalists, Abbey is best known for his novel, *The Monkey Wrench Gang,* the purported inspiration for the militant Earth First! Organization. *Desert Solitaire* is Abbey's provocative and heartfelt meditation on the desolate beauty of Arches National Monument near Moab, Utah, where he worked as a park ranger for three years in the late 1950s.

2. ***Walden; Or Life in the Woods*** by Henry David Thoreau, 1854 – Thoreau's memoir of the two years, two months and two days he spent living alone in a cabin on Walden Pond outside Concord, Massachusetts is a landmark of nineteenth century American letters.

3. ***A Sand County Almanac*** by Aldo Leopold, 1949 – A seminal text in the environmental movement, Leopold's illustrated collection of personal essays reveals how his work for the U.S. Forest Service informed his pro-conservation stance.

4. ***Pilgrim at Tinker Creek*** by Annie Dillard, 1974 – Winner of the 1975 Pulitzer Prize, Dillard's exquisitely written study of the everyday wonders of the natural world is a must-read. Keenly observed and spiritually satisfying, *Pilgrim at Tinker Creek* urges the reader to experience nature in all its amazing and sometimes terrible beauty.

excerpt: ***PILGRIM AT TINKER CREEK:***
Where Tinker Creek flows under the sycamore log bridge to the tear-shaped island, it is slow and shallow, fringed thinly in cattail marsh. At this spot an astonishing bloom of life supports vast breeding populations of insects, fish, reptiles, birds, and mammals. On windless summer evenings I stalk along the creek bank or straddle the sycamore log in absolute stillness, watching for muskrats. The night I stayed too late I was hunched on the log staring spellbound at spreading, reflected stains of lilac on the water.

5. ***Silent Spring*** by Rachel Carson, 1962 – A polarizing book to this day, Carson's influential best-seller sent a shock wave through the scientif-

ic and industrial community with its claims about the harmful effects of pesticides.

6. ***Refuge: An Unnatural History of Family and Place*** by Terry Tempest Williams, 1991 – In elegiac and deeply moving prose, Utah writer/activist Williams draws a haunting parallel between the decline of bird populations around the Great Salt Lake, and her mother's and grandmother's deaths from cancer, which may have been caused by radioactive fallout from nuclear testing in the 1950s and 1960s.

7. ***New and Selected Poems: Volume One*** by Mary Oliver, 1992 – Luminous poems celebrating nature from Oliver, who won the National Book Award for this astonishing collection of her work, much of it inspired by the flora and fauna of Cape Cod.

8. ***Arctic Dreams: Imagination and Desire in a Northern Landscape*** by Barry Lopez, 1986 – During a five-year period, Lopez made several trips into the farthest reaches of the Arctic to study the wildlife and Eskimo culture. The result is a magnificent book of grace and sensitivity that deservedly won the National Book Award.

9. ***The Solace of Open Spaces*** by Gretel Ehrlich, 1985 – Leaving the city for the vastness of Wyoming, poet/naturalist Ehrlich found emotional and spiritual succor in ranch life, which she describes in this radiant memoir.

10. ***The Outermost House: A Year of Life on the Great Beach of Cape Cod*** by Henry Beston, 1928 – As invigorating as a blast of Atlantic sea air, Beston's utterly captivating and transcendently beautiful memoir is one of the most beloved works of nature writing in American literary history.

New York City Books

New York Times' *Ten Best About the "Big Apple"*

On February 5, 1995, Sam Roberts published an article in the *New York Times* introducing a suggested "canon" of books about New York City. With apparent pride in New Yorkers' opinionated and individualistic spirit, he admits that residents are certain to take issue with the list. In any case, each of the ten selections will help you understand one facet of the lively, contradictory, creative metropolis

that is one of history's great cities. Here they are, with our brief descriptions, as listed by Roberts.

1. ***The Power Broker*** by Robert A. Caro, 1974 – This is a biography of Robert Moses, who between the 1930s and the 1960s managed to transform the political and physical landscape of New York City, despite the objections of the city's residents and even its leaders.

2. ***The Bonfire of the Vanities*** by Tom Wolfe, 1987 – A classic satire on the 1980s, this novel follows a wealthy stockbroker's foray from his own world of complacency and greed into the parallel world of the poor.

excerpt: THE BONFIRE OF THE VANITIES:
The more grim the subways became, the more graffiti those people scrawled on the cars, the more gold chains they snatched off girls' necks, the more old men they mugged, the more women they pushed in front of the trains, the more determined was John Campbell McCoy that they weren't going to drive him off the New York City subways. But to the new breed, the young breed, the masterful breed, Sherman's breed, there was no such principle. Insulation! That was the ticket. That was the term Rawlie Thorpe used. "If you want to live in New York," he once told Sherman, "you've got to insulate, insulate, insulate," meaning insulate yourself from those people. The cynicism and smugness of the idea struck Sherman as very au courant. If you could go breezing down the FDR Drive in a taxi, then why file into the trenches of the urban wars?

3. ***Beyond the Melting Pot*** by Nathan Glazer and Daniel P. Moynihan, 1963 – This is an analysis of the power of ethnicity in New York politics and daily life, arguing against the idea that immigrants to the city quickly assimilate into a homogeneous whole.

4. ***The W.P.A. Guide to New York City,*** reissued in 1982 – Much in the city has changed since the *Works Progress Administration Guide* was originally published, but it's still a wonderfully evocative source of information about the diversions, institutions, and atmosphere of the city in the 1930s.

5. ***Manchild in the Promised Land*** by Claude Brown, 1965 – The autobiography of a young black man describes his childhood in Harlem and how he survived the destructive forces all around him.

6. ***The Great School Wars: New York City, 1805–1973*** by Diane Ravitch, 1974 – As the range of years in the title shows, there is a long history of conflicts between the people running the public school

system in New York and the families it serves. This is a thoughtful account of these "wars" and the reasons behind them.

7. ***Down These Mean Streets*** by Piri Thomas, 1967 – Based on the author's youth in East Harlem (and later in prison), *Down These Mean Streets* paints a picture of the hardships and joys of life in the Hispanic ghetto.

8. ***World of Our Fathers*** by Irving Howe, 1976 – From Eastern Europe to the New World, from immigrant to first-generation offspring, and from city to suburbs, the Jewish New Yorkers Howe writes about have undergone sometimes difficult transformations in this city of constant change.

9. ***Time and Again*** by Jack Finney, 1970 – Part novel, part charming picture book, this is the story of a modern New Yorker who travels back in time to the nineteenth century and explores his home city anew (or a-old).

10. ***Here Is New York*** by E.B. White, 1949 – The man who wrote so movingly of the delights of being a pig in a quiet, cozy barn in *Charlotte's Web* writes equally movingly here of the noisy, crowded, passionate island of Manhattan.

New Yorker Contributors

Books by Parker, Thurber & Co.

In 1925, the *New Yorker* magazine founder/editor Harold Ross summed up his vision for the fledgling magazine in the following, oft-quoted prospectus: "The *New Yorker* will be a reflection in word and picture of metropolitan life ... It is not edited for the old lady in Dubuque." To realize his dream of publishing a sophisticated, urbane weekly dedicated to culture and current events, Ross hired many charter members of the legendary Algonquin Round Table as contributors. While Dorothy Parker, S. J. Perelman, and James Thurber brought their wit to the pages of the *New Yorker*, journalists and essayists like Joseph Mitchell and E.B. White regularly contributed articles on the unique flavor and idiosyncratic characters of the Big Apple. Later, during World War II, the *New Yorker* would gain international renown for its war reportage; Ross devoted an entire issue to John Hersey's *Hiroshima*.

Today, eighty-one years after Ross incurred the wrath of little old ladies in Dubuque, the pages of the *New Yorker* now feature the essays and articles of such literary lights as Woody Allen, Susan Orlean (*The Orchid Thief*), David Sedaris, and John Updike. Here are eight books by some of the most famous *New Yorker* contributors from the magazine's first fifty years.

1. ***Here at the New Yorker*** by Brendan Gill, 1997 – No tell-all, Gill's affectionate yet irreverent memoir of his sixty years at the *New Yorker* is a treasure trove of colorful anecdotes about the magazine and some of its most famous contributors.

2. ***Hiroshima*** by John Hersey, 1946 – Ross devoted an entire issue of the magazine to Hersey's stunning, four-part account of the atomic bomb blast that decimated this Japanese city.

3. ***Joe Gould's Secret*** by Joseph Mitchell, 1965 – A compassionate, haunting portrait of an eccentric, downtrodden Greenwich village character, whose claims of writing the definitive oral history of New York turned out to be bogus.

4. ***Most of the Most of S.J. Perelman*** by S.J. Perelman, 2000 – A side-splittingly funny collection of Perelman's writings from 1930 to 1958. When not penning essays for the *New Yorker*, Perelman wrote screenplays for the Marx Brothers.

excerpt: MOST OF THE MOST OF S.J. PERELMAN:
I have always been the mildest of men, but you remember the old saying, "Beware the fury of a patient man." (I remembered it very well and put my finger on it instantly, page 269 of Bartlett's book of quotations). For years I have let dentists ride roughshod over my teeth; I have been sawed, hacked, chopped, whittled, bewitched, bewildered, tattooed and signed on again; but this is cuspid's last stand. They'll never get me in that chair again. I'll dispose of my teeth as I see fit, and after they're gone, I'll get along. I started off living on gruel, and, by God, I can always go back to it again.

5. ***Paris Was Yesterday, 1925–1939*** by Janet Flanner, 1972 – For fifty years, Flanner wrote the *New Yorker*'s "Letter from Paris" feature. This collection of her articles takes the reader on a glittering tour of Paris, with frequent stops to the watering holes and salons of the "Lost Generation."

6. ***The Portable Dorothy Parker*** by Dorothy Parker, 2006 – More "fresh hell" from the endlessly quotable Algonquin Round Table wit, whose

verse, short stories, and essays crackle with wit and gimlet-eyed intelligence in this updated edition.

7. ***The Road Back to Paris*** by A. J. Liebling, 1944 – Wartime dispatches from England, France, and North Africa from the masterful journalist.

8. ***The Thurber Carnival*** by James Thurber, 1945 – A priceless collection of Thurber's essays, short stories, and sketches for the *New Yorker*.

Nineteenth Century Novels

Joanna Trollope's Favorites

Both a literary and literal descendant of the great Victorian-era novelist Anthony Trollope, writer Joanna Trollope typically focuses on the everyday lives of middle-class English families in such novels as *The Rector's Wife* and *Next of Kin*. Her frequent choice of subject matter mirrors her passion for the realistic classics of nineteenth century literature like George Eliot's *Middlemarch,* which weaves together the disparate stories of several English villagers into a brilliantly nuanced epic narrative. Famously hailed by Virginia Woolf as "one of the few English novels written for grown up people," *Middlemarch* is truly a monumental achievement in literary realism that Trollope named her favorite nineteenth century novel. Here are Trollope's ten favorites, as she ranked them for the British newspaper *The Guardian*.

1. ***Middlemarch*** by George Eliot, 1871 – Trapped in a loveless marriage to a pompous clergyman, an intelligent and passionate young woman struggles to find happiness in the provincial village of Middlemarch. Eliot skillfully juxtaposes the heroine's search for true love against the experiences of friends and family in what Trollope calls "a marvelous portrait of 19th century provincial life."

2. ***The Last Chronicle of Barset*** by Anthony Trollope, 1867 – Trollope concluded his renowned Chronicles of Barsetshire literary sextet with this remarkably even-handed portrait of a proud and mercurial curate whose mounting debts bring him and his family to the brink of ruin. Joanna Trollope pronounces *The Last Chronicle of Barset* "a masterpiece."

3. ***Persuasion*** by Jane Austen, 1818 – The ubiquitous Austen's last

novel, published two years after her untimely death at forty-two, is another gem of a love story about a woman pining for the man she rejected seven years earlier. Trollope calls *Persuasion* "a subtle and elegiac novel—more heartfelt than some of her earlier romances."

excerpt: PERSUASION:
A few years before, Anne Elliot had been a very pretty girl, but her bloom had vanished early; and as even in its height, her father had found little to admire in her, (so totally different were her delicate features and mild dark eyes from his own), there could be nothing in them, now that she was faded and thin, to excite his esteem.

4. ***Vanity Fair*** by William Makepeace Thackeray, 1848 – With cunning, guile, and bewitching charm, Becky Sharp claws her way into the rarefied world of English society during the Napoleonic Wars era. Subtitled "A Novel Without a Hero," *Vanity Fair* satirizes the snobbery and hypocrisy endemic to English society in a sprawling narrative that Trollope praises as "sharp, brilliant, touching, clever and cruel."

5. ***The Mayor of Casterbridge*** by Thomas Hardy, 1886 – A fatalist with a singularly gloomy perspective, Hardy set this novel and many others in the fictitious county of Wessex, England. In this emotionally wrenching story—"a tale of true tragedy," per Trollope—the title character's alcoholism hastens his downfall.

6. ***The Moonstone*** by Wilkie Collins, 1868 – A young woman inherits a fabled Indian diamond, the Moonstone, which is stolen the night of her eighteenth birthday in Collins' epistolary novel. Most critics point to this convoluted yarn with multiple narrators and ample red herrings as the first modern English detective novel. As for Trollope, she calls *The Moonstone* "a great, bold, theatrical mystery."

7. ***Bleak House*** by Charles Dickens, 1852-1853 – First published in serial form, Dickens' sweeping novel depicts an epic legal battle that ensnarls the lives of a cast of characters in a book that Trollope says "has everything—joy, grief, success, failure, wealth, poverty, comedy, tragedy."

8. ***North and South*** by Elizabeth Gaskell, 1854 – Championed by Dickens, Gaskell wrote ghost stories, a biography of Charlotte Brontë, and novels set in the industrialized north of England. In *North and South,* Gaskell examines the plight of the working class in what Trollope

describes as "a really remarkable picture of the reality ...of northern industrial life."

9. ***The Portrait of a Lady*** by Henry James, 1881 – The sole book by an American author on Trollope's list, *The Portrait of a Lady* follows an independent-minded American heiress encountering her "destiny" abroad, where she fells prey to the scheming of fellow expatriates. Alluding to James' psychologically astute use of interior monologue, Trollope finds *The Portrait of a Lady* "subtle and sophisticated."

10. ***Rob Roy*** by Sir Walter Scott, 1818 – The literary antithesis of *The Portrait of a Lady, Rob Roy* is a grand, larger-than-life yarn loosely based on the eigtheenth century Scottish folk hero Rob Roy MacGregor. While not a critical darling like the other books on her list, *Rob Roy* earns Trollope's admiration as "a true adventure story."

Nonfiction Favorites

Critics/Readers Picks for the Modern Library's "100 Best"

Sometimes critics adore a book that many readers find hard to finish—James Joyce's *Finnegans Wake,* for example. In other cases, critics pass severe judgments on authors with huge followings. Then there are those lucky writers whose works stand the test of time with both experts and the public.

In the late 1990s, the Modern Library embarked on a project to rank the hundred best works of fiction and nonfiction published since 1900. There were two versions of each list: one drawn up by the members of the Modern Library board, and one determined by popular vote. Nearly 200,000 readers weighed in on the best nonfiction books. Here are the fifteen that found their way onto both the readers' and the board's lists, listed in descending order by their averaged ranking on the lists. The one nonfiction selection that got the same ranking on both lists was Orwell's *Homage to Catalonia,* at number 42. While nothing can be guaranteed in the realm of literature, it's a good bet that you will find any of these books to be memorable reads.

1. ***A Room of One's Own*** by Virginia Woolf, 1929 – Woolf addresses the challenges facing women writers and the conditions they need to achieve greatness. Averaged ranking: 14.5.

2. ***Speak, Memory*** by Vladimir Nabokov, 1951, revised 1966 – A look backward at the author's childhood in late Czarist Russia. Averaged ranking: 18.

3. ***The Varieties of Religious Experience*** by William James, 1902 – This exploration of mankind's religious life is a seminal work in psychology. Averaged ranking: 22.5.

4. ***The Education of Henry Adams*** by Henry Adams, 1918 – A vivid recounting of the life of a member of one of America's great political families. Averaged ranking: 26.

5. ***The Double Helix: A Personal Account of the Discovery of the Structure of DNA*** by James D. Watson, 1968 – One of the most exciting books on molecular science chronicles the race to solve the mystery of DNA. Averaged ranking: 30.5.

6. ***Silent Spring*** by Rachel Carson, 1962 – A warning about the environmental consequences of the use of DDT and other modern pesticides. Averaged ranking: 33.

7. ***Homage to Catalonia*** by George Orwell, 1938 – A tale of heroism and disillusionment—Orwell's experience as one of thousands of international volunteers fighting to save democracy in the Spanish Civil War. Averaged ranking: 42.

8. ***The Art of Memory*** by Frances A. Yates, 1966 – The author examines how people kept their traditions alive in the days before the printing press and widespread literacy. Averaged ranking: 47.

9. ***Out of Africa*** by Isak Dinesen, 1937 – A Danish woman's life as a coffee farmer in British East Africa in the years before World War II. Averaged ranking: 47.

10. ***The Elements of Style*** by William Strunk and E.B. White, 1959 – Still one of the most influential books on the art and craft of writing. Averaged ranking: 48.

11. ***The Great Bridge*** by David McCullough, 1972 – All about the building of the Brooklyn Bridge—a saga of political rivalries, endurance, love, and brilliant engineering. Averaged ranking: 50.

12. ***The Golden Bough*** by James George Frazer, 1922 – A colorful in-

vestigation into the origins of magic, myth, and religion. Averaged ranking: 60.5.

13. ***The Gnostic Gospels*** by Elaine Pagels, 1979 – The history of an early branch of Christianity that was declared heretical by the second century AD. Averaged ranking: 64.

14. ***The Autobiography of Malcolm X*** by Alex Haley and Malcolm X, 1965 – A story of struggles and transformations over the course of this remarkable man's life. Averaged ranking: 71.

15. ***Pilgrim at Tinker Creek*** by Annie Dillard, 1974 – Meditations on the beauty and strangeness of nature, inspired by the author's experiences in the Blue Ridge Mountains of Virginia. Averaged ranking: 75.5.

Orphans in Literature

Graduates of the School of Hard Knocks

Children who have lost their parents are familiar characters in literature. In some ways, their stories are common to everyone. As they grow up, they have to forge their own identities and find belonging, love, and purpose in their lives. But their circumstances are often especially difficult; they have to rely on themselves more than the average child in real life or in fiction; their adventures are more dramatic; and their triumphs are all the more inspiring.

While several of the books listed below were originally written for children, all of them have proved popular with adults as well. The orphaned protagonists are listed in alphabetical order.

1. **Jane Eyre: *Jane Eyre*** by Charlotte Brontë, 1847 – Jane lives at the home of her unfeeling aunt until they send her away to a poorly run boarding school, where she grows to maturity. Though her troubles are far from over when she leaves the school to become a governess for a child in the care of the enigmatic Mr. Rochester, it is a crucial turning point in her life.

2. **Kimball O'Hara: *Kim*** by Rudyard Kipling, 1901 – This poverty-stricken, yet in his way remarkably cosmopolitan little boy is the orphaned son of an Irish soldier; Kimball O'Hara lives as a street child in Lahore, India. The book follows his adventures as he befriends a wise

Tibetan lama, is discovered by his father's regiment, and becomes involved in a dangerous secret mission that takes him into the Himalayan mountains.

3. **Tom Sawyer: *The Adventures of Tom Sawyer*** by Mark Twain, 1876 – Twain's classic picaresque chronicles the life and times of an orphan raised by his aunt. Aunt Polly is not a mean woman, like some of the other caretakers in our list, but she is a bit too pious and orderly for her rambunctious nephew's taste. Set in a small town in Missouri, this American classic depicts murder, treasure, and romance, as well as the simple joys of childhood.

4. **Anne Shirley: *Anne of Green Gables*** by L.M. Montgomery, 1908 – In Montgomery's beloved novel, an elderly brother and sister apply for an orphan boy to help them with chores. Instead, they end up with a sensitive, imaginative, and somewhat wild little girl named Anne in this heartfelt and occasionally hilarious book. Sadly, the author had personal experience with her heroine's loneliness: her mother died of tuberculosis when Montgomery was just a toddler.

5. **James Henry Trotter: *James and the Giant Peach*** by Roald Dahl, 1961 – Of all our orphans, James probably has the strangest life. His parents are killed by a marauding rhinocerous, and he goes to live with two nasty, selfish aunts in a lonely house on the top of a hill in his native England. A visit from a mysterious stranger leads to the appearance of a massive peach, which James manages to float and fly over the Atlantic with an assortment of human-sized garden bugs who turn out to be friendly and charming.

6. **Oliver Twist: *Oliver Twist*** by Charles Dickens, 1837-1838 – Originally published in installments, Dickens' classic novel is the tale of an orphan born into a workhouse in London, where poverty and neglect are the children's lot. Honest by nature, Oliver falls into the hands of a criminal gang leader who tries to make him into a thief. It eventually transpires that Oliver still has living relatives, and he is finally rescued from his sordid life.

7. **Homer Wells: *The Cider House Rules*** by John Irving, 1985 – Homer Wells grows up in an orphanage run by a kindly but ether-addicted doctor. His life continues among the workers of an apple orchard, but years later he returns to run the orphanage after the doctor's death.

Questions of the politics and morality of parenthood, abortion, and birth control run through Irving's compelling novel.

Pen Names

Famous Noms de Plume

Les Krantz, the co-author of *The Book of Books,* once published a book under the name Jay Kaye. In fact, you might be surprised by how many of the items on the shelves of your local bookstore are credited to people who technically don't exist. There are lots of reasons for writers to use pseudonyms, or pen names: to exchange an unwieldy name for something snappier; to evade prejudice by disguising ethnicity or gender; and to express controversial opinions from the safety of anonymity. Noms de plume are a rich tradition in literature and politics. *The Federalist Papers* (1787–1788) were originally published in New York newspapers under the dignified pseudonym Publius; the real authors were Alexander Hamilton, James Madison, and John Jay. Here are some more well-known pen names, listed in alphabetical order.

1. **Lewis Carroll** (1832–1898) – The real name of the creator of *Alice's Adventures in Wonderland* (1865) and *Through the Looking-Glass* (1872) was Charles Lutwidge Dodgson.

2. **Joseph Conrad** (1857–1924) – The author of *Heart of Darkness* (1902) was born Jozef Teodor Konrad Nalecz Korzeniowski.

3. **George Eliot** (1819–1880) – The pen name is very masculine, but the author of *The Mill on the Floss* (1860) and *Middlemarch* (1871) was really Mary Ann Evans.

4. **Pablo Neruda** (1904–1973) – The great Chilean poet, the author of *Twenty Love Poems and a Song of Despair* (1924, translated 1969) was really named Ricardo Eliecer Neftalí Reyes Basoalto.

5. **George Orwell** (1903–1950) – The true name of the author of *Homage to Catalonia* (1938), *Animal Farm* (1945), and *1984* (1949) was Eric Arthur Blair.

6. **George Sand** (1804–1876) – The author of *Elle et Lui* (1859) and lover of both the writer Alfred de Musset and the composer Frédéric Chopin was actually named Amandine-Aurore-Lucile Dupin. In addition to us-

ing a male pseudonym, she shocked society by dressing as a man.

7. **Dr. Seuss** (1904–1991) – The whimsical writer and illustrator of *The Cat in the Hat* (1957) and *Oh, the Places You'll Go!* (1990) was Mr. Theodor Seuss Geisel in everyday life.

8. **Mark Twain** (1835–1910) – The real name of the man who spun the great American yarns *The Adventures of Tom Sawyer* (1876) and *The Adventures of Huckleberry Finn* (1885) was Samuel Langhorne Clemens.

9. **Voltaire** (1694–1778) – The single-word name is very grand, but the author of the novel *Candide* (1759) and various plays and philosophical treatises was named François-Marie Arouet in real life.

10. **Nathanael West** (1903–1940) – The true name of the author of *The Day of the Locust* (1939) was Nathan Wallenstein Weinstein.

Photography Collections

Capturing the World for Posterity

Photography revolutionized the way we see the world. The "mechanical eye" has allowed us to share visual reality (or some version of it) with people thousands of miles away, recording great moments in human history, fleeting moments of light over a seascape, and every wrinkle of a single person's face for posterity. Whether you are an amateur photographer looking for inspiration, or you just want something fascinating for your coffee table, these books, alphabetically listed, include some of history's most indelible images.

1. ***100 Photographs That Changed the World*** by the editors of *Life* magazine, 2003 – This collection brings together memorable images in four categories: "The Arts," "Society," "War and Peace," and "Science and Nature." From wartime Normandy and Iwo Jima to the Beatles arriving in the United States, these remarkable—and sometimes shocking—photos will grab your attention.

2. ***The American Wilderness*** by Ansel Adams, edited by Andrea Stillman, 1990 – Ansel Adams produced awe-inspiring landscapes, capturing the grandeur of mountains and clouds and the shimmering

beauty of trees in leaf. This volume offers large, fine reproductions of his work, along with some of the artist's writings on conservation.

3. ***Earth from Above*** by Yann Arthus-Bertrand, 2002 – Unless you have your own private helicopter, it's unlikely you'll see any of these amazing sights on your own. The complex interactions of land, sea, plants, animals, and humans are spread out in front of your eyes in rich and vivid color.

4. ***L'Amour Fou: Photography and Surrealism*** by Rosalind Krauss, Dawn Ades, and Jane Livingston, 1985 – Long before digital cameras gave amateurs the ability to manipulate their pictures at will, the surrealists of the 1920s and 1930s were creating strange and dreamlike images that blended eroticism and the bizarre. This relatively small volume, with its photos by Brassaï, Man Ray, Salvador Dalí, and others, would provide a field day for a Freudian analyst—or for a photography lover interested in the outer boundaries of the form.

5. ***The Photography Book*** by the editors of Phaidon Press, 1997 – This impressive book provides a sort of survey course (though not in chronological order) on the history of photography. Five hundred photographers are each represented by one work, with a net effect of stunning diversity and endless surprises.

6. ***Richard Avedon Portraits*** by Richard Avedon, Mia Fineman, Maria Morris Hambourg, and Philippe de Montebello, 2002 – Half a century of portraits of creators and celebrities, from painters to movie stars, are brought together in this stylish book. Whether you are interested in the personalities or in the artistic medium, you will find this an absorbing collection.

7. ***Through the Lens: National Geographic Greatest Photographs*** edited by Leah Bendavid Val, 2003 – Pick up any issue of *National Geographic* magazine and you're likely to find photographs that wow you. Here are 250 of the very best of the renowned magazine's images from its more than century-old history, capturing everything from outer space to the arresting green eyes of an Afghan refugee.

8. ***Women*** by Annie Leibovitz and Susan Sontag, 1999 – Leibovitz is a famed celebrity photographer, but this book is not restricted to portraits of the stars. It also depicts ordinary women in a remarkable variety of roles, no less interesting to look at for their obscurity.

Poet Laureates

Library of Congress Appointees, 1990-2006

Each year, the Library of Congress appoints a notable poet to the position of Poet Laureate Consultant in Poetry. In addition to giving an annual lecture and reading, each poet laureate creates events and programs to bring poetry to a wider public. Robert Pinsky, for example, created the "Favorite Poem Project," soliciting readers all across the country for their favorite poems and collecting them into an anthology. Here is a list of our poet laureates since 1990, along with some collections of their works. We have also included information on the Special Bicentennial Consultants who served in 1999–2000.

1990–1991: Mark Strand, born 1934 – Collections include *Sleeping with One Eye Open,* 1964, *The Story of Our Lives,* 1973, and *Blizzard of One,* 1998.

1991–1992: Joseph Brodsky, 1940–1996 – Collections include *Joseph Brodsky: Selected Poems,* 1973, *A Part of Speech,* 1980, and *Less Than One, a collection of essays,* 1986.

1992–1993: Mona Van Duyn, 1921–2004 – Collections include *To See, To Take,* 1970, and *Near Changes,* 1990.

1993–1995: Rita Dove, born 1952 – Collections include *The Yellow House on the Corner,* 1980, *Museum,* 1983, and *Thomas and Beulah,* 1986.

1995–1997: Robert Hass, born 1941 – Collections include *Field Guide,* 1973, *Praise,* 1979, and *Twentieth Century Pleasures, a collection of essays,* 1984.

1997–2000: Robert Pinsky, born 1940 – Collections include *Sadness and Happiness,* 1975, and *History of My Heart,* 1984.

1999–2000, Special Bicentennial Consultants:

- **Louise Glück** (see below, 2003–2004).
- **W.S. Merwin,** born 1927 – Collections include *A Mask for Janus,* 1952, *The Carrier of Ladders,* 1970, and *Feathers from the Hills,* 1978.
- **Rita Dove** (see above, 1993–1995).

2000–2001: Stanley Kunitz, 1905–2006 – Collections include *Selected Poems 1928–1958,* 1958, *The Testing-Tree,* 1971, and *Passing Through: The Later Poems, New and Selected,* 1995.

2001–2003: Billy Collins, born 1941 – Collections include *The Art of*

Drowning, 1995, *Picnic, Lightning,* 1998, and *Sailing Alone Around the Room: New and Selected Poems,* 2001.

2003–2004: Louise Glück, born 1943 – Collections include *Firstborn,* 1968, *Descending Figure,* 1980, and *The Wild Iris,* 1992.

2004–2006: Ted Kooser, born 1939 – Collections include *Sure Signs,* 1980, *One World at a Time,* 1985, and *Delights and Shadows,* 2004.

2006–Present: Donald Hall, born 1928 – Collections include *Exiles and Marriage,* 1955, *The One Day,* 1988, and *White Apples and the Taste of Stone,* 2006.

Poetry

Top Ten Anthologized Poems

William Harmon, a poet, editor, and teacher, published an anthology called *The Top 500 Poems* in 1992. The poems were selected on the basis of how many times they had been included in other modern anthologies, as recorded in the ninth edition of *The Columbia Granger's Index to Poetry* (which lists the contents of 400 such collections). Here are the ten most anthologized poems from the list of 500, ranked in descending order. We include a few lines from each one.

1. **"The Tiger"** by William Blake (1757–1827)

   Tiger, Tiger, burning bright
   In the forests of the night;
   What immortal hand or eye,
   Could frame thy fearful symmetry?

2. **"Sir Patrick Spens"** (anonymous, circa 1400–1600)

   "I saw the new moon late yestreen
   Wi' the auld moon in her arm,
   And if we gang to sea, master,
   I fear we'll come to harm."

3. **"To Autumn"** by John Keats (1795–1821)

   Season of mists and mellow fruitfulness,
   Close bosom-friend of the maturing sun…

4. **"That Time of Year Thou May in Me Behold"** by William Shakespeare (1564–1616)

   In me thou see'st the twilight of such day
   As after sunset fadeth in the west,

Which by and by black night doth take away,
Death's second self, that seals up all in rest.

5. **"Pied Beauty"** by Gerard Manley Hopkins (1844–1899)
   Glory be to God for dappled things—
   For skies of couple-color as a brinded cow;
   For rose-moles all in stipple upon trout that swim…
6. **"Stopping by Woods on a Snowy Evening"** by Robert Frost (1874–1963)
   The woods are lovely, dark and deep,
   But I have promises to keep,
   And miles to go before I sleep…
7. **"Kubla Khan"** by Samuel Taylor Coleridge (1772–1834)
   And all should cry, Beware! Beware!
   His flashing eyes, his floating hair!
8. **"Dover Beach"** by Matthew Arnold (1822–1888)
   …we are here as on a darkling plain
   Swept with confused alarms of struggle and flight
   Where ignorant armies clash by night.
9. **"La Belle Dame Sans Merci"** by John Keats (1795–1821)
   I met a Lady in the Meads
   Full beautiful, a fairy's child;
   Her hair was long, her foot was light,
   And her eyes were wild.
10. **"To the Virgins, to Make Much of Time"** by Robert Herrick (1591–1674)
    Gather ye rosebuds while ye may,
    Old Time is still a-flying;
    And this same flower that smiles today,
    Tomorrow will be dying.

Poets

Masters of the "Confessional" School

After decades of relatively impersonal, formal, and difficult verse, a new movement appeared in American poetry in the late 1950s. It was dubbed "Confessional," because its writers dug into the experiences and suffering of their own lives and laid everything bare in their poems. Like many other movements, this one thrived on its members encouraging, inspiring, and competing with one another. Their work discussed trauma, mental illness, and the underside of domestic life with startling frankness and the energy of discovery. Several of the leading members of the "school" died by suicide, and the confessional poets' work is often gloomy, but it also contains great humor. And it can be comforting to read when you're down—you're not the only one! Here are five of the most prominent confessional poets, listed alphabetically, and some snippets of their work.

1. **John Berryman** (1914–1972) – Berryman authored *The Dream Songs* (1969), a collection about the life of an imaginary man named Henry, a touching antihero. Somehow, alcoholic drinks have the power of speech; and stars get mixed in with Henry's struggles. A line from "Dream Song number 14:" "Life, friends, is boring. We must not say so."

2. **Robert Lowell** (1917–1977) – Lowell was nicknamed "Cal" for his bad temper, after the Roman emperor Caligula and Caliban in Shakespeare's *The Tempest*. But he brought many of the poets in the movement together, teaching them in poetry workshops and influencing them with his own work, especially the groundbreaking collection *Life Studies* (1959). From a later poem, "Notice":

    The resident doctor said,
    "We are not deep in ideas, imagination or enthusiasm—
    how can we help you?"
    I asked,
    "These days of only poems and depression—
    what can I do with them?
    Will they help me to notice
    what I cannot bear to look at?"

3. **Sylvia Plath** (1932–1963) – The death of her father when she was a girl, and her stormy relationship with her husband, the poet Ted Hughes, inform much of Plath's verse. Here is the beginning of "Daddy:"

    You do not do, you do not do
    Any more, black shoe
    In which I have lived like a foot
    For thirty years, poor and white,
    Barely daring to breathe or Achoo.

4. **Anne Sexton** (1928–1974) – Sexton was a beautiful but troubled

woman who wrote about her childhood, family life, and many loves with searing honesty in poems collected in *All My Pretty Ones* (1962), *Live or Die* (1966), and several other volumes. From "The Truth the Dead Know," written for her deceased parents:

And what of the dead? They lie without shoes
in their stone boats. They are more like stone
than the sea would be if it stopped. They refuse
to be blessed, throat, eye and knucklebone.

5. **W.D. Snodgrass** (born 1926) – The 1959 book *Heart's Needle,* with its poems about the author's relationship with his daughter after his divorce from her mother, was a poignant collection that inspired other poets to use their family lives as material. Two lines from his poem "April Inventory": "The blossoms snow down in my hair, / The trees and I will soon be bare."

Political Novels

Corruption, Conspiracies and Cronyism

Drawing upon a seemingly bottomless well of cynicism, H.L. Mencken, aka the "Sage of Baltimore," passed scathing judgment on all facets of American culture in essays and reviews that cut to the bone. Turning his jaundiced gaze on the American political landscape, he famously quipped, "Democracy is the art and science of running the circus from the monkey-cage."

Mencken's withering assessment of politics certainly resonates in many of the following novels, listed alphabetically, which depict the American political system on the local and national levels as rife with corruption, conspiracies, and cronyism. It's enough to put the founding fathers on the spin cycle in their graves!

1. ***Advise and Consent*** by Allan Drury, 1959 – To ease cold war tensions with the Soviet Union, a sickly U.S. president nominates a former Communist party official to be the Secretary of State. Drury's Pulitzer Prize winning classic was inspired by the experiences of Alger Hiss, the U.S. Department of State official accused of being a Communist spy in 1948.

2. ***All the King's Men*** by Robert Penn Warren, 1946 – Warren's monu-

mental account of the rise and dizzying fall of charismatic Louisiana governor Willie Stark draws brilliantly from the real-life story of populist legend Governor Huey Long, "The Kingfisher."

3. ***Democracy: An American Novel*** by Henry Adams, 1880 – A caustically observed satire that skewers the rich and power-hungry who scheme and claw their way to the top of the political food chain.

4. ***Echo House*** by Ward Just, 1997 – A finalist for the National Book Award, Just's novel is a masterfully drawn, century-spanning family saga about three generations of a political dynasty.

excerpt: ECHO HOUSE:
They've got him now, Willy said. They've got his actual language, the language of a race-baiting roughneck. And that will become the issue. He's finished. Washington cannot abide the common speech, the words that people actually use, the petty evasions and nuance and exaggeration and resentment and hatred of the other. They want all Presidents to talk like Lincoln or FDR. They want words you can chisel in marble. He's let them down, you see. Just as they knew he always would. Poor bastard; they'll ride him out of town on a rail. It's a matter of revenge, Willy said. So they can think better of themselves.

5. ***The Last Hurrah*** by Edwin O'Connor, 1956 – Determined to go out with a bang, not a whimper, wily Boston mayor Frank Skeffington launches his final reelection bid in O'Connor's compelling novel about the Irish political machine in Beantown.

6. ***Primary Colors*** by Anonymous, 1996 – Barely veiled roman a clef about Bill Clinton's 1992 presidential campaign is a sophisticated, witty and penetrating novel from "Anonymous," aka Joe Klein, a longtime political journalist.

7. ***Wag the Dog*** by Larry Beinhart, 1995 – Uproariously funny, razor-edged political satire about the extreme lengths spin doctors will go to when a president is caught in a very compromising situation.

8. ***Washington, DC: A Novel*** by Gore Vidal, 1967 – A contemporary H.L. Mencken, Vidal begins his six-volume Narratives of Empire series of novels with this acutely observed, unsparing overview of the American political scene from the Depression through World War II.

Political Science Books

The Globalization Debate

More than at any other time in history, our world is interconnected—in terms of security, the economy, climate, and culture—and this raises all kinds of difficult issues. Can liberal democracy succeed in traditionally authoritarian countries? Are the West and the Muslim worlds doomed to endless conflict? How will rapid advances in communications affect the economy? Should we take responsibility for preventing atrocities in other nations? Here are some influential books, listed alphabetically, from the last fourteen years that tackle these questions and more, illuminating the dangers and opportunities of the contemporary world.

1. ***The Clash of Civilizations and the Remaking of World Order*** by Samuel P. Huntington, 1996 – The author argues that the religious, ethnic, and cultural sentiments of a few distinct civilizations will replace ideological concerns (such as capitalism vs. socialism) as the main source of international conflict in the post–cold war era.

2. ***The End of History and the Last Man*** by Francis Fukuyama, 1992 – Fukuyama argues that capitalist democracy will take hold in most of the world's countries, spreading prosperity and stability and eliminating many of the sources of international conflict. While 9/11 and its aftermath have made his thesis seem less convincing now than in 1992, the yearning for democracy remains a major force even in the most troubled parts of the world.

3. ***The Future of Freedom: Illiberal Democracy at Home and Abroad*** by Fareed Zakaria, 2003 – Why have some democracies self-destructed, while others remain stable and free? Zakaria argues that democracy rarely survives without the development of liberal institutions such as free markets and the rule of law—and sometimes these institutions have to come first.

4. ***Globalization and Its Discontents*** by Joseph E. Stiglitz, 2002 – The author is a winner of the Nobel Prize in economics. Here, he describes his views of how the institutions of globalization, the World Bank and the IMF, need to change in order to help developing nations join the world economy.

5. ***In Defense of Globalization*** by Jagdish Bhagwati, 2004 – In this short and witty book, the renowned economist counters claims that globalization has failed to benefit developing nations and explains how they can make the most of its opportunities.

6. ***Jihad vs. McWorld: How Globalism and Tribalism Are Reshaping the World*** by Benjamin R. Barber, 1995 – Barber explores the uneasy coexistence, competition, and interdependence of the forces of consumerism and fundamentalism across the world.

7. ***A Problem from Hell: America and the Age of Genocide*** by Samantha Power, 2002 – A number of genocides and "ethnic cleansings" have taken place in the last century. As a matter of basic human values, the author argues, the U.S. needs to be much more willing to intervene in such cases.

excerpt: *A PROBLEM FROM HELL:*
When word of the gas attacks began spreading to other villages, terrified Kurds began fleeing even ahead of the arrival of Iraqi air force bombers. Al-Majid's forces were fairly predictable. Jets began by dropping cluster bombs or chemical cocktails on the targeted villages. Surviving inhabitants fled. When they reached the main roads, Iraqi soldiers and security police rounded them up. They then often looted and firebombed the villages so they could never be reoccupied. Some women and children were sent to their deaths; others were moved to holding pens "where many died of starvation and disease. The men were often spirited away and never heard from again. In the zones that Hussein had outlawed, Kurdish life was simply extinct.

8. ***The World Is Flat*** by Thomas L. Friedman, 2005 – The *New York Times* columnist follows up on his previous book on globalization, *The Lexus and the Olive Tree,* with a survey of how telecommunications are revolutionizing the global economy and increasing competition. Toward the end of the book, he also discusses some of the economic aspects of international Islamic fundamentalism.

Post-World War II Novels

Gore Vidal's "Useful" Picks

Essayist, novelist, playwright, and full-time provocateur, Gore Vidal is known as much for his vitriolic tongue as his literary talents. In the sixty years since he burst on the literary scene with his acclaimed debut novel,

Williwaw, inspired by his World War II-era service in the Alaskan Harbor Detachment, Vidal has famously tangled with everyone from William F. Buckley to Truman Capote to his macho nemesis, Norman Mailer. In 1971, Vidal compared Mailer to Charles Manson—and got head-butted by Mailer in reply.

But if Vidal is notorious for his withering dismissal of some writers, he's been a surprisingly passionate and generous champion of others, like Dawn Powell, whom he pronounced "a comic writer as good as Evelyn Waugh and better than Clemens" in a 1981 issue of the *Antioch Review.* Powell, whose satirical novels about the Manhattan literary and bohemian scenes were then out of print, eventually enjoyed a posthumous renaissance, due in large part to Vidal's effusive praise for her work. One of her fifteen novels, *The Golden Spur,* comes in fourth on Vidal's 1999 Salon.com list of five "useful" novels published since World War II.

1. ***Doctor Faustus*** by Thomas Mann, 1948 – Topping Vidal's list is this staggeringly complex masterwork by the 1929 Nobel Prize winning novelist. Mann's protagonist is a musical prodigy who forges a Faustian pact that seals his downfall, which mirrors Germany's intellectual and moral collapse with Hitler's rise to power. An ambitious, demanding novel that Vidal succinctly describes as a "powerful metaphor, great novel."

2. ***Good as Gold*** by Joseph Heller, 1979 – Never one to toe the party line, Vidal bypasses Heller's *Catch-22* in favor of this tragicomic 1979 novel about a frustrated middle-aged college professor reinventing himself as a Washington, DC political broker. To that end, protagonist Bruce Gold ditches his loudly dysfunctional family and reclaims his Jewish heritage, solely for political expediency. Vidal calls Heller "a superb comic novelist with an eye and ear for American idiocies."

3. ***Cosmicomics*** by Italo Calvino, 1965 – Wrapping your mind around Calvino's densely layered, self-reflexive prose can be daunting for even the most adventurous reader. That said, if your tastes run to Kafka, Jorge Luis Borges, and Umberto Eco, you'll probably share Vidal's admiration for Calvino's heady work, like this 1965 collection of short stories, inspired by various scientific facts and theories, and narrated by a being known as Qfwfq. "Total fireworks," according to Vidal.

4. ***The Golden Spur*** by Dawn Powell, 1962 – One of Powell's last novels, *The Golden Spur* follows an impressionable young man from the 'burbs

stumbling his way into the Greenwich Village art scene, where he hopes to find his long-lost father. For Vidal, *The Golden Spur* may be "the New York novel."

5. ***Creation*** by Gore Vidal, 1981 – Modesty in any form has never been one of Vidal's virtues, so it should come as no surprise that he picks one of his own books to round out the list. In *Creation*, a fifth century BC Persian diplomat embarks on a tour of the ancient world's political and religious systems; en route he has pivotal meetings with such figures as Socrates, Buddha, Confucius, and Zoroaster. Vidal includes *Creation* on his list because it "tells us things we ought to know but don't."

Psychopaths in Literature

Great Villains in Novels and Short Stories

What would literature be without villains? Terribly boring—and perhaps unrealistic. Although evil comes in all kinds of varieties and guises, one of its most unsettling causes is a psychological disorder that allows many of the people who suffer it to live in the world as normal, even charismatic and successful members of society. Underneath the civilized veneer, however, psychopaths are heartless manipulators, devoid of conscience or human feeling. Serial killers, war criminals, fanatical dictators, or everyday folk, they are part of society in the world and in fiction.

Now, far be it from us to officially diagnose fictional characters with what they now call sociopathy or anti-social personality disorder. We're just speculating from our reading armchairs. But here are a few who seem to fit the pattern, culled mainly from books beyond the genre of crime fiction. Prepare to be chilled as you read about the following psychopathic characters, listed according to the source material's publication date.

1. **Rhoda Penmark: *The Bad Seed*** by William March, 1954 – Rhoda is a peculiarly tidy, well-behaved eight year-old girl whose mother begins to suspect her of murdering a classmate. Charming on the outside but ugly on the inside, Rhoda is a precocious specimen of evil no less dangerous for her tender age.

2. **Tom Ripley: *The Talented Mr. Ripley*** by Patricia Highsmith, 1955 – Young Tom's drab life as a minor swindler in New York comes to a welcome end when a father sends him to Europe to bring home a

wayward son. But instead of convincing Dickie Greenleaf to return to New York, Tom murders him and adopts his identity. A talented actor and a shrewd planner, he manages his horrific business very well.

3. **Sarah Ham: "The Comforts of Home"** by Flannery O'Connor, 1960 – A young man, named Thomas, finds life unendurable when his kind-hearted mother takes a petty criminal named Sarah Ham into their home. The girl, who goes by the name Star Drake, makes Thomas terribly uneasy: "He needed nothing to tell him he was in the presence of the very stuff of corruption, but blameless corruption because there was no responsible faculty behind it." The author of this short story was a religious woman who often wrote with great originality about the complex relationship between good and evil.

4. **Annie Wilkes: *Misery*** by Stephen King, 1987 – Annie is a retired nurse whose dream comes true when she finds her favorite author, Paul Sheldon, in a car wreck. She imprisons him in her remote Colorado home, feeds him painkillers, keeps him in line with brutal violence, and forces him to write a new novel according to her specs. At one point Paul thinks she is manic-depressive, but people with manic depression (aka bipolar disorder) are more apt to distinguish themselves as poets than as serial killers. Yes, that's why she's retired—her employers finally caught on that she was murdering her patients at every opportunity.

5. **Patrick Bateman: *American Psycho*** by Bret Easton Ellis, 1991 – Bateman is a New York investment banker who looks like the boy next door. He's utterly conformist in most things, but has a penchant for murder. The book is perhaps more of a satire on the superficial consumer culture of the 1980s than a character study, but its clinical descriptions of graphic violence made it extremely controversial.

Real-Life Disasters

From Krakatoa to 9/11

Ever since Pliny the Younger wrote his eyewitness account of the cataclysmic eruption of Mount Vesuvius in 79 AD, historians have chronicled the world's worst disasters, often in harrowing, graphic detail. There's something morbidly irresistible about catastrophes, both natural and man-made, that draw readers back to certain events like moths to the proverbial flame.

Case in point: the 1912 sinking of the legendary luxury liner *RMS Titanic* has spawned a publishing cottage industry, with hundreds of books devoted to that tragic April night, when over 1,500 passengers went down with the supposedly "unsinkable" ship in the freezing waters of the North Atlantic. Given the staggering number of books about the ill-fated luxury liner, you'd think that there'd be nothing further to add about history's most famous maritime disaster, yet the coming months will bring still more books about the *Titanic*.

The sinking of the *Titanic* is just one of the disasters historians have tackled in the following, critically lauded books, listed in alphabetical order, that cover everything from earthquakes to hurricanes to 9/11.

1. ***102 Minutes: The Untold Story of the Fight to Survive Inside the Twin Towers*** by Jim Dwyer and Kevin Flynn, 2005 – A finalist for the 2005 National Book Award for nonfiction, this suspenseful and emotionally shattering book reconstructs the final moments inside the World Trade Center towers, that terrible September morning in 2001.

2. ***The Circus Fire: A True Story of an American Tragedy*** by Stewart O'Nan, 2001 – Faint-hearted readers be warned: O'Nan's engrossing recreation of the horrific, 1944 Ringling Brothers and Barnum & Bailey Circus fire is gruesomely detailed. But if you have the stomach for it, *The Circus Fire* is well worth a look, thanks to O'Nan's immensely readable prose style and the wealth of fascinating information.

excerpt: THE CIRCUS FIRE:
High up, the guyropes parted, the rigging gave way, and the poles by the northeast corner slumped inward, then the center of the canvas. The tent sagged—slowly, not all at once, the flags on top bending almost horizontal—and then with a hissing, swishing sound, the big top collapsed on itself, the heavy centerpoles falling one after another, smashing the animal cages, crushing people. The quarters—thick as phone poles—banged into the grandstands, denting the railings.

3. ***A Crack in the Edge of the World: America and the Great California Earthquake of 1906*** by Simon Winchester, 2005 – Just in time for the centennial of the San Francisco Earthquake, the seemingly tireless British author/journalist turns his attention to the quake and its fiery aftermath. While some critics fault Winchester for his overly digressive approach, he nonetheless cranks out one compelling, albeit tan-

gent-laden book after another—*A Crack in the Edge of the World* is no exception.

4. ***Five Past Midnight in Bhopal: The Epic Story of the World's Worst Industrial Disaster*** by Dominique Lapierre and Javier Moros, 2002 – The heartbreaking and infuriating story of the deadly gas leak that killed thousands of poor Indian villagers in Bhopal comes tragically to life in this profoundly haunting book.

5. ***Isaac's Storm: A Man, A Time and the Deadliest Hurricane in History*** by Erik Larson, 1999 – For the people of Galveston, Texas, the twentieth century got off to a devastating start, when a hurricane laid waste to this Gulf of Mexico community. In Larson's vivid book, meteorologist Isaac Cline emerges as the prototypical tragic hero: a short-sighted yet courageous man whose pregnant wife was among the hurricane's estimated 10,000 fatalities.

6. ***Krakatoa: The Day the World Exploded: August 27, 1883*** by Simon Winchester, 2003 – The book's subtitle is only a slight exaggeration. When the Indonesian volcano Krakaota erupted in apocalyptic fury, it spewed more than six cubic miles of rock, ash, and pumice into the atmosphere and killed over 36,000 people. Ranging far and wide on geology, Indonesian politics, and survivor stories, Winchester's book makes for lively, intellectually stimulating reading.

7. ***A Night to Remember*** by Walter Lord, 1955 – Obsessed with the *Titanic* since childhood, Lord pored over archival information and interviewed more than sixty survivors to write what many regard as the definitive account of the sinking. Thirty-odd years after *A Night to Remember* became a best-seller, Lord wrote a well-received sequel, *The Night Lives On*.

8. ***Triangle: The Fire That Changed America*** by David Von Drehle, 2003 – Von Drehle examines the sociopolitical factors that precipitated the deadly fire at the Triangle Shirtwaist Factory in 1911. Nearly 150 factory workers, most of them poor, immigrant women, died when flames engulfed this sweatshop. Famed *Washington Post* journalist Bob Woodward hailed *Triangle* as "a riveting history written with flare and precision."

Revolutionary War Nonfiction

All About Our Founding Fathers

Called "a one-man historical machine" by fellow Revolutionary War scholar Gordon S. Wood, historian Joseph J. Ellis has maintained a regular berth on the nonfiction best-seller list of late, thanks to such critical and commercial favorites as *Founding Brothers: The Revolutionary Generation* and his latest, *His Excellency: George Washington*. Ellis, along with John Adams biographer David McCullough, deserves the lion's share of the credit for whetting the general public's appetite for serious yet accessible nonfiction books about the Revolutionary War. Although Ellis came under fire in 2001 for lying about serving in the Vietnam War—the very same year he won a Pulitzer Prize for *Founding Brothers*—he has weathered the scandal with his reputation for top-notch scholarship intact. Whatever his personal failings, there's never been a question raised about the veracity of any of his prize-winning Revolutionary War histories, three of which appear on the following, alphabetical list of nonfiction titles about the founding of the United States.

1. ***1776*** by David McCullough, 2005 – Confining his focus to a pivotal year in the Revolutionary War, McCullough crafts another impeccably researched and compelling book that sheds light on both George Washington and his nemesis across the pond, King George III.

2. ***American Sphinx: The Character of Thomas Jefferson*** by Joseph J. Ellis, 1997 – No fan of verbosity, Ellis writes concise yet richly drawn popular histories appealing to general readers and scholars alike. His 1997 National Book Award winning biography of the America's third president is a triumph.

3. ***Benjamin Franklin: An American Life*** by Walter Isaacson, 2003 – A marvelously erudite and entertaining biography of the charming, witty, and brilliant Franklin.

4. ***Founding Brothers: The Revolutionary Generation*** by Joseph J. Ellis, 2000 – Ellis struck literary gold again with his Pulitzer Prize winning examination of six key moments in the lives of the "Founding Fathers."

5. ***His Excellency: George Washington*** by Joseph J. Ellis, 2004 – Engaging and insightful biography that succeeds in humanizing Washington, whom Ellis dubs "the original marble man."

6. ***John Adams*** by David McCullough, 2001 – Long overshadowed by Washington and Jefferson, Adams has finally been recognized for the vital role he played in the creation of the United States of America, thanks to this magnificent biography from McCullough that topped the best-seller list for a year.

excerpt: JOHN ADAMS:
John Adams was also, as many could attest, a great-hearted, persevering man of uncommon ability and force. He had a brilliant mind. He was honest and everyone knew it. Emphatically independent by nature, hardworking, frugal—all traits in the New England tradition—he was anything but cold or laconic as supposedly New Englanders were. He could be high-spirited and affectionate, vain, cranky, impetuous, self-absorbed, and fiercely stubborn; passionate, quick to anger, and all-forgiving; generous and entertaining. He was blessed with great courage and good humor, yet subject to spells of despair, and especially when separated from his family or during periods of prolonged inactivity.

7. ***The Traitor and the Spy: Benedict Arnold and John Andre*** by James Thomas Flexner, 1953 – One of America's foremost historians, Flexner separates fact from fiction regarding the infamous Benedict Arnold in this absorbing book, as dramatic as any novel.

8. ***Washington's Crossing (Pivotal Moments in American History)*** by David Hackett Fisher, 2004 – The 2005 winner of the Pulitzer Prize for history, *Washington's Crossing* is a wonderfully thorough and smartly-paced account of Washington leading his men to decisive victories at Trenton and Princeton.

Road Trips in Literature

Into the Great Unknown

Suffering a bout of wanderlust, but don't want to leave the comforts of home for the uncertainty of the open road? Or endure fresh pain at the pump? Relax—you only need to go as far as your bookshelf to experience the glory of the great outdoors, albeit vicariously, in the pages of the following memoirs about getting away from it all. By turns meditative, witty, elegiac, and philosophical, these chronicles of epic, life-changing road trips—some taken on foot—should quench your desire for adventure as you nestle deeper into your Barcalounger. Featuring books by everyone from

John Muir to John Steinbeck, here are eight literary road trips, listed alphabetically.

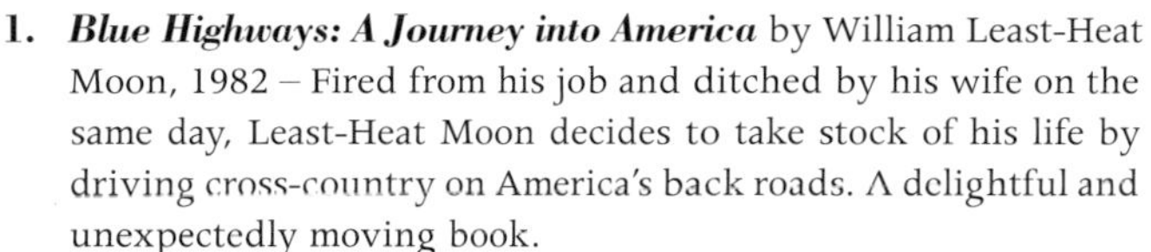

1. ***Blue Highways: A Journey into America*** by William Least-Heat Moon, 1982 – Fired from his job and ditched by his wife on the same day, Least-Heat Moon decides to take stock of his life by driving cross-country on America's back roads. A delightful and unexpectedly moving book.

2. ***Road Angels: Searching for Home Down America's Coast of Dreams*** by Kent Nerburn, 2001 – Longing to revisit the West Coast where he spent his twenties, Nerburn leaves frozen Minnesota for an extended trip down memory lane in this poetic, beautifully written journey of self-discovery.

3. ***Road Fever*** by Tim Cahill, 1991 – Talk about your crazy ideas! Cahill and a professional long-distance driver drove from Chile to Alaska in just under twenty-four days—and lived to tell about it. *Road Fever* is a funny and engaging account of their wild and woolly misadventures en route.

4. ***Route 66: The Mother Road*** by Michael Wallis, 1990 – You'll get your kicks from *Route 66: The Mother Road,* Wallis' lively and fact-filled history of America's most famous highway.

5. ***A Thousand Mile-Walk to The Gulf*** by John Muir, 1916 – The founder of the Sierra Club left his Indiana home in 1867 to wind his way across the post-Civil War South, sketching plants that caught his eye and recording his impressions of the people he met en route to the Gulf of Mexico. Published two years after Muir's death in 1914, *A Thousand Mile-Walk to the Gulf* is an exhilarating memoir of his trek.

excerpt: *A THOUSAND MILE-WALK TO THE GULF:*
October 23. To-day I reached the sea. While I was yet many miles back in the palmy woods, I caught the scent of the salt sea breeze which, although I had so many years lived far from sea breezes, suddenly conjured up Dunbar, its rocky coast, winds and waves; and my whole childhood, that seemed to have utterly vanished in the New World, was now restored amid the Florida woods by that one breath from the sea. Forgotten were the palms and magnolias and the thousand flowers that enclosed me. I could see only dulse and tangle, long winged gulls, the Bass Rock in the Firth of Forth, and the old castle, schools, churches, and long country rambles in search of birds' nests.

6. ***Travels With Charley in Search of America*** by John Steinbeck, 1962 – With his standard poodle Charley for company, Steinbeck drove a camper all over America for three months in 1960. His memoir of that trip succeeds as both a charming travelogue and a profound assessment of the American character.

7. ***A Walk Across America*** by Peter Jenkins, 1979 – His ideals tarnished by the Vietnam War and Watergate, a twenty-two year-old college graduate decides to walk from New York City to New Orleans. *A Walk Across America* is the touching memoir of the people and places Jenkins met over the course of his nearly two-year journey.

8. ***A Walk in the Woods: Rediscovering America on the Appalachian Trail*** by Bill Bryson, 1998 – Irresistibly witty account of Bryson hiking the Appalachian Trail with his equally out-of-shape, middle-aged buddy.

Russian Novels

Daniel Burt's All-Time Best

Of the literary classics that comprise Daniel Burt's *The Novel 100: A Ranking of the Greatest Novels of All Time,* eight were penned by Russian writers. Tolstoy and Dostoevksy, those two grand old men of Russian letters, each contribute two titles to Burt's list, which skews heavily towards books written during the nineteenth century, the acknowledged "Golden Age of Russian Literature." In fact, the only twentieth century Russian novel to make Burt's list is Andrey Bely's *Petersburg,* a symbolist narrative of brewing political unrest in turn-of-the century Russia, which eerily anticipates the Russian Revolution of 1917. Conspicuously missing from Burt's list are such acknowledged masterpieces as Boris Pasternak's *Doctor Zhivago,* Mikhail Bulgakov's *The Master and Margarita,* and Alexandr Solzhenitsyn's *One Day in the Life of Ivan Denisovich.* And while Vladimir Nabokov's *Lolita* came in #47 on Burt's rankings, it takes place primarily in the United States—and therefore does not qualify as a Russian novel per se.

Weighty tomes all, both thematically and literally (the shortest comes in just under 300 pages), here are Burt's eight greatest Russian novels, per his ranking.

1. ***War and Peace*** by Leo Tolstoy, 1869 – If you only read one Russian epic, make it Tolstoy's *War and Peace*. Yes, it's a HUGE undertaking, but his spellbinding saga of Russian aristocrats during the Napoleonic era is a monumental achievement.

2. ***The Brothers Karamazov*** by Fyodor Dostoevsky, 1880 – Brooding, gloom-laden novel from the novelist many consider the father of existentialism. The title characters must wrestle with the profound consequences of killing their hated father.

3. ***Anna Karenina*** by Leo Tolstoy, 1877 – The novel's legendary first sentence sets the tone of Tolstoy's other masterpiece: "Happy families are all alike; every unhappy family is unhappy in its own way." A mercurial, passionate aristocratic beauty embarks on an ill-fated affair with a handsome nobleman in this tragic, sweeping romance.

excerpt: ANNA KARENINA:

Anna, in that first period of her emancipation and rapid return to health, felt herself unpardonably happy and full of the joy of life. The thought of her husband's unhappiness did not poison her happiness. On one side that memory was too awful to be thought of. On the other side her husband's unhappiness had given her too much happiness to be regretted. The memory of all that had happened after her illness: her reconciliation with her husband, its breakdown, the news of Vronsky's wound, his visit, the preparations for divorce, the departure from her husband's house, the parting from her son—all that seemed to her like a delirious dream, from which she had waked up alone with Vronsky abroad.

4. ***Crime and Punishment*** by Fyodor Dostoevsky, 1866 – Considering himself beyond moral reproach, a poverty-stricken St. Petersburg student murders a despised money-lender and her feeble sister, only to succumb to paranoia and guilt in Dostoevsky's influential novel.

5. ***Dead Souls*** by Nikolai Gogol, 1842 – Contrary to its morbid title, Gogol's *Dead Souls* is a rollicking, over-the-top satire of Russian provincial life. A rabidly ambitious young man of limited means attempts to scheme and spend his way towards prosperity in a village populated by neurotic, larger-than-life characters.

6. ***Fathers and Sons*** by Ivan Turgenev, 1862 – An insightful examination of the generation gap, vis-à-vis the philosophical divide between nihilism and spirituality that arose in mid-nineteenth century Russia.

Amid growing political unrest, a political revoluntionary plots to assassinate a high ranking Czarist official: his father.

7. ***Petersburg*** by Andrey Bely, 1913 – First translated into English in 1959, Bely's innovative symbolist novel has been compared to James Joyce's *Ulysses* for its allusive text and dense wordplay.

8. ***Oblomov*** by Ivan Goncharov, 1859 – Content to daydream his life away, a fallen member of the Russian aristocracy nearly loses everything, including his one true love, due to his paralyzing apathy, in Goncharov's tragicomic classic.

Satirical Novels

From Voltaire to Vonnegut

Lampooning human folly and tipping sacred cows with gleeful relish, satirists have been ridiculing leaders, organizations, and cultural norms since at least the beginnings of civilization. Classical scholars trace the origins of satire in Western literature back to ancient Greece, citing the plays of Aeschylus and Aristophanes, who in turn may have looked to primitive curses and rituals for inspiration. In the centuries since Aristophanes' anti-war satirical comedy "Lysistrata" first played to packed amphitheaters, satirists ranging from Voltaire to Jonathan Swift to Gore Vidal have taken aim and fired at targets with stinging accuracy—often at great risk. Just ask Salman Rushdie, whose 1988 satirical novel *The Satanic Verses* was considered so blasphemous, Iran's Ayatollah Khomeni issued a fatwa for Rushdie's execution.

Here are eight classic satirical novels, listed alphabetically, that go right for the jugular, often by way of the funny bone.

1. ***Breakfast of Champions*** by Kurt Vonnegut, 1973 – Hilariously off-kilter gem from Vonnegut, who casts a jaundiced eye on the malaise gripping 1970s-era America in this story about "two lonesome, skinny, fairly old white men on a planet which was dying fast."

2. ***Candide: Or, Optimism*** by Voltaire, 1759 – Taking the form of a picaresque, Voltaire's pithy classic follows an idealistic young man stripped of his rose-colored glasses through a series of misadventures.

3. ***The Gilded Age: A Tale of Today*** by Mark Twain & Charles Dudley Warner, 1873 – The only novel Twain ever wrote with a collaborator,

The Gilded Age: A Tale of Today is a sharp and ever timely indictment of wretched excess, greed, and corruption in post-Civil War America.

excerpt: ***BREAKFAST OF CHAMPIONS:***
Everybody in America was supposed to grab whatever he could and hold onto it. Some Americans were very good at grabbing and holding, were fabulously well-to-do. Others couldn't get their hands on doodley-squat.

Dwayne Hoover was fabulously well-to-do when he met Kilgore Trout. A man whispered those exact words to a friend one morning as Dwayne walked by: "Fabulously well-to-do."

And here's how much of the planet Kilgore Trout owned in those days: doodley-squat.

4. ***Gulliver's Travels*** by Jonathan Swift, 1726 – Lilliput is just one of four mythical lands sea captain Lemuel Gulliver visits in Swift's subversive and bitingly funny classic. Swift was a major influence on George Orwell, who called *Gulliver's Travels* "one of six indispensable books in world literature."

5. ***Lucky Jim*** by Kingsley Amis, 1954 – Caustic satire of British academia about a disaster-prone young history teacher is the barbed antithesis of *Goodbye, Mr. Chips.*

6. ***Money*** by Martin Amis, 1984 – The raunchy and rollicking misadventures of a drunken and debauched British commercials director running amok in New York while making his first film.

7. ***Myra Breckinridge*** by Gore Vidal, 1968 – Vidal's scathingly funny send-up of the sexual revolution and Hollywood kitsch takes the form of a diary written by Myra Breckinridge, a gorgeous transsexual with a score to settle.

8. ***Scoop*** by Evelyn Waugh, 1938 – England's notorious Fleet Street press get a taste of their own medicine in Waugh's priceless satire about journalists chasing the next sensational headline.

Scariest Books

CNN Interactive's Chilling Picks

Forget Lestat or any of the vampire dandies who walk the night in Anne Rice's phenomenally popular novels about the undead. For the academics, writers, and media types polled by CNN Interactive regarding the scariest

books ever written, the philosophy-spouting bloodsuckers in Rice's *Interview with the Vampire* and *The Vampire Lestat* lack the bite of Bram Stoker's immortal creation, Count Dracula.

Since its publication in 1897, Stoker's *Dracula* has been imitated, parodied, and filmed countless times, but few, if any of its subsequent incarnations conjure the nightmarish dread of Stoker's epistolary novel, which draws heavily upon Central European folklore. Initially regarded as just a Gothic potboiler—albeit a supremely chilling example of the genre—*Dracula* is now considered a bona-fide literary classic. That the respondents to CNN Interactive's 2000 poll ranked *Dracula* the scariest book of all time proves that Stoker's novel has lost none of its power to keep readers awake long past bedtime, listening for things that go bump in the night.

Here are the five scariest books of all time, ranked in descending order of votes received in the CNN Interactive poll.

1. ***Dracula*** by Bram Stoker, 1897 – Best read with the lights on, Stoker's most acclaimed novel (he wrote thirteen in all, including *The Lair of the White Worm*), remains an atmospheric and genuinely frightening work that set the bar for all novels of the supernatural that followed. Leaving a trail of corpses stretching from Transylvania to London, Dracula meets his match in the Dutch vampire hunter, Van Helsing.

excerpt: ***DRACULA:***
Somewhere high overhead, probably on the tower, I heard the voice of the Count calling in his harsh, metallic whisper. His call seemed to be answered from far and wide by the howling of wolves. Before many minutes had passed a pack of them poured, like a pent-up dam when liberated, through the wide entrance into the courtyard.

There was no cry from the woman, and the howling of the wolves was but short. Before long they streamed away singly, licking their lips.

I could not pity her, for I knew now what had become of her child, and she was better dead.

2. ***The Shining*** by Stephen King, 1977 – The undisputed king of modern horror, King is a veritable writing machine, turning out books with an astonishing speed that would give even the prolific Joyce Carol Oates pause. His third novel, *The Shining,* is a triumphant blend of ghost story and psychological drama. Jack Torrance, an alcoholic, frustrated writer (and reported King alter ego), falls under the supernatural influence of a haunted Colorado resort, The Overlook, where he's working as the winter caretaker.

3. ***The Exorcist*** by William Peter Blatty, 1971 – Faithfully adapted for the screen by Blatty and director William Friedkin in 1973, *The Exorcist* has a visceral intensity, even on the page, that's not for the easily spooked. Based on an actual exorcism performed in 1949, Blatty's disturbing novel pits two priests against an ancient demon who's taken possession of a movie star's adolescent daughter.

4. ***Complete Tales and Poems*** by Edgar Allan Poe, 2002 edition – This compilation of the nineteenth century American master's writings contains forty-eight poems and seventy-three short stories, including such macabre classics as "The Fall of the House of Usher," "The Black Cat," and "The Masque of the Red Death." Poe's gorgeously ornate and moodily effective prose continues to cast an eerie spell on readers.

5. ***The Haunting of Hill House*** by Shirley Jackson, 1959 – A team of parapsychologists investigate a haunted, supposedly cursed New England mansion, with unnerving results, in Jackson's elegant, psychologically acute novel. Jackson, the author of the creepy short story "The Lottery," turns the traditional ghost story upside down in this novel, which depicts the emotionally fragile heroine's struggle to hold onto her sanity as all matter of supernatural hell breaks loose.

Science Books

Science in Unexpected Places

There are lots of science books about black holes, DNA, and the like, many of them excellent. But sometimes it's fun to learn about science from an unpredictable angle—to discover how the laws of physics determine what happens in your favorite sport, or how penguins' physiology allows them to walk across expanses of Antarctic ice without suffering frostbite. Listed alphabetically, these books are entertaining and can illuminate all kinds of little mysteries—and they also provide fresh perspectives to spark new questions about ourselves and the world around us.

1. ***Life at the Extremes: The Science of Survival*** by Frances Ashcroft, 2000 – Ashcroft's book explains clearly and precisely how the bodies of humans and animals manage (or fail) to withstand intense heat and cold, high water pressure and low air pressure, and other extreme situations. Astronauts, athletes, whales, birds, and the author herself all illustrate the marvels of biology and the power of conditioning.

2. ***Life's Matrix: A Biography of Water*** by Philip Ball, 2000 – Dew, clouds, tears, living cells, oceans, snow, steam, glaciers ... water in its myriad forms is just about everywhere, and life as we know it would be impossible without it. This book covers the physics and chemistry of this essential substance, as well as the history of our understanding of it, and current ecological issues.

3. ***The Physics of Baseball*** by Robert K. Adair, 1990, third edition, 2002 – A fun way to learn more about physics and to gain a deeper understanding of the game—Adair explains players' neurophysiology, the finer points of wind resistance, and much more. If this kind of thing intrigues you, you might also enjoy *The Physics of Golf* by Theodore P. Jorgensen (1999), *The Physics of Hockey* by Alain Haché (2002), and *The Physics of Football: Discover the Science of Bone-Crunching Hits, Soaring Field Goals, and Awe-Inspiring Passes* by Timothy Gay (2004).

4. ***Radar, Hula Hoops, and Playful Pigs: 67 Digestible Commentaries on the Fascinating Chemistry of Everyday Life*** by Joe Schwarcz, 1999 – A popular lecturer in chemistry, Schwarcz discusses the uses and misuses of science, the chemical reasons for everyday phenomena, and what the three items in the title all have in common. You'll come away from the book with a bit more insight, wisdom, and savvy.

5. ***Universal Foam: From Cappuccino to the Cosmos*** by Sidney Perkowitz, 2000 – There's a dizzying array of types of foam in our world—including sea foam, latte foam, shaving cream, cheese soufflés, pumice from volcanoes, and possibly even "quantum foam," to name just a few. But Perkowitz makes sense of them all in this delightful book.

6. ***What Einstein Told His Cook: Kitchen Science Explained*** by Robert L. Wolke, 2002 – A funny and eloquent writer, dedicated gourmand, and professor of chemistry, Wolke explains some of the mysteries of cooking, as well as familiar processes that you might never have thought of in a scientific light before. There are also a few tempting recipes, so you can see and taste how things work for yourself.

7. ***Why We Hurt: The Natural History of Pain*** by Frank T. Vertosick Jr., 2000 – Whether you are coping with a painful condition or just curi-

ous about the neurology and physiology of pain, this is a fascinating and surprisingly uplifting book. Vertosick, a neurosurgeon, shares case studies and his personal experiences about nature's formidable messenger.

8. ***Why We Love: The Nature and Chemistry of Romantic Love*** by Helen Fisher, 2004 – Why does love make us feel so rapturous? Why do so many couples divorce after just a few years, while others manage to stay together their whole lives? Do animals experience romantic love? Neurochemistry, evolutionary theory, and love poetry all come together in this thought-provoking and appealing book.

Science Fiction Novels

Alien Invasions

If only the aliens who invade the Earth in many of these science fiction novels followed the benign lead of Klaatu, the extraterrestrial emissary of peace in the classic film *The Day the Earth Stood Still*. Whereas Klaatu comes to Earth to save us from ourselves in Robert Wise's still-potent cold war parable, the Martians in H.G. Wells' *War of the Worlds* pursue an intergalactic form of "scorched earth policy" after landing outside London. And then there's the more insidious threat to mankind posed by the interstellar pods in Jack Finney's *Invasion of the Body Snatchers*. They're simply taking over our bodies and minds while we sleep. It's enough to make you welcome chronic insomnia!

Here are eight science fiction novels, listed alphabetically, that depict our first contact with aliens— none of whom even vaguely resemble little green men.

1. ***Childhood's End*** by Arthur C. Clarke, 1953 – An alien race initially brings peace and prosperity to Earth, but over time, reveal themselves to have a sinister ulterior motive for mankind. An unnerving and provocative classic from the visionary author of *2001: A Space Odyssey*.

2. ***Day of the Triffids*** by John Wyndham, 1951 – Wyndham's taut apocalyptic thriller depicts a world overrun by predatory, mobile plants, "triffids," who attack and devour their human victims.

3. ***Ender's Game*** by Orson Scott Card, 1985 – Trained by the govern-

ment in the art of war, boy genius Ender Wiggin puts his skills to the test when hostile aliens lay siege to the Earth. The first in a series of seven Ender novels, *Ender's Game* won both the Hugo and the Nebula Awards for science fiction.

4. ***The Forge of God*** by Greg Bear, 1987 – The arrival of two groups of aliens on Earth is greeted as a sign of the imminent apocalypse. The *Los Angeles Times* praised Forge's novel as "profound and unusual."

5. ***This Immortal*** by Roger Zelazny, 1968 – An expanded version of Zelazny's Hugo Award winning 1966 novella *...And Call Me Conrad, This Immortal* takes place following nuclear war, when the Earth is run by blue-skinned aliens known as Vegans.

6. ***Invasion of the Body Snatchers*** by Jack Finney, 1955 – Finney's chilling, oft-filmed story of aliens replacing people with emotionless replicas.

7. ***The Puppet Masters*** by Robert Heinlein, 1951 – Secret agents in a shadowy, government organization known only as "The Section" face a deadly, seemingly unstoppable foe in the repellant form of mind-controlling, slug-like aliens. Heinlein skillfully plays on cold war-era jitters about the Soviet Union in *The Puppet Masters*.

8. ***War of the Worlds*** by H. G. Wells, 1898 – The sun nearly sets on the British Empire, and everywhere else for that matter, when Martians unleash hell on mankind in Wells' classic, Victorian era version of alien Armageddon.

excerpt: WAR OF THE WORLDS:

Those who have never seen a living Martian can scarcely imagine the strange horror of its appearance. The peculiar V-shaped mouth with its pointed upper lip, the absence of brow ridges, the absence of a chin beneath the wedgelike lower lip, the incessant quivering of this mouth, the Gorgon groups of tentacles, the tumultuous breathing of the lungs in a strange atmosphere, the evident heaviness and painfulness of movement due to the greater gravitational energy of the earth—above all, the extraordinary intensity of the immense eyes—were at once vital, intense, inhuman, crippled and monstrous.

Seafaring Novels

Classic Literature, Ahoy!

Even the most committed landlubbers will find it hard to resist the romance of the high seas once they dive into Patrick O'Brian's grand and glorious *Master and Commander* series of historical novels. In twenty vividly rendered and scrupulously authentic books, O'Brian envelops readers in the seafaring adventures of Royal Navy Captain Jack Aubrey and ship surgeon/confidante Steven Maturin, as they navigate the globe during the Napoleonic Wars. With these novels, O'Brian took his place alongside Joseph Conrad, Herman Melville, and Robert Louis Stevenson as one of the greatest writers about the sea in the English language. Here are eight novels, listed alphabetically, that transport you to a bygone era of nautical adventure and exploration, when pirates sailed the seven seas and the South Pacific islands beckoned like a tropical siren.

1. ***An Eye of the Fleet*** by Richard Woodman, 1981 – The first in Woodman's fourteen-book series of Nathaniel Drinkwater novels about a British Royal Navy officer during the Napoleonic Wars. In *An Eye of the Fleet,* Drinkwater is a midshipman aboard the *HMS Cyclops,* circa 1779. Charged with capturing American privateers, the crew of the *Cyclops* sets sail for the swamps of South Carolina, where Drinkwater gets a crash course in warfare.

2. ***Hornblower: Beat to Quarters*** by C.S. Forester, 1937 – Forester's dashing Royal Navy captain, Horatio Hornblower, plots a course for Central America, where he locks horns with a crazy leader who calls himself El Supremo. Most fans regard *Beat to Quarters* as the strongest book in Forester's Hornblower series.

3. ***Master and Commander*** by Patrick O'Brian, 1969 – The first novel in the series introduces us to Captain Jack Aubrey and naval surgeon Stephen Maturin—temperamental opposites who form an unlikely bond over a shared love of music.

4. ***Mutiny on the Bounty*** by Charles Nordhoff and James Norman Hall, 1932 – A fictionalized account of the legendary mutiny led by *Bounty* master mate Fletcher Christian against Captain Bligh in 1789. While the authors take a few liberties with the facts, *Mutiny on the Bounty*

remains a stirring, albeit romanticized depiction of the mutiny that's inspired several movies and a musical.

excerpt: MUTINY ON THE BOUNTY:
Christian placed the point of his bayonet at Bligh's throat with a look in his eye there was no mistaking. "Slit the dog's gullet!" someone shouted; and there were cries of "Let him have it, Mr. Christian!" "Throw him overboard!" "Feed the bastard to the sharks!" and the like. It was only then, I think, that Captain Bligh realized his true situation. He stood for a moment breathing hard, looking about him with an expression of incredulity on his face.

"Mr. Christian, allow me to speak!" he begged hoarsely. "Think what you do! Release me — lay aside your arms! Let us be friends again, and I give you my word that nothing more shall be said of this matter."

"Your word is of no value, sir," Christian replied. "Had you been a man of honour things would never have come to this pass."

5. ***Rites of Passage*** by William Golding, 1980 – The first novel in Golding's seafaring trilogy (the others being *Close Quarters* and *Fire Down Below*), *Rites of Passage* is a splendid, Booker Prize winning novel about a young Englishman's epic voyage to Australia in the early nineteenth century.

6. ***The Sea Wolf*** by Jack London, 1904 – The tyrannical captain of a seal-hunting schooner named *The Ghost* pushes a shipwrecked literary scholar to the breaking point in London's taut psychological thriller.

7. ***Treasure Island*** by Robert Louis Stevenson, 1883 – A rip-roaring adventure yarn/coming-of-age novel of pirates and buried treasure that continues to enthrall new generations of readers young and old alike.

8. ***Typhoon*** by Joseph Conrad, 1902 – The captain of a Siamese steamer sets a course right into the path of a deadly storm in Conrad's stunningly realized novella.

Self-Help Books

Stress Relief

Ordinary life in our society has become a bit crazy. Each day, we're confronted with a whirlwind of information both important and trivial, and many of us have more responsibilities than we can easily handle. All too often our attention is fragmented, our bodies are tense, and our lives feel out of control. There are lots of quick fixes available (fast food to solve the eating problem, mindless television to relax, sleeping pills for insomnia) but in the long run these don't give us vitality and joy.

Are there straightforward solutions to these problems? Sometimes there are, even if you can't spend the rest of your life at a spa. These books, listed alphabetically, provide alternative perspectives on contemporary life. They offer a wealth of practical ways to cut down on stress and respond better to the stressful circumstances that remain, giving you more time and energy for the things and people you value most.

1. ***Clear Your Clutter With Feng Shui*** by Karen Kingston, 1999 – Even if you're skeptical about some of the esoteric aspects of feng shui—the traditional Chinese practice of arranging objects and buildings to optimize energy flow—this lovely book can inspire you to let go of the clutter in your home (and mind and body) that may be "clogging" your life.

2. ***Conscious Breathing: Breathwork for Health, Stress Release, and Personal Mastery*** by Gay Hendricks, 1995 – One of the most profound influences on our mental and emotional states is hidden right under our noses (or flowing right through them, to be more precise). This book explains the physiology of breathing and provides illustrated exercises to help you experience the difference that conscious breathing can make.

3. ***Finding Flow: The Psychology of Engagement With Everyday Life*** by Mihaly Csikszentmihalyi, 1997 – Written by a cutting-edge researcher, this book teaches us how we can have "peak experiences" of consciousness more often and how to live richly at work, in our leisure time, and even when doing our least favorite chores.

4. ***How to Stop Worrying and Start Living*** by Dale Carnegie, 1944 – With his talent for getting at the heart of a matter, the author of *How to Win Friends and Influence People* offers timeless wisdom about prioritizing, effectiveness, and authenticity.

5. ***Life Is Not a Stress Rehearsal: Bringing Yesterday's Sane Wisdom Into Today's Insane World*** by Loretta LaRoche, 2001 – LaRoche presents a clear-headed look at the excesses, misplaced values, and unnecessary complications that are rampant in our culture—all with a healthy dose of humor.

6. ***The Simple Living Guide*** by Janet Luhrs, 1997 – The editor of *Simple Living* magazine shares realistic ideas and useful resources for enjoying a well-planned, relaxed, and vibrant lifestyle. The book includes inspiring examples of people who've radically changed their lives in the direction of simplicity.

7. ***The Wellness Book: The Comprehensive Guide to Maintaining Health and Treating Stress-Related Illness*** by Herbert Benson and Eileen M. Stuart, 1992 – Benson is the renowned author of *The Relaxation Response;* here, he and his co-author discuss that topic and many others, covering both physical and psychological aspects of health.

8. ***Wherever You Go, There You Are: Mindfulness Meditation in Everyday Life*** by Jon Kabat-Zinn, 1994 – This is a clear, friendly introduction to different types of meditation and their benefits from the founder of the Stress Reduction Clinic at the University of Massachusetts Medical Center. It even shows you how parenting—often one of the most stressful experiences as well as one of the most rewarding—can be a route to mindfulness.

Shakespeare's Immortal Lines

To Quote or Not To Quote

Here are the Bard's most-quoted works in *Bartlett's Familiar Quotations,* with fifty or more citations each, listed in descending order.

TITLE	ENTRIES IN BARTLETT'S
1. ***Hamlet***	221
2. ***MacBeth***	123
3. ***King Lear***	105

1. ***Hamlet*** — 221

"Neither a borrower, nor a lender be"; "This above all: to thine own self be true, / And it must follow, as the night the day, / Thou canst not be false to any man"; "Brevity is the soul of wit"; "To be, or not to be: that is the question"

2. ***MacBeth*** — 123

"Double, double toil and trouble; / Fire burn and cauldron bubble"; "Angels are bright still, though the brightest fell"; "Out, damned spot! out, I say!"

3. ***King Lear*** — 105

"More sinn'd against than sinning"; "As flies to wanton boys, are we to the gods; / They kill us for their sport"

4. ***Othello*** 103
"For I am nothing if not critical"; "O! beware, my lord, of jealousy; / It is the green-eyed monster"
5. ***Henry IV, Part I*** 95
"Sink or swim"; "Play out the play"
6. ***The Merchant of Venice*** 94
"Your mind is tossing on the ocean"; "It is a wise father that knows his own child"
7. ***As You Like It*** 83
"Sweet are the uses of adversity"; "All the world's a stage, / And all the men and women merely players"
8. ***Julius Caesar*** 75
"Beware the ides of March"; "Friends, Romans, countrymen, lend me your ears; / I come to bury Caesar, not to praise him"; "Et tu, Brute!"
9. ***Romeo and Juliet*** 66
"A pair of star-cross'd lovers"; "What's in a name? that which we call a rose / By any other name would smell as sweet"
10. ***Henry VI*** 59
"Fight till the last gasp"; "Small things make base men proud"
11. ***Sonnets*** 58
"Shall I compare thee to a summer's day?"; "Let me not to the marriage of true minds / Admit impediments"; "Lilies that fester smell far worse than weeds"
12. ***Antony and Cleopatra*** 56
"My salad days, / When I was green in judgment"
13. ***A Midsummer-Night's Dream*** 54
"Though she be but little, she is fierce"

Short Story Collections

Masters of the Short Story, Past and Present

Short story writers can create a world in just a few pages. Although they can be read in a brief period of time, the best works of short fiction give you much to think about long afterward. Here are eight short story collections, listed alphabetically, from masterful practitioners of the form, past and present.

1. ***The Complete Stories*** by Flannery O'Connor, 1971 – The ailing young woman from Georgia who kept peacocks on her lawn wrote

some of America's most haunting and strange fiction. There are always unexpected moral dimensions to the portraits she drew of a wide range of people in her native South.

2. ***The Essential Tales of Chekhov*** by Anton Chekhov, translated by Constance Garnett and edited by Richard Ford, 1998 – The Russian playwright was also a master of the short story, revealing the internal dramas in his characters' lives with both humor and gravity.

3. ***High Lonesome: Stories 1966–2006*** by Joyce Carol Oates, 2006 – The stories in this collection were chosen by the author herself from four decades of work. Oates has a distinct vision of contemporary American life often expressed in tightly wound tales of dysfunctional families and individuals. As edgy and dark as they can be, they achieve a believability that makes them compelling.

4. ***Interpreter of Maladies*** by Jhumpa Lahiri, 1999 – Set in India and the United States, these stories offer a gentler look at contemporary life and its often perplexing, unmoored experiences. They explore the nuances of marriages and other relationships, including the relationships between different cultures.

5. ***Paris Stories*** by Mavis Gallant, 2002 – Gallant is a Canadian writer who has spent many years living in Paris, the setting for some of her best fiction. Her sharp powers of observation join forces with a strong awareness of the past, which often seems to haunt the people and places she writes about.

6. ***The Short Stories*** by Ernest Hemingway, 1938 – Hemingway's famous prose style—spare and understated yet vivid, tough yet moving—has stood up well through the years and continues to inspire other writers. This collection contains classics such as "The Snows of Kilimanjaro," which is about a writer's encounter with death while he is on safari, and "Hills Like White Elephants," a brief story of a couple conversing over drinks that manages to be fraught with realistic tension.

7. ***The Stories of John Cheever*** by John Cheever, 1978 – Cheever writes about troubled characters trapped in normal suburban life. His narratives describe ominous, surreal events and reveal buried inner struggles and discordancies. You'll find favorites such as "The Enormous Radio" and "The Swimmer" in this collection.

8. ***Where I'm Calling From: Selected Stories*** by Raymond Carver, 1988 – In contrast to Cheever's portrayals of middle-class America, Carver's home terrain is working-class America. His writing is simple but sophisticated, and wonderfully heartfelt as well.

Slave Stories

The Age of Slavery in American Literature

When Abraham Lincoln met Harriet Beecher Stowe in 1862, he reportedly said, only half in jest, "So you're the little woman who wrote the book that started this Great War!"

The "book" was Stowe's classic novel *Uncle Tom's Cabin,* which had first appeared in serialized form in the abolitionist newspaper *The National Era,* in 1851. Later published in book form, Stowe's harrowing tale of slaves enduring brutal abuse and abject cruelty at the hands of their masters was an immediate cause célèbre that polarized readers and became a huge best-seller. While its melodramatic plot and egregious racial stereotypes don't hold up very well, *Uncle Tom's Cabin* nonetheless remains the most influential novel about slavery ever written for its galvanizing effect on the abolition movement. It therefore rates a place on the following, alphabetical list of novels about the age of slavery in the United States.

1. ***The Bondwoman's Narrative*** by Hannah Crafts, 1850s – Discovered by Harvard historian Henry Louis Gates, Jr. at an auction, *The Bondwoman's Narrative* may be the first novel written by an African-American woman. Melodramatic and stilted, this story about a young slave woman escaping to freedom nevertheless holds your interest.

2. ***Clotel: Or The President's Daughter*** by William Wells Brown, 1853 – One of the first novels written by an African-American writer, *Clotel* tackles a controversial subject head-on: the rumored mulatto offspring of Thomas Jefferson and his slave mistress. In Brown's compelling, swiftly-paced narrative, the heroine escapes slavery, only to risk capture when she attempts to rescue her daughter from Jefferson's home.

3. ***The Confessions of Nat Turner*** by William Styron, 1967 – Based on the actual jailhouse confession of Turner, who led a slave revolt in Virginia in 1831, Styron's Pulitzer Prize winning novel has polar-

ized African-American critics over its portrait of the title character, an educated slave whose long-simmering rage explodes in bloody violence.

4. ***Jubilee*** by Margaret Walker, 1966 – Inspired by her grandmother's stories, Walker transforms the true story of a Mississippi slave woman born to her master and his slave mistress into a riveting and sensitively wrought piece of historical fiction.

5. ***The Known World*** by Edward P. Jones, 2003 – Jones' superb, Pulitzer Prize winning novel addresses a subject that's rarely discussed: freed slaves who became slaveholders themselves. Set in antebellum Virginia, this mesmerizing and brilliantly nuanced novel depicts the social and psychological repercussions of black-on-black ownership from multiple points of view.

excerpt: THE KNOWN WORLD:
It took Moses more than two weeks to understand that someone wasn't fiddling with him and that indeed a black man, two shades darker than himself, owned him and any shadow he made. Sleeping in a cabin beside Henry in the first weeks after the sale, Moses had thought that it was already a strange world that made him a slave to a white man, but God had indeed set it twirling and twisting every which way when he put black people to owning their own kind. Was God even up there attending to business anymore?

6. ***Middle Passage*** by Charles Johnson, 1990 – On the run from creditors and a lovelorn schoolteacher, a freed slave stows away aboard a ship, unaware that he's boarded an illegal slave trader bound for Africa under the erratic command of a sadistic taskmaster. The winner of the National Book Award, *Middle Passage* has the sweep and emotional heft of the seafaring novels of Conrad and Melville.

7. ***Uncle Tom's Cabin*** by Harriet Beecher Stowe, 1851 – Yes, it's clichéd and painfully overwrought, but *Uncle Tom's Cabin* has an undeniably raw power and sincerity that nearly compensates for Stowe's problematic depiction of the slave characters.

8. ***Walk Through Darkness*** by David Anthony Durham, 2002 – Durham beats the sophomore slump with this terrific follow-up to his well-received debut novel, *Gabriel's Story*. He skillfully balances the parallel storylines of two men in the antebellum South: a runaway slave and the old Scottish immigrant tracking him down.

Southern Literature

Classics of the Modern Era

Few regions in the United States exert a more enduring hold on the popular imagination than the American South. Alternately romanticized and reviled, the South remains haunted by a tumultuous, often terrible past that continues to shape and inform the culture of the region to this day, over 140 years after the Civil War ended with Lee's surrender to Grant at Appomattox.

One of the legacies of the South's unique culture has been a rich literary tradition that's produced many of America's greatest writers and historians: William Faulkner, Civil War historian Shelby Foote, and Eudora Welty immediately spring to mind. Along with scores of other Southern writers, they cast a light on this misunderstood and often maligned region that's lent itself to caricature and stereotyping.

In 2000, while researching his three-part documentary series on twentieth century Southern literature, *Tell Us About the South: Voices in Black and White,* filmmaker Ross Spears polled book editors, publishers, scholars, and reviewers regarding their selections for "the most remarkable works of modern Southern literature." Spanning fiction and nonfiction, here are the top ten vote-getters, ranked in descending order.

1. ***Invisible Man*** by Ralph Ellison, 1952 – Winner of the 1953 National Book Award, Ellison's magisterial novel follows the unnamed African-American narrator on his journey of self-discovery from the South to Harlem, where he becomes involved with a black nationalist group called The Brotherhood. A startling, provocative novel that burns itself in your memory.

2. ***Let Us Now Praise Famous Men*** by James Agee, 1941 – Taking its title from Ecclesiasticus, this landmark work in photojournalism documents the lives of impoverished, white sharecropping families in the Depression-era South. Novelist/film critic James Agee wrote the text that complements Walker Evan's stark, almost unbearably sad black-and-white photographs.

3. ***The Sound and the Fury*** by William Faulkner, 1929 – Arguably the greatest of all the Southern novelists, Faulkner immerses you in the tumultuous lives of the Compson family in this demanding, stream-of-consciousness novel divided into four sections. Set in Yoknapatawpha

County, Mississippi, the fictional setting for many of Faulkner's novels, *The Sound and the Fury* was selected the sixth greatest English-language novel of the twentieth century by Modern Library.

4. ***The Mind of the South*** by Wilbur Cash, 1941 – This groundbreaking sociological analysis of Southern culture presents a lucid and informed overview of the region and its peculiar characters, stripped of myth and misconceptions.

5. ***Look Homeward, Angel*** by Thomas Wolfe, 1929 – Although some critics now regard it as overwrought and hyperbolic, Wolfe's first, unabashedly autobiographical novel remains a pivotal work of modern Southern literature. His sprawling, coming-of-age narrative follows Eugene Gant as he flees his North Carolina hometown for the sophisticated world of Harvard University.

6. ***To Kill a Mockingbird*** by Harper Lee, 1960 – A perennial favorite that's brought generations of readers to tears, Lee's elegiac, sensitively written coming-of-age novel is set against the backdrop of a racially-charged rape trial in Depression-era Alabama. Lee's only novel, *To Kill a Mockingbird* won the 1961 Pulitzer Prize.

7. ***The Color Purple*** by Alice Walker, 1982 – Walker's epistolary novel tells the heartbreaking yet finally uplifting story of Celie, a poor, downtrodden African-American woman trapped in an abusive marriage to a widower with several children. Gradually, through her relationship with a fiery blues singer, Celie finds the strength to take charge of her destiny in Walker's feminist classic, written in the black vernacular of her uneducated heroine.

8. ***Their Eyes Were Watching God*** by Zora Neale Hurston, 1937 – A key figure of the "Harlem Renaissance," novelist/folklorist Hurston achieved her greatest success with this vivid and evocative novel about a strong-willed woman chafing under the status quo in the all-black community of Eaton, Florida. Although some of Hurston's fellow "Harlem Renaissance" writers criticized this novel for reinforcing negative racial stereotypes, *Their Eyes Were Watching God* has influenced such writers as Maya Angelou and Alice Walker.

9. ***Absalom, Absalom!*** by William Faulkner, 1936 – Peripherally connected to *The Sound and the Fury, Absalom, Absalom!* is a quintessential Southern Gothic saga of three Mississippi families before, during

and after the Civil War. Told in flashback form, Faulkner's mesmerizing novel paints a disturbing portrait of the American South at its most degenerate.

excerpt: ***ABSALOM, ABSALOM!:***
There was a wistaria vine blooming for the second time that summer on a wooden trellis before one window, into which sparrows came now and then in random gusts, making a dry vivid dusty sound before going away: and opposite Quentin, Miss Coldfield in the eternal black which she had worn for forty-three years now, whether for sister, father, or nothusband none knew, sitting so bolt upright in the straight hard chair that was so tall for her that her legs hung straight and rigid as if she had iron shinbones and ankles, clear of the floor with that air of impotent and static rage like children's feet...

10. ***Lanterns on the Levee: Recollections of a Planter's Son*** by William Alexander Percy, 1941 – Described by his cousin, novelist Walker Percy, as "the most extraordinary man I have ever known," William Percy was a poet/lawyer who oversaw the Red Cross during the catastrophic Mississippi River flood of 1927. His eloquent autobiography provides readers a fascinating glimpse of the American South emerging from the ashes of the Civil War.

Sports Books

Sports Illustrated's *Top Ten*

When the *New Yorker* journalist A. J. Liebling quipped, "I can write better than anybody who can write faster, and I can write faster than anybody who can write better," it wasn't just idle boasting on his part. A dazzling writer of pungent wit and brilliant insight who could turn a phrase that made his peers sigh with envy, Liebling could write on everything from Louisiana politics to food to boxing with equal authority. Hailed by no less than Tom Wolfe as one of the pioneers of "new journalism," Liebling is probably best remembered today for *The Sweet Science*, his superb collection of essays on boxing.

In 2002, the editors of *Sports Illustrated* declared Liebling's *The Sweet Science* the all-time best sports book. Here are the *Sports Illustrated* editors' top ten nonfiction sports books, ranked in descending order.

1. ***The Sweet Science*** by A. J. Liebling, 1956 – A knockout collection of essays on boxing that *SI's* editors pronounce "timeless." Pugilists

famous (Rocky Marciano) and obscure duke it out, figuratively speaking, in the essays of *The Sweet Science,* which the *SI* editors compare to the novels of Henry James for the extraordinary richness of detail.

2. ***The Boys of Summer*** by Roger Kahn, 1971 – A monumental portrait of the Brooklyn Dodgers, whose relocation to Los Angeles in 1958 plunged the team's Brooklyn fans into mourning. Kahn's superbly written account of the players' lives on and off the baseball diamond is as dramatic as any novel. According to *SI's* editors, "No book is better at showing how sports is not just games."

3. ***Ball Four*** by Jim Bouton, 1970 – Bouton's controversial, hilarious warts-and-all memoir of the 1969 Yankee season spares no one, least of all himself, in airing the players' dirty laundry. According to *SI's* editors, Bouton's "biting observations" rendered him persona non grata in the Yankee dugout.

4. ***Friday Night Lights*** by H.G. Bissinger, 1990 – In the flat, dusty towns of West Texas, high school football is practically a religion. Bissinger's masterful and socially acute portrait of an Odessa, Texas high school football team in the late 1980s is a "brilliant look at how Friday-night lights can lead a town into darkness," per *SI's* editors.

5. ***A Season on the Brink*** by John Feinstein, 1986 – To say that former Indiana University basketball coach Bobby Knight is "volatile" would be an understatement. A polarizing figure whose remarkable record is frequently overshadowed by his notorious, sometimes violent fits of rage, Knight gave Feinstein unlimited access to watch his every move over the course of a season. Called "unsparing" by *SI's* editors, *A Season on the Brink* was a huge best-seller.

6. ***Paper Lion*** by George Plimpton, 1965 – Not many rank amateurs would test their mettle against professional football players, but that's just what Plimpton did in 1963, when he participated in the Detroit Lions' training camp. Not only did Plimpton survive the bone-crunching experience, he also wrote about it—"brilliantly," per *SI's* editors—in *Paper Lion,* his insider account of the NFL.

7. ***The Game*** by Ken Dryden, 1983 – Now a politician in his native Canada, former Montreal Canadien goalkeeper Dryden sheds light on the rough-and-tumble world of professional hockey in *The Game,* his perceptive memoir about the Canadiens' 1979 Stanley Cup-winning

season that *SI's* editors call "well-crafted."

8. ***Seabiscuit*** by Laura Hillenbrand, 2001 – Hillenbrand's exhilarating, prize winning book about the knobby-kneed Depression-era racehorse who dominated the nation's headlines is a modern day classic. "Irresistible," according to *SI's* editors.

excerpt: SEABISCUIT:
When they returned to the scales, Seabiscuit wasn't even breathing hard. He had eclipsed another track record, running less than a second off the world record. His time was so fast that in the following year, no horse in Bay Meadows would come within three seconds of it. Pollard suddenly found himself in a sea of reporters. If he met the same field again, he sang out, he'd have time to ride Seabiscuit right off the track, canter him down to San Mateo for some Christmas shopping, swing by the post office for their fan mail, and still trot back in time to win the race.

9. ***Loose Balls*** by Terry Pluto, 1990 – Julius "Doctor J" Erving, Rick Barry, and Mel Daniels are just some of the basketball greats reminiscing about the long-gone American Basketball Association in this oral history teeming with anecdotes that *SI's* editors call "almost too-good-to-be-true."

10. ***Heaven is a Playground*** by Rick Telander, 1976 – Telander's "intriguing account of inner-city hoops," per *SI's* editors, will appeal to anyone who loved the 1994 documentary, *Hoop Dreams.*

Terrorism Studies

Making Sense of the Senseless

It's hard to believe that human beings would choose to air their grievances by deliberately targeting civilians for slaughter. But the ideologies that celebrate this behavior are attractive to enough people to make this a pressing issue not just in Washington, DC, and New York City, but around the world. We need to understand the whys and hows of fanaticism and terror in order to fight it. Here are some insightful books, listed alphabetically, about the problem and how to counter it.

1. ***Dying To Kill: The Allure of Suicide Terror*** by Mia Bloom, 2005 – The author traces the use of suicide attacks throughout history in

places as diverse as Japan, Ireland, and the West Bank. Drawing on contemporary research in the field, as well as historical analysis, she examines the motivations of attackers and the ways their decisions are influenced by attitudes within their communities. She finds that harsh counterattacks often lead to a cycle of violence, and discusses ways to avoid this. The book also includes a chapter on female suicide bombers.

2. ***Dying to Win: The Strategic Logic of Suicide Terrorism*** by Robert Pape, 2005 – Pape collects information about suicide attacks around the world since the 1980s and subjects the data to rigorous analysis, coming up with some surprising conclusions. Many suicide bombers, for example, are well educated and middle class. Pape shows how the strategic goals of the organized groups that are responsible for most suicide attacks can both drive them forward and rein them in. He also notes a striking similarity among contemporary suicide terrorist campaigns—all are aimed at expelling the military forces of a democracy from land they consider theirs.

3. ***Ghost Wars: The Secret History of the CIA, Afghanistan, and bin Laden, from the Soviet Invasion to September 10, 2001*** by Steve Coll, 2004 – During the cold war, America supplied arms to Islamists in Afghanistan to fight the Soviets. Unfortunately, this support came back to haunt us in the form of an extremist Taliban that sheltered Osama bin Laden. Coll recounts this history, along with the experiences and ideas that have shaped the Clinton and Bush administrations in their fight against terror.

4. ***Nuclear Terrorism: The Ultimate Preventable Catastrophe*** by Graham Allison, 2004 – Nuclear weapons—whether in the form of airborne missiles or "dirty bombs"—represent the basis of the most horrifying terror scenarios. A number of violent groups below the level of statehood may be interested in acquiring such weapons, and now with Iran making moves toward going nuclear, the need to halt proliferation is even more urgent. Allison outlines the dangers, as well as a strategy for keeping nukes from falling into the wrong hands, including more aggressive action to secure Russian nuclear materials.

5. ***Osama: The Making of a Terrorist*** by Jonathan Randal, 2004 – This book looks into the life and times of Osama bin Laden. It follows the

development of the mysterious but influential terrorist leader, along with the changes across the Middle East that have led to the current state of affairs, from Algeria's culture of violence to the unification of Yemen.

6. ***Terrorism and U.S. Foreign Policy*** by Paul R. Pillar, 2001 – The author suggests that successfully fighting terrorism is not only a matter of taking drastic actions, but also of serious dedication to the everyday work of monitoring and preventing terrorist activity. His detailed knowledge of intelligence comes from years with the CIA.

7. ***Understanding Terror Networks*** by Marc Sageman, 2004 – Sageman explores the psychology of the alienated young men—often living in the West—who form groups of Muslim extremists bent on jihad (holy war). The men who attacked the United States on September 11, 2001, are one example of this sort of clique. Preventing these tight-knit groups from being coached by members of al Qaeda, he argues, is one of the ways to reduce the threat they pose.

Tiny Things

Books About the Microscopic World

In the daily rush of life, it's all too easy to forget how magical everything is. There are marvels both visible and invisible all around us, and even inside us. You may not have looked through a microscope since high school biology, but the books in this alphabetical list will remind you just how amazing little things can be—helping you "see a world in a grain of sand," as William Blake put it.

1. ***The Ants*** by Bert Hölldobler and Edward O. Wilson, 1990 – Ants—so much more than picnic pests! This book, which won a Pulitzer Prize in general nonfiction, will show you why. It explores ants' altruistic behavior, how they divide labor, their communication by the aromatic chemicals known as pheromones, and many other aspects of their society. There are special chapters on such interesting varieties as army ants, ants that cultivate fungus, and weaver ants. It's also a lovely book with captivating photos and illustrations.

2. ***Atom: Journey Across the Subatomic Cosmos*** by Isaac Asimov, 1991 – Getting tinier still, as tiny, in fact, as it's possible to get—how far can

you divide matter? The great science fiction writer Isaac Asimov addresses this question, explaining the world of the infinitesimal with such clarity that you won't need to be a physics whiz to understand such mysteries as fission, fusion, leptons, antiparticles, and the beginning and end of the universe.

3. ***Nanofuture: What's Next For Nanotechnology*** by J. Storrs Hall, 2005 – This book offers both a realistic and an imaginative assessment of the prospects for nanotechnology—tiny machines engineered at the molecular level. The field is still at an early stage, but it holds great potential for future advances in medicine and other areas.

4. ***The Nature of Diamonds*** edited by George E. Harlow, 1998 – Get your science and your social history together in this book about the little rocks that mean so much. Enticingly illustrated, it will teach you how diamonds form in nature, why they come in different colors, how we cut them, and much more.

5. ***The Secret Life of Germs: What They Are, Why We Need Them, and How We Can Protect Ourselves Against Them*** by Philip M. Tierno Jr., 2001 – Moving on to a somewhat less pleasant but no less fascinating subject than diamonds, germs—they're all over. (Yes, even at the engagement-ring counter at Tiffany's—the author takes a sampling there.) The author explains how normally "friendly" germs can cause disease, the prospects for bioterrorism, and other unsettling matters, but mostly, it is a comforting book.

6. ***Secrets of Saffron: The Vagabond History of the World's Most Seductive Spice*** by Pat Willard, 2001 – Saffron is a colorful and richly perfumed spice madc from thc stigma of a purple crocus. Unlike less precious spices that are sold by the jar, you'll find saffron sold in vials containing just a pinch of the wee, but powerful threads. Enjoy the legends and history of saffron, along with the author's own experiences with the spice, and lots of recipes.

7. ***The Tipping Point: How Little Things Can Make a Big Difference*** by Malcolm Gladwell, 2000 – This is a more abstract discussion of the importance of tiny things—subtle nonverbal signals that people make during conversations, for example, and small numbers of people with particular skills that make them influential—and how they can create social change on a grand scale.

8. ***The World of the Hummingbird*** by Robert Burton, 2001 – Learn about the unusual flying skills, nectar-sipping ways, and social lives of the world's smallest birds. In addition to all the fascinating facts, this book is appealing for its stunning photos of the beautiful little creatures. Even in close-ups their feet look unbelievably tiny.

True Crime Classics

Ripped from the Headlines

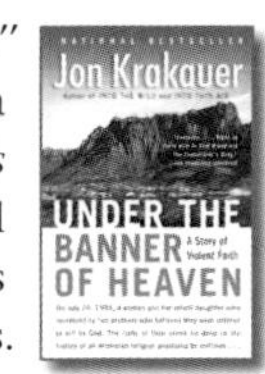

When Truman Capote unveiled his self-proclaimed "nonfiction novel" *In Cold Blood* in 1966, critics and readers were astonished. Although he'd won wide acclaim for such novellas as *Breakfast at Tiffany's* and *The Grass Harp,* nothing in Capote's literary oeuvre suggested that he was capable of pulling off such an ambitious project as this mesmerizing, fact-based account of a mass murder in rural Kansas. But the elfin, much-imitated Southern-born writer with the instantly recognizable voice confounded skeptics with this brilliantly textured and piercingly observed book. With remarkable insight, Capote delves into the hearts and minds of the two drifters who slaughtered four members of a family in 1959. An instant classic, *In Cold Blood* effectively set the literary template for all true crime sagas that followed. Fascinating, lurid, and deeply disturbing, the following true crime books, listed alphabetically, make for powerful reading.

1. ***The Devil in the White City: Murder, Magic and Madness at the Fair that Changed America*** by Erik Larson, 2003 – Set against the backdrop of Chicago's 1893 World's Fair, Larson's best-seller reveals the nightmarish underside to this celebration of progress. As architect Daniel Burnham supervised construction on the fairgrounds, serial killer H.H. Holmes preyed upon tourists staying in his World Fair's Hotel, which contained a gas chamber and crematorium.

2. ***The Executioner's Song*** by Norman Mailer, 1979 – Often compared to *In Cold Blood,* Mailer's epic "nonfiction novel" examines the tragic, violent life and controversial execution of Utah inmate Gary Gilmore, who rejected his lawyers' attempts to appeal his death sentence—and sparked intense debate over capital punishment. A mammoth accomplishment, *The Executioner's Song* won Mailer his second Pulitzer Prize.

excerpt: THE DEVIL IN THE WHITE CITY:
Darker forces marshaled in the smoke. Somewhere in the heart of the city a young Irish immigrant sank still more deeply into madness, the preamble to an act that would shock the nation and destroy what Burnham dreamed would be the single greatest moment of his life.

Closer at hand a far stranger creature raised his head in equally intent anticipation. "I was born with the devil in me," he wrote. "I could not help the fact that I was a murderer, no more than the poet can help the inspiration to sing."

3. ***Fatal Vision*** by Joe McGinnis, 1983 – In 1970, Dr. Jeffrey MacDonald's pregnant wife and two young daughters were viciously murdered by hippies strung out on acid—or so MacDonald loudly maintains. And for awhile, McGinnis believed him, until he began poring over the evidence and interviewing the charming yet ice-cold doctor. Although some balk at McGinnis' theory that MacDonald killed his family in an amphetamine-fueled rage, *Fatal Vision* remains a haunting book.

4. ***Helter Skelter: The True Story of the Manson Murders,*** by Vincent Bugliosi with Curt Gentry, 1974 – Few crimes have gripped the American public like the Tate-LaBianca murders in Los Angeles, circa 1969. The definitive book on this horrific mass murder remains *Helter Skelter* by Bugliosi, the Los Angeles assistant district attorney who successfully prosecuted the killers, Charles Manson and four members of his hippie "family."

5. ***In Cold Blood*** by Truman Capote, 1966 – Capote's masterpiece, *In Cold Blood* would sadly turn out to be the writer's swan song. He would never write another book of comparable scope and artistry.

6. ***The Onion Field*** by Joseph Wambaugh, 1973 – A former LAPD sergeant, Wambaugh became a best-selling novelist in the 1970s, with such hard-hitting crime dramas as *The New Centurions* and *The Blue Knight*. He took a detour into true crime with *The Onion Field,* about the 1963 kidnapping/murder of a Los Angeles police officer by two robbers, pulled over on a routine traffic stop.

7. ***The Stranger Beside Me: The Twentieth Anniversary Edition*** by Ann Rule, 2000 – The doyenne of true crime writing, Rule first burst onto the scene in 1980 with this riveting book about the notorious serial

killer Ted Bundy, whom Rule knew as a fellow volunteer at a Seattle suicide hotline. Gruesomely detailed but never exploitative, this updated version of *The Stranger Beside Me* packs a real wallop, thanks to Rule's firsthand experience with the sexual psychopath, thought to have killed upwards of thirty-five women.

8. ***Under the Banner of Heaven: A Story of Violent Faith*** by Jon Krakauer, 2003 – The Mormon Church lambasted Krakauer for this study of religious extremism taken to homicidal lengths in contemporary Utah. Although the primary focus is on the religiously motivated slaying of a woman and her toddler by her Mormon fundamentalist brothers-in-law, *Under the Banner of Heaven* also explores the rise and spread of Mormonism in America.

True-Life Adventures

Hold onto Your Armchair

Ever since legendary explorer Marco Polo dictated his memoirs to a fellow prisoner in thirteenth century Genoa, the true-life adventure has been one of the most enduring genres in nonfiction. By turns triumphant and tragic, these incredible, often first-person accounts of men and women pushing the limits take readers to the farthest reaches of the planet, without ever leaving their armchairs.

To select twelve "must-reads" from the scores of gripping true-life adventures, we turned to no less an authority than the National Geographic Society for guidance. In the July/August 2001 issue of *National Geographic Adventure,* a panel of experts chose the "100 All-Time Best Adventure Books." The following list reflects their top ten picks, plus two others deserving of mention. The list below is alphabetical.

1. ***Annapurna*** by Maurice Herzog, 1952 – Three years before Sir Edmund Hillary and Tenzing Norgay reached the summit of Mount Everest, mountain climber Maurice Herzog joined the French Alpine Club in an attempt to climb the 26,493-foot Himalayan mountain Annapurna. With only a rough map of the mountain and no clear route to the summit, Herzog and teammate Louis Lachenal somehow reached the top of Annapurna. But as he reveals in this riveting account of the 1950 expedition, they nearly died on their hellish descent to the base camp.

2. ***Arabian Sands*** by Wilfred Thesiger, 1959 – A romantic, larger-than-life figure cut from the same mold as T. E. Lawrence, aka Lawrence of Arabia, Sir Wilfred Thesiger spent five years exploring the Empty Quarter of Saudi Arabia, where he lived among the Bedouins and twice crossed the Rub-al-Kahli deserts. In *Arabian Sands,* the Oxford-educated Englishman describes how he was often forced to wear disguises to find acceptance among the suspicious and hostile tribes, who have lived in this bleak and unforgiving region for thousands of years.

3. ***Desert Solitaire: A Season in the Wilderness*** by Edmund Abbey, 1968 – One of the most colorful and paradoxical figures in the environmentalist movement, Edmund Abbey was a beer-swilling, gun-touting naturalist who opposed what he called "industrial tourism" in America's national parks. *Desert Solitaire* is an irreverent, passionate memoir of Abbey's tenure as a park ranger in Utah's Arches National Monument.

4. ***Exploration of the Colorado River and Its Canyons*** by John Wesley Powell, 1895 – In 1869, John Wesley Powell headed a 1,000-mile expedition down the Colorado River and into the Grand Canyon. Neither Powell nor his men knew the terrain or how the Native Americans would receive them. The lack of supplies, the punishing heat, and the Colorado's dangerous rapids took their toll on some of Powell's men, who eventually turned on their commander. Powell survived and turned his field writings into a dramatic account of the expedition that has lost none of its punch for contemporary readers.

5. ***In the Heart of the Sea*** by Nathaniel Philbrick, 2000 – Winner of the 2000 National Book Award for nonfiction, Philbrick's book documents the real-life incident that inspired Herman Melville's *Moby Dick*. When an enraged sperm whale rams and sinks the *Essex* in the South Pacific in 1819, the captain and his crew take to the lifeboats. Adrift for the next three months, the sailors resort to any means possible, including cannibalism, to survive.

6. ***Into Thin Air: A Personal Account of the Mount Everest Disaster,*** by Jon Krakauer, 1998 – A fixture on the nonfiction best-seller list in the late 1990s, Krakauer's first-person account of a disastrous 1996 Mount Everest expedition is a compelling tale of fatal hubris at the highest place on Earth. In addition to the graphic and suspenseful account of the climb, Krakauer also sheds much needed-

light on what drives people to risk their lives by climbing Mount Everest.

excerpt: ***IN THE HEART OF THE SEA:***

With its huge scarred head halfway out of the water and its tail beating the ocean into a white-water wake more than forty feet across, the whale approached the ship at twice its original speed – at least six knots. ...With a tremendous cracking and splintering of oak, the whale struck the ship just below the anchor...the force of the collision caused the whalemen's heads to jounce on their muscled necks as the ship lurched to a halt on the slablike forehead of the whale. The creature's tail continued to work up and down, pushing the 238-ton ship backward until – as had happened after the knockdown in the Gulf Stream – water surged up over the transom. ...No longer going backward, the Essex was now going down.

7. ***Journals*** by Meriwether Lewis and William Clark, 1814 – From 1804 to 1806, explorers Meriwether Lewis and William Clark led an expedition into the vast uncharted territory of the Louisiana Purchase. In addition to mapping rivers and staking claim to the Idaho, Washington, and Oregon territories, Lewis and Clark collaborated on a meticulous journal of their "Voyage of Discovery" from the banks of the Missouri River to the Pacific Northwest. Both a fascinating travel narrative and invaluable source of data on the plants, animals, and terrain of the frontier, *Journals* continues to enthrall new generations of readers.

8. ***The Perfect Storm: A True Story of Men Against the Sea*** by Sebastian Junger, 1997 – In October 1991, the Massachusetts fishing boat *Andrea Gail* disappeared beneath the hundred-foot waves of a terrific storm dubbed "perfect" by meteorologists. Junger's best-selling account of the *Andrea Gail's* final hours is a haunting and unforgettable reminder of man's vulnerability to nature's fury.

9. ***Travels*** by Marco Polo, 1298 – The book that started it all, Marco Polo's *Travels* remains a fascinating and fantastic account of the merchant-traveler's thirteenth century trek from Venice across Asia. Although some historians initially dismissed Polo's *Travels* as fictitious, time has proven that many of his observations of Asian life and customs are grounded in fact.

10. ***West With the Night*** by Beryl Markham, 1942 – No less a writer than Ernest Hemingway hailed Markham's memoir of her life as an aviatrix as "bloody wonderful." A glamorous blonde who grew up on a

Kenyan farm, Markham was the first woman in Africa to hold a pilot's license. In 1936, she made history by becoming the first pilot to fly solo across the Atlantic Ocean from east to west. *West With the Night* is an entertaining account of Markham's remarkable African upbringing and aviation career.

11. ***Wind, Sand & Stars*** by Antoine de Saint-Exupery, 1939 – Best known in the United States as the author of *The Little Prince,* French aviator, novelist, and bon vivant Antoine de Saint-Exupery thrived on adventure. His memoir *Wind, Sand & Stars* is widely regarded as Saint-Exupery's finest work, an epic and thrilling account of his experiences flying solo over the Andes and crash-landing in the Sahara Desert.

12. ***The Worst Journey in the World*** by Apsley Cherry-Garrard, 1930 – Cherry-Garrard's absorbing account of Robert Falcon Scott's ill-fated 1911 expedition to the South Pole plunges the reader into the frozen landscape of the Antarctic, where perpetual darkness reigns and temperatures regularly drop seventy degrees below zero. The sole survivor of the expedition, Cherry-Garrard vividly describes the extreme hardship and emotional anguish he and other members of Scott's team endured during this nightmarish trek into the unknown.

Urban Histories

Books About Cities

Every great city has its own history, flavor, and way of life—sometimes developed in relative seclusion, like Tokyo, and sometimes a composite of lots of cultures all melded together, like New York. Whether you live in a great city or love to visit them, there are some fascinating books out there written by people who know the cities well and love them passionately. Listed in alphabetical order, these seven books offer illuminating portraits of cities that are rich in vivid detail and colorful anecdotes.

1. ***Alexandria: A History and a Guide*** by E.M. Forster, 1922 – The ancient and mysterious city in northern Egypt comes to life in Forster's account. Founded by and named after Alexander the Great, the city was important in Jewish, Hellenistic, and early Christian culture, and was restored to importance in the nineteenth century by the viceroy Muhammed Ali.

2. ***Barcelona*** by Robert Hughes, 1992 – Hughes is an enthusiastic chronicler of this independent-minded city in Spain's northeastern region of Catalunya. Discover its long and lively history from Roman times to the creation of the fanciful, undulating buildings of the modern architect Gaudí and beyond.

3. ***Empire City: New York Through the Centuries*** edited by Kenneth T. Jackson and David S. Dunbar, 2002 – New York is a cacophony of voices. This is not a conventional history book, but an anthology of writings about the city starting in the early seventeenth century and going right through the fateful year of 2001.

4. ***London: A History*** by A.N. Wilson, 2004 – The author, also a novelist and biographer, traces 2000 years of London's history, encompassing royal intrigues, plague, extraordinary literary productions, brave resistance to the Nazis, and the contemporary scene.

5. ***New Orleans: A Cultural History*** by Louise McKinney, 2006 – For much of its history, the Big Easy, home of wild Fat Tuesday celebrations, jazz, and beautiful architecture, has seemed exotic and alluring to the rest of America. Its reconstruction after Hurricane Katrina is a perfect time to learn more about its remarkable melting-pot history that both sets it apart from other cities, and makes it distinctively American.

6. ***Seven Ages of Paris*** by Alistair Horne, 2002 – This is a delightful narrative of a delightful city that has nurtured culture, philosophy, high art, and the arts of living for centuries—though its history has been tumultuous at times. The Calvinist Henry IV became Catholic for the city, calling it "well worth a Mass." Horne describes the conquerors, dreamers, and remakers of the city over the course of "seven ages."

7. ***The World of Venice*** by Jan Morris, 1960 – Past and present in the city of great artists and craftsmen, commerce and theater, and streets made of water come to life in this charming book. Morris shares her profound appreciation of the city's dazzling history and its unique way of life.

Vietnam War Nonfiction

Dispatches from the Quagmire

Hired to be *Esquire* magazine's Vietnam bureau chief, journalist Michael Herr arrived in the war-torn country just before the Tet Offensive—and went right into the field to cover the fire fights and night attacks that American soldiers faced daily. When he wasn't dodging enemy fire or joining the fight against the Viet Cong in the Mekong Delta, Herr jotted down his impressions of battle and snatches of soldiers' conversation in his notebook. Years later, after he'd returned to the United States, Herr shaped his notes into a book that became an instant classic of war reportage: *Dispatches*. Novelist John Le Carre praised *Dispatches* as "the best book I have ever read on men and war in our time." Herr would go on to work with Francis Ford Coppola and Stanley Kubrick on their respective Vietnam War films, *Apocalypse Now* and *Full Metal-Jacket*. Although he continues to write, albeit sporadically, Herr remains best known for his acid trip of a book, one of eight justly acclaimed nonfiction books about the Vietnam War, listed below alphabetically.

1. ***The Best and the Brightest*** by David Halberstam, 1972 – A masterful and thorough account of the foreign policy decisions and other factors that led to the U.S. involvement in the Vietnam War.

2. ***Born on the Fourth of July*** by Ron Kovic, 1976 – A gung-ho, patriotic soldier becomes an anti-war activist after combat injuries leave him paralyzed from the chest down.

3. ***A Bright Shining Lie: John Paul Vann and America in Vietnam*** by Neil Sheehan, 1988 – Pulitzer Prize winning, warts-and-all biography of the highly controversial, larger-than-life Vann, an army field adviser who dared to speak openly to the press about U.S. military setbacks in Vietnam.

4. ***Chickenhawk*** by Robert C. Mason, 1983 – Powerful memoir by an army helicopter pilot who flew more than 1,000 missions in Vietnam between 1964 and 1968.

5. ***Dispatches*** by Michael Herr, 1977 – Herr's electrifying, mind-bending prose plunges you headlong into the insanity of the Vietnam War.

6. ***Fire in the Lake: The Vietnamese and the Americans in Vietnam*** by Frances Fitzgerald, 1972 – Fitzgerald examines the war from a sociological perspective in this study of two cultures on a deadly collision course. Winner of both the Pulitzer Prize and the National Book Award.

7. ***A Rumor of War*** by Philip Caputo, 1977 – The *New York Times* called Caputo's gripping memoir of his six-month tour of duty as a platoon leader in Da Nang "a marvelous and singular work."

8. ***We Were Soldiers Once...And Young: Ia Drang—The Battle That Changed the War in Vietnam*** by Lt. General H.G. Moore and Joseph L. Galloway, 1992 – A compelling story of uncommon valor and self-sacrifice in the first major battle between the United States and the North Vietnamese.

Vietnam War Novels

Fiction from the Quagmire

Like so many men of the baby boom generation, novelist Tim O'Brien received his college diploma and his Vietnam War-era draft notice in rapid succession. Serving in the U.S. Army's Fifth Battalion, Forty-Sixth Infantry from January 1969 to March 1970, he returned home with a Purple Heart and memories of combat seared into his brain. His experience of the "quagmire" that was the Vietnam War informs his fiction, like *The Things They Carried* and the National Book Award winner, *Going After Cacciato.* Arguably the preeminent American novelist writing about the Vietnam War and its aftermath, O'Brien is one of four combat veterans whose novels appear on the following alphabetical list of essential titles about the war that claimed the lives of nearly 60,000 American soldiers and millions of Vietnamese.

1. ***Dog Soldiers*** by Robert Stone, 1974 – A Vietnam War correspondent cajoles his best friend into smuggling heroin back to the United States, but all hell breaks loose in Stone's darkly powerful National Book Award winner.

2. ***Fields of Fire*** by James H. Webb, 1978 – Three, idealistic young men from wildly different backgrounds are shattered by the madness of

jungle warfare in this intense novel by Webb, a former U.S. Marine who also served as Ronald Reagan's Secretary of the Navy.

3. ***Going After Cacciato*** by Tim O'Brien, 1978 – O'Brien's second novel is a highly original mixture of deadpan absurdist comedy and harrowing scenes of combat. When Private Cacciato goes AWOL to walk from Vietnam to Paris, the site of peace talks, his squad sets off in dogged pursuit—following his trail of chocolate M&Ms.

excerpt: ***GOING AFTER CACCIATO:***
Liquid and shiny, a mix of rain and clay, the trail took them higher. Out of radio range, beyond the reach of artillery.

Cacciato eluded them but he left behind the wastes of his march: empty ration cans, bits of bread, a belt of gold-cased ammo dangling from a shrub, a leaking canteen, candy wrappers, worn rope. Hints that kept them going. Luring them on, plodding along the bed of a valley; once they saw his fire on a distant hill. Straight ahead was the frontier.

"He makes it that far," Doc said on the morning of the sixth day, pointing to the next line of mountains, "and he's gone, we can't touch him. He makes the border and it's bye-bye Cacciato."

4. ***Meditations in Green*** by Stephen Wright, 1983 – Compared to the work of James Joyce and Michael Herr's *Dispatches* for its dazzling language and hallucinatory imagery, *Meditations in Green* is an intense, fever dream of a novel about a young soldier teetering on the brink of madness.

5. ***Novel Without a Name*** by Duong Thu Huong, 1995 – A comparative rarity in Vietnam War fiction: a novel told from the point of view of the North Vietnamese. Mentally and physically spent, a North Vietnamese soldier returns to his village, where everyone is mired in despair and cynicism prevails.

6. ***Paco's Story*** by Larry Heinemann, 1986 – The sole survivor of a Viet Cong attack returns home to rebuild his life, but he's unable to shake the lingering nightmares of combat experience. Narrated by the ghost of one of the survivor's fellow soldiers, *Paco's Story* is a devastating, National Book Award winning novel from Heinemann, who served with the U.S. Army's 25th Infantry Division in Vietnam.

7. ***The Short-Timers*** by Gustav Hasford, 1979 – Former Marine Hasford drew upon his combat experiences for this ambitious, three-part novel that inspired Stanley Kubrick's *Full-Metal Jacket*.

8. ***The Things They Carried*** by Tim O'Brien, 1990 – A powerful amalgam of fiction and personal reminiscence that can be read either as a novel or series of short stories about the men of Alpha Company in Vietnam.

Western Novels

Cowboy Classics

Published in 1902, Owen Wister's *The Virginian* is generally regarded as the literary template for the "modern" western novel. All the elements that have become genre standards—the stoic cowboy meting out frontier justice to the cowardly villain before the lovestruck gaze of the schoolmarm heroine—are present and accounted for in Wister's novel, which he dedicated to old chum, Teddy Roosevelt.

The success of *The Virginian* paved the way for Zane Grey, Louis L'Amour, and A.B. Guthrie, who in turn fueled the imagination of the modern masters of the genre, Larry McMurtry and Cormac McCarthy. Their psychologically complex and viscerally charged novels like *Lonesome Dove* and *Blood Meridian* bear only the faintest resemblance to *The Virginian,* which looks downright quaint in comparison. Here are eight classics, listed alphabetically, in this most American of literary genres.

1. ***All the Pretty Horses*** by Cormac McCarthy, 1992 – Far less bleak than McCarthy's graphically violent masterpiece *Blood Meridian,* this National Book Award winner is a twentieth century western about a naïve young cowboy's ill-fated romance with the beautiful daughter of a wealthy Mexican landowner.

excerpt: ***ALL THE PRETTY HORSES:***
He rode among the horses on the mesa and he walked them up out of the swales and cedar brakes where they'd gone to hide and he trotted the stallion along the grassy rims for the wind to cool him. He rode up buzzards out of a draw where they'd been feeding on a dead colt and he sat the horse and looked down at the poor form stretched in the tainted grass eyeless and naked.

2. ***The Big Sky*** by A.B. Guthrie, Jr., 1947 – An enthralling saga from the Pulitzer Prize winning novelist of *The Way West.* Caught up in the romance of the wide open spaces, a young Kentucky man joins his two friends on life-changing journey into the land of *The Big Sky.*

3. ***Hondo*** by Louis L'Amour, 1953 – L'Amour's first novel and still one of his best. In a remote corner of nineteenth century Arizona, a former U.S. Cavalry scout becomes the sworn protector of a woman and her young son amidst rising tensions between settlers and the Apache Indians.

4. ***Lonesome Dove*** by Larry McMurtry, 1985 – No other western has ever captivated critics and readers to the same degree as McMurtry's Pulitzer Prize winning epic about two retired Texas Rangers on a cattle drive to Montana. A spellbinding, bona-fide classic.

5. ***The Ox-Bow Incident*** by Walter Van Tilburg Clark, 1940 – A profound and troubling morality play about the consequences of mob violence in the American West. Clark's novel was later turned into a classic film starring Henry Fonda.

6. ***Riders of the Purple Sage*** by Zane Grey, 1912 – A spirited Mormon heroine turns to a handsome, quick-on-the-draw cowboy for help when cattle rustlers descend on her Utah ranch. An unpretentious and enjoyable page-turner that races towards its conclusion.

7. ***The Shootist*** by Glendon Swarthout, 1975 – The Western Writers of America hailed this elegiac character study about a terminally ill gunslinger confronting his mortality as "one of the ten greatest western novels of the twentieth century."

8. ***The Virginian*** by Owen Wister, 1902 – The title character may be a man of few words, but he's too busy battling Wyoming cattle rustlers to talk much in Wister's pioneering western novel.

World War I Novels

Stories of The Great War

When Bosnian Serb Gavrilo Princip assassinated Austria's Archduke Franz Ferdinand in Sarajevo in 1914, he set in motion what would later be known as "The War to End All Wars." Four years of fighting claimed ten million lives, toppled the Austro-Hungarian, German, Ottoman, and Russian Empires, and sowed the seeds of World War II.

The horrific carnage of World War I, and its profound impact on the world order, left many deeply traumatized. Addressing the psychic and physical wounds of trench warfare, these novels, some of them written by

WWI veterans who witnessed the horror firsthand, rank among the greatest about the "Great War" and are listed in alphabetically.

1. ***All Quiet on the Western Front*** by Erich Maria Remarque, 1929 – War is truly hell in Remarque's blistering, psychologically acute novel, based on his own experiences, about a German soldier whose battlefront experiences complicate his return to civilian life at war's end.

2. ***Birdsong*** by Sebastian Faulks, 1996 – The epochal Battle of Somme, which claimed over a million casualties in World War I, is brought to life with unstinting, at times grisly realism in Faulks' novel, which unfolds through the eyes of a young British army lieutenant, fresh from a love affair with a beautiful Parisian.

3. ***A Farewell to Arms*** by Ernest Hemingway, 1929 – A young American ambulance driver falls in love with a beautiful English nurse in Italy, but lasting happiness tragically eludes them in Hemingway's classic World War I romance, inspired by his own love affair with an American Red Cross nurse.

4. ***The Ghost Road*** by Pat Barker, 1995 – The final and greatest chapter in Barker's Regeneration trilogy of novels about shell-shocked British soldiers in World War I. Such real-life figures as poets Siegfried Sassoon and Wilfried Owen appear in *The Ghost Road,* which depicts a psychoanalyst's treatment of a working class officer, whose apparent calm belies his inner torment. Winner of the Booker Prize.

5. ***Johnny Got His Gun*** by Dalton Trumbo, 1939 – Probably better known as one of the "Hollywood Ten" blacklisted screenwriters, Trumbo was also a novelist of the first rank, as this viscerally-charged anti-war classic readily proves. Horribly wounded on the front, an American soldier has been reduced to a blind, deaf, and mute torso, unable to communicate with the outside world. As his mind wanders between the past and the present, the details of his wartime experience gradually come into sharp focus.

6. ***Parade's End*** by Ford Maddox Ford, 1924-1928 – Comprised of four novels, *Parade's End* can be a tough read, due to Ford's liberal, at times off-putting use of interior monologues and its non-linear chronology. That said, if you stick with it, you'll be engrossed in this massive yet emotionally intimate story of an Edwardian England gentleman fighting in the trenches as his marriage falls apart.

excerpt: JOHNNY GOT HIS GUN:
Things began to shoot back and forth in front of his eyes. Rockets and bombs and pinwheels and curves of fire and great white flares whirled through his head and sank into the soft wet part of his brain with a hissing sound. He could hear the hissing very plainly. It was like the escape of steam from a locomotive. He could hear explosions and howls and whines and words that didn't mean anything and whistles so high and shrill; that they cut through his ears like knives. Everything was dazzling and deafening. It hurt so much that he thought all the pain in the world was trapped somewhere between his forehead and back of his skull and trying to hammer its way out.

7. ***A Soldier of the Great War*** by Mark Helprin, 1991 – Dazzling, multi-layered epic flight of imagination from the author of *Winter's Tale*. In 1964, an Italian World War I veteran in his seventies looks back on the war, which brought an abrupt end to his carefree life of privilege.

8. ***Three Soldiers*** by John Dos Passos, 1921 – An ambulance driver in France and Italy during the war, Dos Passos paints a unflinchingly honest portrait of war's toll on his protagonists, three army privates trying to hang onto their humanity in the midst of bloody chaos.

World War II Novels

Stories of G.I. Joe

Ten years after he witnessed the Japanese attack on Pearl Harbor, 27th U.S. Infantry Regiment veteran James Jones burst onto the literary scene with *From Here to Eternity,* his gripping portrait of U.S. soldiers stationed in Honolulu in the days prior and immediately after the attack. Shocking in its day for Jones' frank portrayal of sex and liberal use of profanity, *From Here to Eternity* was an immediate critical and commercial sensation hailed for its authenticity. Jones would later draw upon his combat experiences in Guadalcanal for *The Thin Red Line,* the second book in his World War trilogy of novels. The last novel in the trilogy, *Whistle,* would be published in 1978, a year after Jones' death. All three rank among the great World War II novels about the American soldiers' experiences in Europe and the Pacific—eight of which are listed below, in alphabetical order.

1. ***A Bell for Adano*** by John Hersey, 1944 – Two years before he wrote his classic piece of war reportage, *Hiroshima,* Hersey won the Pulit-

zer Prize for this novel, which depicts an Italian-American U.S. Army major's life-changing experiences in a Sicilian village during the war.

2. ***The Caine Mutiny*** by Herman Wouk, 1951 – A petty dictator of the first rank, Captain Queeg of the *U.S.S. Caine* so alienates his crew that they overthrow him in Wouk's spellbinding novel, set in the Pacific Theater.

3. ***Catch-22*** by Joseph Heller, 1961 – Heller's classic anti-war novel is a scathingly funny and audacious critique of military life. Based on a Mediterranean island off Italy, U.S. Army Air Force bombardier Captain John Yossarian runs up against the impossible paradox of "Catch-22" in his efforts to get out of duty.

4. ***From Here to Eternity*** by James Jones, 1951 – The first novel in Jones' WWII trilogy essentially depicts the proverbial calm before the storm, i.e., the attack on Pearl Harbor. With unvarnished honesty, Jones portrays the culture of military life—its rigid emphasis on hierarchy and order—and how it alters the fate of Jones' tragic hero, Private Robert E. Lee Prewitt.

excerpt: ***FROM HERE TO ETERNITY:***

And as the last note quivered to prideful silence, and the bugler swung the megaphone for the traditional repeat, figures appeared in the lighted sallyport from inside of Choy's. "I told you it was Prewitt," a voice carried faintly across the quadrangle in the tone of a man who has won a bet. And then the repeat rose to join her quivering tearful sister. The clear proud notes reverberating back and forth across the silent quad. Men had come from the Dayrooms to the porches to listen in the darkness, feeling the sudden choking kinship bred of fear that supersedes all personal tastes. They stood in the darkness of the porches, listening, feeling suddenly very near the man beside them, who also was a soldier, who also must die.

5. ***The Naked and the Dead*** by Norman Mailer, 1948 – Mailer established himself as one of the leading post-war novelists with *The Naked and the Dead,* a pulverizing and profane epic inspired by his own combat experiences in the South Pacific.

6. ***The Thin Red Line*** by James Jones, 1962 – Astonishing and disturbing evocation of the physical and psychological toll of combat on U.S. soldiers in the Battle of Guadalcanal.

7. ***Whistle*** by James Jones, 1978 – Jones died from congestive heart fail-

ure before he could finish *Whistle,* which was completed by writer Willie Morris, using Jones' notes. If *Whistle* pales somewhat in comparison to Jones' earlier books, it's still an intense, viscerally charged narrative about four casualties of Guadalcanal, returning home to a U.S. Army hospital.

8. ***The Young Lions*** by Irwin Shaw, 1948 – Published the same year as *The Naked and the Dead,* Shaw's unjustly neglected novel portrays the wartime experiences of three soldiers, two Americans and a German, whose paths ultimately cross.

Writers in Captivity

Exiled, Imprisoned, and Tortured

While many writers insist that they need peace and quiet to practice their craft, quite a few others have led tumultuous lives. Independence of mind and spirit has led a number of writers over the centuries to run afoul of authority. Here is a small sampling of authors, listed alphabetically, who have found themselves in jail, in exile, or otherwise in trouble—some honorably, some dishonorably, some because of poverty and some just on account of bad luck.

1. **Fyodor Dostoevsky,** 1821–1881 – In the mid-nineteenth century, the future author of *Crime and Punishment* was arrested for his involvement with a circle of young intellectuals. He was jailed for eight months, nearly executed, and then exiled to Siberia for four years.

2. **Václav Havel,** born 1936 – The Czech playwright and poet was imprisoned several times for his political resistance to Soviet domination; one of his arrests led to four years of hard labor. Within a decade of his release, he became president of the Czech and Slovak Republic, and went on to lead the independent Czech Republic.

3. **Niccolò Machiavelli,** 1469–1527 – Considering that his name has become a byword for underhanded power politics, perhaps it should come as no surprise that Machiavelli had his share of trouble. Active in politics in the Florentine republic, he was jailed, tortured, and forced into exile when the Medici family returned to power.

4. **Ezra Pound,** 1885–1972 – For his pro-Mussolini radio broadcasts to American troops in Italy during World War II, the pioneering mod-

ernist poet was indicted for treason. He spent three weeks in an outdoor cage and several more in a medical tent, where he wrote *The Pisan Cantos,* some of his most beautiful verse. Returned to the U.S., he was declared insane and confined in a mental hospital for over a decade.

5. **Aleksandr Isayevich Solzhenitzyn,** born 1918 – Solzhenitzyn was arrested in his late twenties for making a derogatory reference to Stalin in a letter to a friend and spent eight years in prison camps. Later, his novels were received uneasily and subjected to censorship. When his nonfiction account of Soviet prison camps, *The Gulag Archipelago,* was published in 1973, he was arrested again and went into exile for twenty years.

Writers' Guides

Inspirational Titles for Aspiring Authors

Becoming a writer doesn't absolutely require formal training in the way that, say, becoming a concert pianist does. But there are times when a good book by an experienced writer or teacher can provide the inspiration, insights, and motivation that you need to get to work and find your own voice. Here are some recent books and beloved classics, listed alphabetically, to help you do just that.

1. ***Bird by Bird: Some Instructions on Writing and Life*** by Annie Lamott, 1994 – A funny, wise, and practical book on overcoming writer's block and other challenges to experience the joy of writing for its own sake.

excerpt: BIRD BY BIRD:

You are going to love some of your characters, because they are you or some facet of you, and you are going to hate some of your characters for the same reason. But no matter what, you are probably going to have to let bad things happen to some of the characters you love or you won't have much of a story. Bad things happen to good characters, because our actions have consequences, and we do not all behave perfectly all the time. As soon as you start protecting your characters from the ramifications of their less-than-lofty behavior, your story will start to feel flat and pointless, just like in real life.

2. ***The Elements of Style*** by William Strunk, Jr., and E.B. White, 1959 – The all-time classic on writing good prose in English, with advice like

"Prefer the specific to the general, the definite to the vague, the concrete to the abstract" and the pithy "Omit needless words."

3. ***The Elephants of Style*** by Bill Walsh, 2004 – The author, a witty and alert copy editor for the *Washington Post,* shares his well-reasoned, up-to-date views on some of the nuts and bolts of using the English language.

4. ***On Becoming a Novelist*** by John Gardner, 1983 – An uncompromising look at what it takes to write serious fiction, as well as the benefits and dangers of workshops, how to deal with editors and the frustration of rejections, and even how to prepare for a good writing session by using self-hypnosis.

5. ***On Writing*** by Stephen King, 2000 – The hugely successful horror writer discusses how his wife salvaged an early draft of *Carrie* from the trash, the importance of wide-ranging reading, how to revise, and the elements of a good story.

6. ***One Writer's Beginnings*** by Eudora Welty, 1984 – Not a writer's guide per se, but an utterly beguiling and inspiring memoir that offers aspiring writers' invaluable lessons on honing and refining their craft. Culled from a series of lectures that Welty gave at Harvard University in 1983, *One Writer's Beginnings* stresses the importance of writers developing their voices through listening and observation.

7. ***Simple and Direct: A Rhetoric for Writers*** by Jacques Barzun, 1975 – Another advocate of straightforward writing, Barzun shows how "simple" does not mean dull or imprecise. In his view, careful attention to words' sounds and meanings is the path to a truly expressive style.

8. ***Spunk and Bite*** by Arthur Plotnik, 2005 – While no book is likely to topple Strunk and White's *Elements of Style* from the literary pantheon, *Spunk and Bite* is an exhilaratingly different approach to writing. Using excerpts from masters of vivid prose to illustrate his points, Plotnik reminds us of the value of invention, rule-breaking, and even wildness in literature.

Young Adult Novels

Michael L. Printz Award Winners, 2000-2006

Sponsored by *Booklist*, a magazine published by the American Library Association, the Michael L. Printz Award is given yearly to a book that "exemplifies literary excellence in young adult literature." (Printz was a school librarian involved with YALSA, the Young Adult Library Services Association, a division of the ALA; he had a knack for discovering compelling new books.) Here are the winners since the prize was first given in 2000, listed chronologically, with our summaries. For more good choices, have a look at YALSA's annual Teens' Top Ten List drawn up by teenage readers at www.ala.org/yalsa.

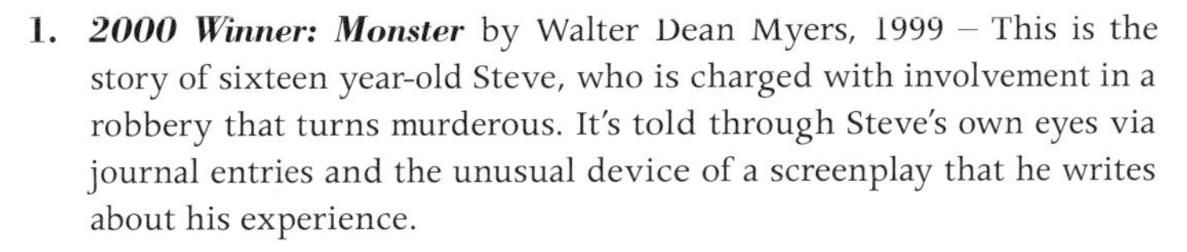

1. ***2000 Winner: Monster*** by Walter Dean Myers, 1999 – This is the story of sixteen year-old Steve, who is charged with involvement in a robbery that turns murderous. It's told through Steve's own eyes via journal entries and the unusual device of a screenplay that he writes about his experience.

2. ***2001 Winner: Kit's Wilderness*** by David Almond, 2000 – Thirteen-year-old Kit moves with his parents to an old coal-mining town in Northern England where his family has roots and where a death-haunted past seems quite alive. A thirteen-year-old relative with his own full name, Christopher Watson, in fact, perished in a mining disaster in 1821, bringing Kit even closer to the dark local history.

3. ***2002 Winner: A Step from Heaven*** by An Na, 2001 – Young Ju, a Korean girl who moves to California at the age of four, grows up caught between her family's traditional values and the life of an American schoolgirl. She eventually finds her way, even as her family struggles and eventually dissolves.

4. ***2003 Winner: Postcards from No Man's Land*** by Aidan Chambers, 2002 – Chambers gracefully weaves together two narratives, set fifty years apart in Amsterdam, in this sophisticated novel that touches on everything from war to euthanasia to bisexuality. In 1990s-era Amsterdam, a moody, sexually confused English teenager visits the Dutch woman who nursed his grandfather during World War II. Their stories gradually mesh in Chambers' challenging and richly textured prose.

4. ***2004 Winner: The First Part Last*** by Angela Johnson, 2003 – A teenage boy becomes a father in this moving and serious story. Bobby's girlfriend Nia, for reasons that don't become clear until late in the book, has no part in taking care of their child. He makes the decision on his own to raise little Feather, accepting the burdens and rewards of parenthood.

5. ***2005 Winner: how i live now*** by Meg Rosoff, 2004 – Fifteen-year-old Daisy leaves her home in New York and goes to England to stay in the country with her aunt and cousins. Her life there is emotionally intense, but outwardly tranquil—until terrorists invade England and everything changes in this captivating story of love, war, and growth.

6. ***2006 Winner: Looking for Alaska*** by John Green, 2005 – Miles Halter flees his lackluster life at home to look for the "Great Perhaps" at boarding school. For the first time he makes what he considers real friends, connecting with his roommate Chip and the beautiful but troubled Alaska on a level he's never experienced before. But his new life offers grief as well as joy.